CARDINAL MANNING 1865-1892

CARDINAL MANNING

His Public Life and Influence
1865–1892

VINCENT ALAN McCLELLAND

LONDON
OXFORD UNIVERSITY PRESS
NEW YORK   TORONTO
1962

Oxford University Press, Amen House, London E.C.4

GLASGOW NEW YORK TORONTO MELBOURNE WELLINGTON
BOMBAY CALCUTTA MADRAS KARACHI LAHORE DACCA
CAPE TOWN SALISBURY NAIROBI IBADAN ACCRA
KUALA LUMPUR HONG KONG

Printed in Great Britain

TO MY FATHER

PREFACE

IN 1956 the present writer began research into the workings of the Cross Commission and the reports which it issued in 1888. The Commission had been set up by Salisbury before the return to power of Gladstone in February 1886 and its purpose was to enquire into the efficiency of the 1870 Education Act. Henry Edward Manning was invited to be a member of this Commission and in a very short time he became the dominant figure. It was as a result of this work that the present writer began to develop a wider interest in the history of this powerful personality.

Through a series of incredible blunders, after the death of Manning in 1892, part of his personal papers fell into the hands of a journalist, Edmund S. Purcell. The latter, who was trying to recuperate after a serious failure in a literary venture which he had undertaken at the instigation of the Cardinal, produced a two-volume *Life* which was hurriedly written and which was based on only a fraction of the total documents available. The picture thus produced was so distorted that Wilfrid Ward tried to get the executors to obtain an injunction against the publication of the book. Purcell's book, however, remained the sole source of information concerning this 'Eminent Victorian' until Sir Shane Leslie published his *Life and Labours* in the early 1920's. Leslie's book, while being of a 'popular' character, did attempt to give a more balanced account of its subject. Sufficient time has now elapsed for an historical approach in estimating the impact upon this country of one who may be called England's last great 'Churchman'. Much new documentary evidence has come to light which helps to disprove a number of traditional attitudes, and use has been made of the Gladstone and Newman Papers in addition to the Manning Papers. The writer has explored a number of diocesan archives, hitherto ignored, and has received every consideration from the ecclesiastical authorities in tracing elusive material.

In order not to overburden the pages of the text with footnotes these have been confined to points which may be of interest to the reader in passing, and the details of sources are given in the numbered notes to each chapter which appear following the text on pp. 222–232. Abbreviations used in the latter are listed on p. 222, and these may occasionally be found in the footnotes also.

No excuse is made for limiting the scope of this work to the twenty-seven years when Manning was the occupant of the See of Westminster. The work does not purport to be a biography and more than sufficient has already been written on the Oxford Movement and its protagonists. In reality, the attraction of the nineteenth century in English history lies not so much in the religious revival (important as that may be) but in the great social changes, in education, in labour, in Ireland. These were the great issues of the century and to a certain extent the religious turmoil was but an offshoot of these changes. It is, however, impossible to appreciate these developments fully if the part played by Henry Edward Manning in their formation is not understood. In this book an attempt is made to indicate the nature and extent of this influence; whether the attempt is successful or not is for the reader to decide.

V. A. M.

Bardsley, Lancs. 1961

CONTENTS

		PAGE
Preface	. . . .	vii
Acknowledgements	. . . . . .	xi
I. The 'Old Catholics' and Practical Christianity	. .	1
II. The Schools	. . . . . .	26
III. The Act of 1870 and its Consequences	. . .	61
IV. Higher Education	. . . . . .	87
V. The Condition of the People	. . . .	129
VI. Ireland and Gladstone	. . . . .	161
VII. Philanthropy	. . . . . .	199
VIII. Epilogue	. . . . . .	213
A Note on the Sources	. . . . .	218
Notes to Chapters I–VIII	. . . . .	222
Bibliography	. . . . . .	233
Appendixes		
I: Newman-Manning Correspondence at Bayswater	.	238
II: Gladstone Papers	. . . . .	241
III: Manning-Newman Letters at Birmingham	.	242
IV: Manning Letters at Bristol	. . . .	243
Index	. . . .	245

ACKNOWLEDGEMENTS

My grateful thanks are due to the Father Superior of the Oblates of St. Charles for permission to use the Manning Papers and to the Rev. Professor Alphonse Chapeau of the University of Angers for his great kindness in guiding me through the relevant documents at Bayswater and for his invaluable help and friendship. I am indebted to the University of Birmingham for permitting me to conduct the research within the University and to Mr. Philip Styles, M.A., Reader in English History in the University, for his patient examination of the work and his sensible and scholarly advice. His Grace the Archbishop of Birmingham and their Lordships the Bishops of Clifton and Salford have granted access to their archives and for this along with many personal favours I am deeply grateful. I wish to record my thanks to the Provincial of the Redemptorist Fathers and the Superior of the Birmingham Oratory for permission to consult the Coffin and Newman Papers respectively and for their hospitality. Mr. A. C. F. Beales has advised on the education question and Professor John Tracy-Ellis on the American labour problems. Mr. C. Brackwell, the Assistant Registrar of Birmingham University, and Mr. R. B. Grove of Nottingham University have allowed me to quote from their unpublished theses and I am indebted for help of various kinds to Sir Philip Magnus-Allcroft, Bt., Professor J. M. Cameron, the late Professor G. D. H. Cole, Professor Denis Gwynn, Dr. J. W. Battersby, Dr. J. M. Handley, Mr. H. O. Evennett of Trinity College, Cambridge, and Mr. C. H. D. Howard of King's College, London University. Finally I record my appreciation for Professor Moody's bringing to my notice in Dublin a hitherto unpublished letter of Manning of considerable importance.

For permission to quote from various books published by Burns, Oates I am especially grateful. These books include W. J. Battersby, *Brother Potamian : Educator and Scientist* (1953), G. A. Beck (ed.), *The English Catholics, 1850–1950* (1950), J. Fitzsimons (ed.), *Manning, Anglican and Catholic* (1950), S. Leslie, *Henry Edward Manning : His Life and Labours* (1921). Sir Arnold Lunn has granted me leave to quote from his *Roman Converts* (1924) and Professor Tracy-Ellis to quote from his *Life of James, Cardinal Gibbons, Archbishop of Baltimore* (1952). Finally I am especially grateful to Sheed and

Ward for allowing me to quote at length from Canon St. John's *Manning's Work for Children* (1929) and to Longmans for permission to make use of letters quoted in P. J. Walsh's *William J. Walsh, Archbishop of Dublin* (1928).

I have received efficient and courteous treatment from the Keeper of the Manuscripts at the British Museum and from the Librarians at Colindale and at Merton College, Oxford, from the Goldsmiths' Librarian in the University of London and from the Borough Librarian at Clitheroe. My deepest gratitude is reserved for my father for his constant encouragement and patience.

If, through an oversight, I have unwittingly offended against anyone's copyright I apologize; and I thank all those who have helped me in any way and whose names have been involuntarily omitted from this list.

Chapter I

THE 'OLD CATHOLICS' AND PRACTICAL CHRISTIANITY

*

On 3 April 1585, Thomas Goldwell, Bishop of St. Asaph and the last of the Marian bishops to remain loyal to Rome under Elizabeth I, died in Rome. Goldwell had been deprived of his see for refusing to take the Oath of Supremacy (1559). With his death the Roman Catholic Hierarchy of England and Wales was considered by Pope Sixtus V to be extinct and Roman Catholics in these countries were without *normal* episcopal government for two hundred and sixty-five years, until by Letters Apostolic (*Universalis Ecclesiae*), 29 September 1850, Pope Pius IX restored the English Roman Catholic Hierarchy under the Primacy of Nicholas, Cardinal Wiseman, Archbishop of Westminster and Metropolitan.

During those two hundred and sixty-five years before the restoration of the Hierarchy, Roman Catholics had many varied forms of government. From 1581 until his death in 1594 William, Cardinal Allen, Archbishop-elect of Mechlin, was 'Prefect of the English Mission', and from 1598 until 1621 Archpriests* were in charge of the Mission. The first Vicar Apostolic in episcopal orders was appointed in 1623 by Pope Gregory XV; he was the Rev. William Bishop and he held the titular see of 'Chalcedon'. After this date the actual government of the Roman Catholic Church was by Vicars Apostolic holding titular sees—first one for the whole of England and Wales (1623–87), then two (1687–8), then four (1688–1840) and finally eight (1840–50).† After the death in prison in 1584 of Thomas Watson, Bishop of Lincoln, there was not a Roman Catholic bishop residing in England or Wales for thirty-nine years (1584–1623) and the Catholics were completely without any form of ecclesiastical government between 1594 and 1598 and again from 1621 to 1623 and from

---

* Rev. George Blackwell (1599–1608) who died in prison; Rev. George Birkhead (1608–14); Rev. William Harrison (1615–21).

† In each of the cases the country was divided into districts or vicariates, each completely under the jurisdiction of its own vicar. Each of the vicars was subject directly to the Congregation 'de Propaganda Fide' as England was classed as a missionary country.

I

1655 to 1685*. During these long stretches of time, amounting to a total of seventy-five years, English Catholics were cut off from the disciplinary influence of the episcopate. In the days when Cardinal Allen was 'Prefect of the English Mission' (1581–1594) it had been impossible for him to reside in England.† The web of ecclesiastical government had therefore been extremely thin and contact with Rome had tended to be spasmodic and irregular. In 1647 a Roman Catholic priest, Father Henry Holden, described the chaos that existed, saying it was 'more like the confusion of Calvin's synagogue than the unity of the Catholic Church'.[1] A state of open feud had arisen between the Regular and Secular clergy and there was no recognized episcopal authority. After the reign of Elizabeth I Roman Catholics were few in number and were convinced that their best chance of survival was to withdraw from public notice and settle down to a life of isolation and to a surreptitious practice of their religion. This was the only possible course of action; the faith lived on, especially in the households of a number of titled families and in the country houses of landowners—such as the Cliffords of Chudleigh, the Vaux of Harrowden, the Vavasours of Yorkshire, the Welds and many others. The Manor of Spinkhill, in Derbyshire, always had a resident Jesuit missioner through-out penal times as also had the Manor of Stonyhurst in Lancashire. These manor-houses served as Mass-centres for their districts.

The inhabitants of these houses were a proud, aristocratic race; they were the race who claimed in the nineteenth century that they had kept the faith alive; they had given martyrs to the faith; they had been impoverished by the fines consequent on refusing to attend the services of the Established Church; they had been in-carcerated for the faith; they had given priests to the Church in the days when to be a priest meant to be a hunted man; they had suffered the injustice of not being able to send their children to the national Universities because of the Tests, but had to send them abroad for their education;‡ they had given up the prospect of leading the nation in politics; they claimed they were of the soil

---

* Bishop Richard Smith died in 1655 and Bishop John Leyburn was not appointed until 1685, leaving a gap of thirty years.

† Most of the dates are taken from *The Catholic Directory*, 1956 (B.O.W.).

[1] Numbered notes will be found at the end of the book, pp. 222–32.

‡ Douay College was established in 1568; English College at Rome in 1575. Colleges were also founded for English students at Valladolid and Seville in Spain.

of England and yet of the blood of martyrs. These were the race of 'Old Catholics', grown old, they would claim, in the sacrifice and love of Faith and Conscience. If one is to understand the opposition to Cardinal Manning and to the Oxford converts, one has to appreciate the feelings and position of the 'Old Catholics'.*

Two great influences were brought to bear upon the Roman Catholics in England before the advent of the Oxford Movement, influences which radically altered the nature and bases of the Church. After the outbreak of the French revolution several thousand French priests fled to England, where they were for the most part welcomed by English Catholics.[2] They were the fellow-persecuted and they had lost property, position, all, for the faith. The 'Old Catholics' thought they recognized in the fate of the French priests a similar one to their own. But the coming of these strangers was important for another reason; they were the first real contact that English Catholics had made with the ideas of continental Catholicism since the Reformation. Their arrival brought with it a more daring Catholicism; one which began to witness the introduction of continental devotions and more external homage to the Virgin Mary; a Catholicism which began to find itself slowly but surely drawn from hiding to face the world once more. These French émigrés were the early precursors of the Oxford converts in the move to deliver the Church 'from the catacombs'.

The second great influence was the impact of Irish Catholicism upon England. In order to show the extent of the Irish immigration prior to the turn of the nineteenth century it is interesting to study the figures of the census of 1841 dealing with the extent of the Irish population in various parts of Great Britain.[3]

Various parts of Gt. Britain	Males	Irish-born Females	Total Irish-born	Percentage of whole	Total Population
England	148,151	135,977	284,128	1·9	14,995,138
Wales	3,080	2,196	5,276	0·6	911,603
Scotland	66,502	59,819	126,321	4·8	2,620,184
The Islands	1,664	1,867	3,531	2·8	124,040
	219,397	199,859	419,256	2·2	18,650,965

* As used here, and throughout this book, the phrase 'Old Catholics' has of course nothing to do with the name used by those who seceded from the Roman Catholic Church on the Continent, and are now known as the 'Old Catholic' Church, with an Archbishop at Utrecht.

Certain general observations may be made on these statistics. The table only concerns those of the population who were born in Ireland and not those children of one or two Irish parents born in England, Wales or Scotland but whose background, culture and sympathies would be Irish. These children are included in the total populations as being native to this country. The total number of Irish males outnumbered the females by 19,538. Many of these excess Irish males would marry English, Welsh or Scottish girls and if they did not make them Roman Catholics they would insist that their children be brought up in that religion. There existed, therefore, in England, Wales and Scotland, not only a convert-making potential but a certainty that the Roman Catholic population was going to increase and increase steadily in the near future. It is true that not all the Irish were Roman Catholics, but the Protestant Irish largely settled in Scotland where the affinities with Ulster were very great, and the Catholic Irish in England.[4] The proportion of Irish to native-born inhabitants in Scotland was in 1841 practically treble the proportion for England, and four times greater than that for Wales. We can, however, estimate that by 1841 the total Roman Catholic population in England, Wales, Scotland and the Isles was about 2·2 of the whole population— the 'Old Catholics' and the Protestant Irish cancelling each other out. But the great influx was yet to come. The Irish immigration 'increased in volume during the nineteenth century until it reached its full flood during and after the terrible famine years from 1845 to 1849'.[5]

The Irish, coming as they did and under the conditions of famine and privation, naturally joined the Highland Scots as the poorest element in these islands. They settled, to a large extent, in the great ugly towns thrown up by the Industrial Revolution—and especially in the north of England, in Lancashire.[6] The Irish, coming from an agricultural country, may have wished to settle in the agricultural districts of England, but finding no dearth of labour there had to move into the manufacturing towns. What shortage of labour there was in the country districts occurred only at harvest time and could be met by casual Irish labour.

The result of the Irish impact on Roman Catholicism in England was to bring it more and more into public view. 'Up to 1840 there had been a steady increase in the Catholic churches, which now numbered between four and five hundred, in Great Britain', declares

Denvir,[7] and he adds: 'But this did not by any means keep pace with the increase in the Irish population.'

The 'Old Catholics' did not view this addition to their numbers with anything like approbation. They felt the old coinage was being debased to an irreparable extent and that the new accretions to their numbers of ignorant and pauperized Catholics would tend to degrade their Church in the eyes of the Anglicans. The alteration was to a certain extent tolerable so long as the government of the Church in this country remained in the hands of native English of the old families. The situation was to become intolerable for them when rulers were appointed who regarded their first duty as being to provide for the spiritual needs of the Irish in Great Britain.

The outward sign of the change in temper was the restoration of the Hierarchy in 1850. By 1851 there were 733,866 Irish in Great Britain, as declared by the census of that year.[8] This increase of numbers had made it imperative that England's position should be regularized in its capacity as an ecclesiastical province of the Roman Catholic Church. Many influential Catholics at Rome had been working for this end and none had worked harder than Nicholas Wiseman, who had been at the English College, Rome, for most of his life and had been a titular bishop in England, assisting the Vicar of the Midland District. He was of Irish descent. The practical result of these efforts was that the Hierarchy was re-established in 1850 (under much clamour from Protestants in scenes reminiscent of the days of the Gordon Riots) with Nicholas Wiseman, now created Cardinal, as first Archbishop of Westminster and Metropolitan of the new Province.

The effect on the 'Old Catholics' of this move was startling; the Duke of Norfolk showed his disapproval by being a strong supporter of Russell's Ecclesiastical Titles Bill, in spite of the fact that his son had opposed the Bill in the House of Commons. Norfolk wrote to Lord Beaumont (28 Nov. 1850): 'I should think that many must feel, as we do, that Ultramontane opinions are totally incompatible with allegiance to our Sovereign and with our Constitution',[9] and Beaumont himself had written to the Earl of Zetland, a member of the Government, that 'the late bold and clearly expressed edict of the Court of Rome cannot be received or accepted by English Roman Catholics without a violation of their duties as citizens'.[10] He added that 'the line of conduct now adopted by Lord John Russell [was] that of a true friend of the British Constitution'. In fact, it seems to have been a family tradition of the Norfolks to have been opposed to the appointment of bishops, for as early as 1667 we find the then Duke opposed to any 'tampering with Rome' about the appointment of a bishop for English Catholics.[11] Other ennobled Catholics, such as Lord Camoys, formally protested to the Pope and the new Cardinal was regarded by the 'Old Catholic' families with as much distrust as he was by his religious opponents.* They felt that this change would mean an increase of 'Irish-ism'† in the Church and they feared a rejuvenation of anti-papalism and anti-Catholic legislation. Their fears seemed to have some justification, with the outburst in the press and the streets against the restoration of the Hierarchy, inflamed by Russell's 'Durham Letter' of 14 November 1850 and by his Ecclesiastical Titles Bill (1851). The excitement died down, however, chiefly through the conciliatory attitude of Wiseman, and Russell's Bill was a dead letter from the beginning. The opposition of the 'Old Catholics' was also due to some extent to their fear of being supplanted by the new elements in the governance of the Church in England.

Wiseman,‡ although of Irish descent on his maternal side, was descended on his father's side from an old English recusant family. He was, however, 'a Roman'; that is, he had spent most of his life in the Eternal City and had imbibed Roman culture and ideas. This was to prove a source of much grievance to the 'Old Catholics' who were Gallican in their ideas.§ It is not surprising that they resented the closer tie with Rome and what it entailed, when their

* There is no justification for the assertion by Dr. Georgina P. McEntee in her book *The Social Catholic Movement in Great Britain* (Macmillan, New York, 1927) that 'the remnant of the Catholic Church in the land was elated' (p. 3) with the restoration of the Hierarchy.

† *The Guardian* of 11 Dec. 1850 hinted at this fear when it declared: 'the strength of Romanism in this country, even as a political power, is no longer confined to noblemen's castles. It is something rougher, more aggressive, less English in its attachments and sympathies.'

‡ Dr. McEntee is again in error when she states that the reason why Wiseman was uninterested in social amelioration was because the tide of Irish immigration had not yet hit the Church (p. 5). The restoration of the Hierarchy was a direct outcome of that immigration. Wiseman had to follow a policy of conciliation and consolidation. Social reforms would have alienated the 'Old Catholics'.

§ Sir John Throckmorton, writing sixty years before the Restoration of the R.C. Hierarchy, spoke of 'the descendants of the Old Catholic families and a respectable portion of the clergy, who true to the religion of their ancestors have uniformly . . . protested against the usurped authority of the Court of Rome.' (*A Letter addressed to the Catholic Clergy of England on the Appointment of their Bishops*. London, publ. by J. P. Coghlan, 2nd. edn. 1792. In B.M.)

long past of virtual independence in ecclesiastical discipline is considered. As Ward[12] in his life of Wiseman contends, the establishing of the new Hierarchy 'entailed the founding of an ecclesiastical polity in England'. He goes on: 'A Church independent of lay control—its priests no longer normally the chaplains of the squire— had to have its constitution accurately defined.'[13] The definition of the new ecclesiastical polity caused much heartbreak in many a stately mansion.

The attitude of the 'Old Catholics' towards the new ecclesiastical settlement might have mellowed and passed into a more favourable aspect, but for the question of the Oxford converts. Nine years before the re-establishment of the Hierarchy there was published *Tract 90*—in 1841. This is regarded as marking the peak of the Oxford Movement. After this it had been but a matter of time before the flood gates were opened and Newman and his Oxford disciples entered the Roman Catholic Church. The converts were welcomed and, particularly after the appointment of Wiseman to Westminster, were much favoured by the Church.[14] Wiseman always believed that he was the one destined to reunite England to the Holy See. He saw in the Oxford converts but an earnest of that general submission which he confidently expected. He was especially anxious to show the converts that they were welcome in the Church of their adoption and that all posts and offices were open to them as they were to cradle-Catholics.[15] But no cradle-Catholic ever enjoyed the favour or respect given to a Newman, a Faber, a Talbot or a Manning. This was a source of bitterness to the 'Old Catholics'. 'The contrast between the culture of the Oxford converts and the lack of culture of the Old Catholics, whose families had been excluded from the Universities by the Penal Laws, was painfully obvious.'[16] This contrast is vividly described by Wilfrid Ward in his Life of his father when he states that the difference between a Catholic of the day meeting a Protestant in controversy was like that of 'a barbarian meeting a civilised man'.[17]

Converts are often more zealous for their new Church than others and they sometimes push their views to extremes. The effect of the Oxford converts on the Catholic Church was that the Church became *more Roman, more Italian* in its appearance—a change greatly encouraged by Wiseman. 'Lives of the Saints' were undertaken by Newman and Faber and pursued to such fantastic lengths that Dr. Ullathorne, O.S.B., Newman's bishop at Birmingham, had to protest.[18] Italianate architecture became the fashion—to the great regret of Pugin. Luscious hymns were written by Faber to replace the old melodies, perhaps reaching their zenith in the stanza:

> For ever climbs that Morning Star
> Without ascent or motion:
> For ever is its daybreak shed
> On the Spirit's boundless ocean.
> Oh marvellous! O worshipful!
> On the Spirit's boundless ocean.
> Oh marvellous! O worshipful!
> No song or sound is heard,
> But everywhere and every hour,
> In love, in wisdom, and in power,
> The Father speaks His dear Eternal Word.

Statues came more into evidence; processions, both indoor and outdoor, once again became popular and many foreign devotions and acts of piety were imported. This aspect of the Oxford Movement is one which is often forgotten.*

The 'Old Catholics' felt that this change was far too radical; that it was likely to revive anti-papalism and that it would keep out rather than encourage more converts. In fact, the Gallicanism of the 'Old Catholics' really dated from the time when the Pope, secure at Rome, had exposed them to persecution by his reckless Bulls,[19] and they feared a repetition of their sufferings.

The converts for their part considered the 'Old Catholics' were 'in a backwater, stagnating, deficient in education, culture, enterprise, and failing in appreciation of the duty of trying to make the Catholic religion appeal to the non-Catholic masses'.[20] Wiseman, wholly on the side of the converts, imported once more the Religious Orders, such as the Redemptorists, the Rosminians and the Oratorians, many of which consisted largely of Italians and intensified the rapid Romanization of the Church. The whole of the fourteen years of Wiseman's episcopate was spent in the endeavour to reconcile the three elements in the Church, the 'Old Catholics', the Irish, and the converts. This reconciliation had only been partly achieved before the succession of Manning in 1865 to Westminster. It was a grave situation that Manning had to face, himself strongly

---

* Lunn considers the revival to be a good thing—one of 'Beauty in many forms, stone, music, in ritual and in art'.

Roman, Ultramontane and a convert, but by his death in 1892 he had done much to remedy the failure of Wiseman.

As already stated, the government of the Roman Catholic Church in England prior to 1850 was by means of Vicars Apostolic in episcopal Orders and holding titular sees. On the restoration of the Hierarchy the ironical problem arose of what to do with the Vicars Apostolic—some of whom had been against the restoration. It was decided that the only way to ensure peace was to appoint the Vicars to the new sees. We therefore find that by 1851, when all the appointments were completed, of the thirteen new sees, eight were occupied by bishops who had previously been Vicars Apostolic.* Only five new elevations were made.† These appointments are very significant. Vicars Apostolic had reigned supreme in their own districts, only being subject directly to Rome, to the Congregation 'de Propaganda Fide'.‡ Now, with the creation of the Hierarchy, the Archbishop of Westminster was also designated Metropolitan of the English Province. As he was the only Metropolitan, his position was equal to that of a Primate. This meant that he was the immediate ecclesiastical superior of all the bishops and that as a consequence of this his policies should be supported, obeyed, and followed by the various Ordinaries. The members of the new Hierarchy who had previously been Vicars Apostolic, and who were in a majority, resented this change in their status; they were no longer the supreme arbiters of affairs in their own domains but were to follow the orders of Westminster—and this was to be especially obnoxious to the suffragans when the Provincial See was occupied by a strong prelate like Manning, a prelate who was unsympathetic to the 'Old Catholic' body from which most of the new Hierarchy had been selected. This situation enables us to understand the reasons why Wiseman's days were to be so engrossed by squabbles over jurisdiction.[21]

When Manning was appointed Archbishop of Westminster, on 8 June 1865, by the personal intervention of Pius IX (who had rejected the 'Old Catholic' nominees—Clifford, Errington and Grant) he found that three (and those his senior bishops) of his

* Ullathorne of Birmingham; Brown of Newport and Menevia; Brown of Liverpool; Hendren of Clifton and later of Nottingham; Hogarth of Hexham; Briggs of Beverley; Wareing of Northampton, and, of course, Wiseman himself.

† Brown of Shrewsbury; Errington of Plymouth; Turner of Salford; Grant of Southwark and in 1851 Burgess of Clifton.

‡ As in all territories where a regular hierarchy is not established.

suffragans were 'Old Catholics' and had been Vicars Apostolic—
Ullathorne, O.S.B., of Birmingham, Brown, O.S.B., of Newport,
and Hogarth of Hexham—and a Hierarchy bitter over quarrels with
Wiseman. The bishops also numbered among their ranks two
members who had been rejected for the succession to Wiseman—
and Dr. Errington. It was a formidable and unenviable situation.
Butler, somewhat naïvely, describes the Hierarchy of the time as
'just a set of hard-working diocesan bishops, good pastors, who
devotedly and successfully gave themselves up to the work
of organizing the new dioceses entrusted to their care'.[22] They
were very English, sturdy, independent and hard-hitting. Clifford
of Clifton* (later to prove Manning's most persistent and zealous
opponent in the Hierarchy), Grant of Southwark, and the redoubtable Errington had constituted the 'Terna' submitted to Rome by
the Westminster Chapter and approved by the suffragan bishops
on the death of Wiseman. Manning's name had never even been
considered. Leslie informs us that Newman was suggested,[23]
Newman who had distinctly allied himself with the 'Old Catholics'.
Manning had been the personal selection of Pio Nono.[24] His was
not a popular appointment; he had been Wiseman's right-hand
man and he represented all that was most obnoxious to the old
families. The situation was well described by Monsignor Talbot
who wrote from Rome to congratulate Manning, on 10 July 1865:
'Your appointment has been a severe blow given to the club theory,
I mean the view that the Catholic body, as it is called in England,
is a kind of club, and that the dignities in it ought to be the
property of the Cliffords and other Catholic families.'[25]

This was, therefore, the situation in the Roman Catholic Church
in England when Henry Edward Manning became its head. It
was narrow, discordant, conservative. In twenty-six years Cardinal
Manning was to transform the outlook and status of the Church
and his influence was to be felt throughout the Empire, Europe
and the United States, an influence now recognized as far-reaching
and essential.

'God forbid that we should be looked upon by the people as
Tories, or of the Party that obstructs the amelioration of their
condition; or as the servants of the plutocracy instead of the guides
and guardians of the poor'[26]—so wrote Cardinal Manning in an

---

* He outlived Manning by a year, and was a bishop eight years before Manning was
consecrated.

autobiographical note two years before his death, and the sentiments expressed here can be said to embody his philosophy of life, his 'practical Christianity'.

If we are to enquire when it was that Manning first became social-conscious, we have to look at the years of his life before 1865. From his days as Anglican Vicar of Lavington and as Archdeacon of Chichester, he had been surrounded by the poverty of his people. The depression of the agricultural labourer was blatantly obvious and the countryside was being depleted, work being sought in the new factories of the large towns. It is in this setting that we first encounter Manning, the social reformer. From 1842 until 1849 his archidiaconal charges reverberate with indictments of social evil and with proposed remedies.

In 1842 he began by attacking certain ecclesiastical privileges of the wealthy, declaring that

the best sites in our Churches are occupied by exclusive pews, and the poor are thrust into inconvenient and remote sittings; [that] in many places the pews have so enclosed and appropriated the whole interior of the Church, that the poor are thrust out altogether from the House of our Common Father; [that] when this is not so, yet in the very presence of God, where all temporal distinctions should be blended in one aspect of brotherhood, the inequalities of our earthly lot are forced upon us with a nakedness, and an obtrusiveness, which galls one's very heart.[27]

He solemnly concludes: 'The truth must be told. Pews are a strong abuse. . . . Private rights have no place in the freehold of God. It is against Him that we commit the trespass.'[28] This policy was to continue after his submission to Rome, and many a poor parish priest was to quake with fear if he thought the Archbishop had noticed he took bench-rents in his Church.

The Charge of 1843 contained a number of instances of how the Archdeacon's sympathies were with the poor. He declared:

It is a high sin in the sight of Heaven for a man to wring his wealth out of the thews and sinews of his fellows, and to think that, when he has paid them their wages, he has paid them all he owes. He owes them a care as broad as the humanity of which he and they alike partake: as he shall answer at the day of judgment, he may not dare to deal with them as less than members of the body of Christ. The dense masses of our manufacturing towns, the poor families of our agricultural villages, are each of them related, by the bond of labour and wages to some employer, and on him they have a claim for alms, both of body and soul.[29]

This same Charge treats of three more matters, with which, as Archbishop of Westminster, Manning was greatly concerned—education, the middle classes, and the personal sanctification of the clergy—and it is interesting to observe that his early opinions on the first and last of these never underwent any radical change. Of education he said:

The function of educating children does not belong to the sacred orders as such, but to all members of the Church, clerical and lay; that is to say, not to a portion of the Church, but to the whole body.[30]

Later in his life as a Roman Catholic this viewpoint was to receive much opposition, for too many Catholics thought the only body to whom education could safely be entrusted was the clergy and the religious communities. But Manning was later to give practical effect to his views when he concerned himself with the establishment of training colleges for lay teachers, with the encouragement of pupil teachers, with the exclusion of the 'monopolistic' teaching Orders from his diocese and with the staffing of his university college at Kensington almost exclusively by laymen. To him a good lay teacher was preferable to a bad clerical teacher. This policy we shall consider later in more detail but it is interesting to record that its roots lay as far back as 1843. Manning had a keen perception of the contemporary scene and he early recognized the growing importance of the middle class of society. 'At this day', he wrote, 'the middle class had attained to a measure of wealth and numbers, and to a vigour of understanding and energy of character, unequalled in earlier times.'[31] His education policy as Archbishop was to be one of provision for the middle classes; one which would give an adequate scientific and technical training to the youths who would earn their living in industry. His university college was to be largely and primarily a middle-class university. He rightly realized, too, that if the Church was to have any impact upon this new, rising, influential class it would do so by its practical sagacity and alliance and not by learning in its narrower sense. His clergy must be equipped with scholarship but at the same time must be willing to forsake a life of seclusion and study for one of active social and religious work. In the Charge of 1843 we discover that, so early, Manning had recognized this truth: 'Learning and study and sacred literature there must be, and they have their due dignity and sphere. . . . What men want is a reality which will solve their own perplexed being. . . . We must be the thing we preach.'[32] Christ, he was never tired of pointing out, 'went about doing good' to all he met; he did not write a book informing others how to do it. In these statements it is not hard to discover the reason why Manning and Newman were to prove incompatibles.

The Charge of 1845 was largely devoted to a plea for greater recreations for the agricultural labourer and the need for longer and more frequent holidays. He spoke of the people as being

straitened by poverty—worn down by toil; they labour from the rising to the setting of the sun; and the human spirit will faint or break at last. It is to this unrelenting round of labour that the sourness so unnatural to our English poor, but now too often seen, is chiefly to be ascribed. There is something in humanity which pines for a season of brighter and fresher thoughts, and becomes sharp and bitter if it be not satisfied. What is the fact? Except Sunday and one or two days—such as Christmas Day, Good Friday and Ascension Day, which, through the Christian kindness of many landlords and farmers in this neighbourhood, has of late, without loss of wages, been given to their labours—our poor have no days of relaxation for mind or body. Time must be redeemed for the poor man. The world is too hard upon him, and makes him pay too heavy a toll out of his short life.[33]

He concluded with a passionate plea, showing how much he loved the agricultural poor:

Those who have lived, as it is our blessing to do, among the agricultural poor, well know that, with some rudeness of address, and with faults not to be denied, they are still a noble-hearted race, whose sincerity, simplicity, and patience we should buy cheap at the cost of our refinements. But little is needed to make their holiday. The green fields, and tools idle for a day, the church-bell, an active game, simple fare, the sport of their children, the kindly presence, and patient ear of superiors, is enough to make a village festival. I am not now speaking of towns, which have difficulties of their own kind, and need a separate treatment.[34]

The Charge of 1846 discussed the problem that was to engross his attention throughout his life and to which so much of his social policy can be related—the search for a 'via media' between scientific development and Christianity. Most of his educational policy as Archbishop can be attributed to his urgent desire to wean the Roman Catholic laity away from the traditional and classical branch of studies, as prescribed at Oxford and Cambridge and advocated by the Jesuits and Newman, towards the scientific and modern branch, and thus he hoped to achieve a reconciliation between the claims of science and those of the Church. In his Charge of 1846, we see that he had early recognized the dangers in store for Christianity. He writes:

The developments of Rationalism, extending to the rejection not only of specific doctrines but even of the original facts of the Christian faith, show us what is preparing for the future. This, and not imperfect forms of Christianity, will be our peril. Strauss' Life of Jesus (a work I will not here describe) has been within a few weeks published in English.[35]

He goes on to indict the inadequacy of Oxford and Cambridge to supply the increasing demand for higher education:

The number of young men residing within the precincts of the two universities at one time may be taken to be about 5,000. Can it be maintained that this is an adequate number upon a population of 20,000,000? . . . What is 5,000 upon the youth of England? Upon the nobles, gentlemen, statesmen, legislators, jurists, clergy of the next generation? What is such a number measured upon the multitude of keen and practised intellects labouring with power upon the public mind and character in every branch of literature and science?[36]

He deplored the lack of scientific education given in these universities: 'it is specially observable, that while the popular intellect has taken so strong a course in the direction of professional and abstract science, our Universities, and especially one of them,[37] have become comparatively unscientific.'[38] He quotes a statement from the *Spectator* of 9 December 1843 to prove his point: 'They still retain the exclusive privilege of conferring the title of "M.D.''; but who would trust his life in the hands of a physician whose medical education has been confined to Oxford and Cambridge?'[39] He concludes his Charge on this matter with the important remark 'There is the great middle class, for whom in the Universities a new and distinct provision is required'.[40] That provision he attempted to make himself, for Roman Catholics, at Kensington, and his prohibition of Oxford and Cambridge was an attempt to change by force the outlook of the Catholics. We shall write of this in more detail when we discuss his university policy; it is, however, clear that his ideas on this problem were firmly established in his Anglican days.

This same Charge of 1846 also illustrates another aspect of Manning's development. That overwhelming sympathy for the underdog, for the worthless, and for the ill-treated that he was wont to refer to as 'practical Christianity' had clearly begun to show itself. This Charge contains a savage indictment of the penal code of the day and its harsh penalties and later, after his conversion to Catholicism, it was to win him the favour of that great opponent of the convict settlements in Australia, Bishop Ullathorne of Birmingham. Referring to these penal settlements, Archdeacon Manning wrote: 'I speak in weighed and measured words when I say that our convict population is a phenomenon of carnal and spiritual wickedness, such as, I believe, the earth has never seen.'[41] He stigmatized the manner by which convicts were 'herded together by thousands in the chain-gang and the crime-class (things and names created for new mysteries of iniquity) without pastors without the means of salvation, making repentance, so far as man can, impossible, and an intense communion of mutual corruption absolutely certain'.[42] He questioned: 'Where are the thousands who from the chain-gang have gone up to meet their Judge and ours? It is not enough to say "This system will henceforward be abandoned". The blood of souls cries to heaven against us. The past is indelible, save by the great Atonement for the sin of the World. And if we could plead this, works meet for repentance must be done.'[43] As a Roman Catholic, Manning was to identify himself with all the leading movements and figures for prison reform and was himself instrumental for getting the appointment of Roman Catholic chaplains in prisons.

No Charge was written in 1847, but instead Archdeacon Manning published a pamphlet entitled: *What One Work of Mercy Can I Do This Lent? A Letter to A Friend.*[44] It is in this pamphlet that we encounter Manning's first references to Ireland, and the appalling conditions caused by famine. It was an attempt to awaken not only a sympathy but a consciousness of the condition of Ireland in the hearts and heads of his people. He wrote:

It seems almost like an imposture to read, under our warm roofs and at our well-spread boards, of the horrors of famine and disease in Ireland and the Highlands. We can hardly persuade ourselves that anywhere in Great Britain people are crying in vain for bread. Our markets are full, and our daily meals return at their hours: we feel no pinch. How then can we believe horrible tales of famine in Cork and Skibbereen? of families on one meal a day; or with no food for two days? How can people be dying on sea-weed?[45]

He goes on to extend his argument to embrace the agricultural poor and their hard lot, declaring:

Before the late rise in the price of bread brought a rise in the rate of wages, the average week's wages of the labouring poor (i.e. in the villages) was perhaps ten shillings a week. By the census it would appear that the average number in a family is five persons. Therefore our labouring poor were living, on an average of five persons, the father, mother and three children, on ten shillings a week. . . . But this is the weekly average of only one person in a moderate household. . . . The father who works has a pound of pork in the week, it may be. The wives and children live on vegetables and bread, *they keep a perpetual Lent*. . . . We need no famines afar off to waken our charity. The poor at our doors are more than enough. . . . There is a sort of sacred personality about the poor, even though unworthy and unthankful, which is to me as Himself. . . .[46]

Often Manning's statements about the poor contained a sharp rebuke to those complacent people who ignored the problem largely by refusing to concede that it existed. 'Let them eat rice if they cannot afford potatoes' was a sentiment not uncommon. This pamphlet was no exception to his general rule, and he concludes:

Let us hear no more of inducing the poor to live on rice instead of potatoes, and to consume coarse flour instead of fine. If equally nutritious, let us do it ourselves. Why force the poor man to change his few simple morsels, or cheat his chastened palate of the only food he knows? Such changes and cheats will do our fastidious palates good. But if not equally nutritious, then how dare any Christian diet a poor brother upon food he shuns himself?[47]

The Charge of 1848 was largely concerned with ecclesiastical topics but again we find him advocating that the clergy should turn their attention and energies to 'the masses in mines and factories, herding in the desolation of crowded cities'.[48] It is, therefore, clear that the majority of Manning's plans for social amelioration can be traced back to his Anglican days in Sussex. These Charges prove beyond any doubt that Manning was fully conscious of the social inequalities of his day and that his heart and mind understood the conditions and difficulties of the poor among whom he ministered. This leaning towards social improvement was nurtured by three major events in his life, his friendship with Florence Nightingale and with William Ewart Gladstone, and his years of residence at Bayswater. 'To rescue the fallen or nurse the sick was considered methodistical and unladylike'[49] and Manning from 1847 onwards was perhaps the only person that did not simply console Florence Nightingale but who urged her on to greater things. She was uncertain of her vocation in life but she realized that it was to serve humanity in some necessary and enduring way. Was it to be a nurse? Or was it to be a nun? It was here that Manning stepped into her life and guided her, almost as if he were her spiritual father. With the outbreak of the Crimean War, the light dawning on her as to her future action, he it was who encouraged her in spite of fearful opposition. While Miss Nightingale was tramping the streets of London in search of nurses, Manning was exhorting the diffident Wiseman and the cautious Bishop of Southwark to send nuns to the Crimea as nurses. 'Make the hospital a cloister and their hearts a choir',[50] Manning had told the Irish nuns who went to the Crimea, and he was invaluable as liaison officer between Miss Nightingale, the nuns and their Superiors on the one hand, and the two prelates and the War Office on the other. In the meantime he was urging Sydney Herbert,* the Minister for War, to increase the number of Roman Catholic chaplains in the Crimea.

Manning's friendship with Gladstone dated from their undergraduate days at Oxford, when they were both members of the Union, Manning being somewhat the more popular debater of the two. He had first met Gladstone in Charles Wordsworth's rooms and it was not long before the acquaintance ripened into a close friendship. In his Oxford days Manning developed Liberal tendencies. At the Union he spoke against an excessive death penalty, against unanimous juries, against slavery (although his father had pecuniary connexions with it), and against the action of the Crown in the Civil War, and he defended Lord Byron in comparison with Shelley. Perhaps the only non-Liberal motion he propounded was one attacking the proposed stability of the American Constitution. The curious fact emerges that he supported the 1832 Reform Bill before Gladstone. Among the Union orators of 1829, Manning was the most conspicuous. 'He spoke "at every meeting, on all subjects, at length, with unfailing fluency and propriety of expression". His manner . . . impressive, his self-confidence mature.'[51] It was in such circumstances that Manning's friendship with Gladstone developed. It was during these days that the future Archbishop was able to take measure of Gladstone's abilities, his innate tendencies

* Herbert was a school friend of Manning at Harrow—see Purcell, op. cit. II, p. 18.

of mind and his characteristics. It was this deep personal knowledge that stood him in great stead in the years to come.

Towards the end of his life, Manning wrote his estimate of
Gladstone's political evolution. Referring to him in an entry of his
diary for 13 December 1882,[52] he claimed: 'His course has been to
me intelligible from the first. He began as a Tory. I was always, as I
said, a Mosaic Radical. His Toryism was only a boyish and Etonian
admiration of Canning, and an intimacy with Lincoln and the like.'
In *Pastime Papers* Manning rather wistfully referred to the vagaries
of Gladstone's political life, declaring: 'Mr. Gladstone began as a
Church-and-State Tory. How he will end, who can tell? He has
disestablished one Church and may have to disestablish two more.
And for his Toryism, Mr. Bright is his godfather.'[53] The friendship
with Gladstone was unbroken, excepting for the years 1853–61 and
in the years consequent on Gladstone's polemical pamphlets against
Papal Infallibility and what he termed 'Vaticanism'.

Unlike Newman, who had never worked or lived among the poor,
Manning had spent all his priestly life among them. We have seen
how his chief concern was for them when he was Vicar of Lavington
and Archdeacon of Chichester. In the years after his conversion
to Roman Catholicism and prior to his appointment as Archbishop
of Westminster he was parish priest and Superior of the Oblates of
St. Charles at St. Mary of the Angels, Moorhouse Road, Bayswater,
London. This was one of the areas in which resided a large number
of Catholic Irish and as a consequence of this was one of the poorest
quarters of the Metropolis. Here it was that he grew to love the rich
brogue and honest sincerity of his poor Irish and it was during this
time that he gained first-hand practical experience of their abject
condition. Bayswater, today, is by no means one of the more
attractive districts of London, and the church where Manning
served, and where he afterwards claimed that he passed the most
happy years of his life,* still stands gaunt, bare and erect among a
chaos of flats, warehouses and coalyards. In the depressing and
barrack-like presbytery, with its spiral staircase and twisting corri-
dors, Manning's room can be seen, small, ordinary and austere.
Here it was that the future Cardinal held dominion over his flock
and it was from this spot that the seeds of his influence over the

---

* Leslie claims that 'they were the happiest eight years of his life'—see p. 122 of his
Life, op. cit. See also Manning's testimony quoted by Purcell, op. cit. II, p. 73, from
the Bayswater Journal for 1879.

Irish were first sown. It was here, too, that he first witnessed the evils of drink and the havoc it caused in many a poor family. It made him into a life-long Temperance advocate. It is the fruit of real personal experience that can issue in the cry '. . . who can speak for the poor? crowded and stifled in hovels where the death rate is double or even three-fold as compared with the houses of the ground landlords in the West End. My politics are social politics. . . . Such is my Radicalism, going down to the roots of the sufferings of the people.'[54] He proceeds to give the remedy—the episcopate must ally itself with the worker—and in thinking of the bishops, in an agony of doubt, he cries: 'Do they see this? Will they deliberate upon it?'[55] Manning tried to galvanize the Christian opinion of his country into action. He was willing and keen to help anybody who thought alike with him on these points, for as Lunn puts it: 'he had none of that sectarian foolishness which is always anxious to depreciate the good work of other Churches.'[56] This is well illustrated by his philanthropic schemes and his admiration for General Booth and the Salvation Army—an admiration frowned upon by his suffragan bishops. It is related [57] how Manning sent Bishop Vaughan of Salford on a tour of the houses run by the Salvation Army in London in order to convince the bishop of its greatness. Vaughan returned with the conviction that proselytism was behind the movement and told Manning so. Manning would not agree. Vaughan then indicated that he was not interested in philanthropy for its own sake; he was interested in souls not bodies; he did not love the world for its own sake. Manning's reply was as sharp as it was characteristic of his greatness: 'God so loved the World, that He sent His only begotten Son—but that is a detail.'[58] Manning had grasped that 'religion could be better served by appealing to the *minds and hearts* of the people'.[59]

Manning, whilst an Anglican, had divined why the Anglican Church seemed to be losing its hold upon the people; it had become too closely identified with the government of the day, the ruling aristocracy and the landlords.* Many of the Anglican clergymen 'were disinclined at the outset to concern themselves with the physical welfare of man; the soul was more important than the body, the future than the present'.[60] Thus the poor 'could not look to the Church for encouragement and sympathy';[61] society was not responsible for the condition of the poor, but God (in which case

* See the general tenor of his Archidiaconal Charges, quoted *passim*.

resignation to the Divine Will was preached) or the poor themselves (in which case they were told to be frugal and to work harder). The Anglican Church had become identified in many areas with 'the oppressor'. Manning had seen this and along with Gladstone had lamented it. Before he became a Roman Catholic he had realized the necessity for disestablishment of the Irish Church because it had become a symbol of oppression.* 'Poverty was divinely ordained so nothing should be done about it'[62] sums up the attitude not only of the *Christian Remembrancer* but of a large number of Anglican divines of the 1840's and 1850's. Manning's sympathies for the poor were accompanied by a belief in the moral degradation that he considered came with the acquisition of wealth. He expressed his views on this, when he wrote 'Few men are both rich and generous. Fewer are both rich and humble. Wealth, unless controlled by moral elevation, generates a mind of its own which is lofty, isolated, and if not contemptuous of others, unconscious of its own mental and moral inferiority to those whom it consciously looks down upon.'[63] Another consequence of wealth was vanity. 'This is true also', he wrote, 'of those who, having thirsted for Grosvenor Square, have at last found themselves admitted to the great world. It is too much for them; their brain reels, and they worship it with a worldliness, not to be found in inveterate worldlings.'[64]

On his conversion to Roman Catholicism, Manning discovered that he had entered into a narrow, withdrawn and aloof circle. Reviewing this condition he wrote at the end of his life the following vigorous indictment of the social awareness of his adopted Church as he had found it:

All the great works of charity in England have had their beginning out of the Church, for instance the abolition of the slave trade and of Slavery. . . . Not a Catholic name so far as I know shared in this. . . . It was a Quaker that made Father Mathew a Total Abstainer. . . . The Act of Parliament to protect animals from cruelty was carried by a non-Catholic Irishman. The Anti-Vivisection Act also. . . . The Acts to protect children from cruelty were the work of Dissenters. On these three Societies there is hardly a Catholic name. On the last mine was for long the only one. . . . There are endless works for the protection of shop assistants, overworked railway and train men, women and children ground down by sweaters, and driven by starvation wages upon the streets. Not one of the works

* 'I do not believe the Irish Established Church can stand long', he had declared to Bishop Wilberforce—see Leslie, op. cit. p. 192.

in their behalf were started by us, hardly a Catholic name is to be found on their Reports. Surely we are in the Sacristy. It is not that our Catholics deliberately refuse, but partly they do not take pains to know, partly they are prejudiced . . . unconscious that Lazarus lies at their gate full of sores.[65]

This condition whereby the Christian Church seemed to be but an *appui* of the ruling class had to be remedied, it seemed to him, in order for Christianity to survive. The Churches, Anglican and Roman Catholic, must learn to ally themselves with the people. This to him was not only a matter of policy, it was but the fulfilment of a divine injunction. He felt that, perhaps, the most certain way to achieve his purpose would be to attract the sons of the middle class and the Irish into the priesthood, instead of relying solely on the sons of the old English families and those of a like background. This broadening of the base of the priesthood had been his policy as an Anglican just as it was as a Roman Catholic. In 1846 he had written: 'The priesthood of the Church is not the inheritance of a tribe, or the heirloom of a family. Still less is it the privilege of a class, or the adjunct of any worldly condition.'[66] The infusion of a new element into the priesthood would make the Roman Catholic Church social-conscious, he felt, and his later policy in establishing a new seminary at Hammersmith instead of sending his students to St. Edmund's, Old Hall, was designed to achieve this purpose. The Roman Catholic Church, he was never tired of stating, must be brought into the full stream of national life. Manning's attitude towards Church-State relationship spread to other churches. We have seen how interested he was in the Salvation Army, and the following note from the diary of the Anglican divine and Archbishop of Canterbury, E. W. Benson, shows that his example was not lost in that direction either. Archbishop Benson recorded in his diary after Cardinal Manning had settled the Dock Strike of 1889: 'Cardinal Manning has done well in London. But why has my dear Bishop of London gone back and left it to him?'[67] Disappointment was general that Frederick Temple had given up so easily. A further Anglican testimony to the social influence of Manning is that of Archdeacon Farrar who wrote in March, 1892: 'He has left behind him a great name and a great example, and it would be well for the Church of England, if she had one or two Bishops who would learn from him how a great ecclesiastic may win the enthusiastic confidence of the working classes, and stamp his influence on the humanitarian progress of the age.'[68]

Hilaire Belloc[69] records how on one of his visits to the Cardinal, a certain phrase of Manning's impressed him by its profundity. He says that this saying 'became a searchlight' for him, and he goes on: 'with the observation of the world, and with the continuous reading of history, it came to possess for me a universal meaning so profound, that it reached to the very roots of political action.' The saying was: 'all human conflict is ultimately theological.' The phrase gives the key to all of Manning's social action and thought. For him nothing, no matter how trivial or weighty, could be divested of its theological significance. His Christianity extended to and embraced all states and conditions of human nature and existence. The remedy for social evil was an application into practice of the principles of Christianity. He had little patience with ecclesiastics, such as Newman, who could keep their Christianity in a kind of watertight compartment and remain oblivious to the world around them.* This attitude of ignoring the existence of evil in society is well illustrated by the reply of Newman to Manning who had tried to enlist the former's support for Temperance Reform. 'Newman replied "As for me, I do not know whether we have too many public houses or too few".'[70] That was the reply of an ecclesiastic living in the heart of an industrial area where the proposed reform was badly needed—Birmingham.† Manning's sermons invariably contained a social theme; Christian doctrine and social reform were for him inseparable from each other. This view pursued to its logical conclusions evoked from him statements such as this:

We must admit and accept calmly and with good will that industries and profits must be considered in second place; the moral state and domestic condition of the whole working population must be considered first. I will not venture to formulate the acts of parliament but here is precisely their fundamental principle for the future. The conditions of the lower classes as are found at present among our people, cannot and must not continue. On such a basis no social edifice can stand.[71]

These wise and far-seeing words were quoted by Cardinal Gibbons of Baltimore to Leo XIII when he was fighting against a possible papal condemnation of the Knights of Labour. They were radical

---

* Newman described London as being 'like a glimpse of the great Babylon. . . . It made me think of the words, "Love not the World nor the things of the World".' See *Letters of Archbishop Ullathorne* (Burns, Oates, 1892), p. 533.

† Newman was later to write to Ullathorne: 'I have been indoors all my life, whilst you have battled for the Church in the World.' *Letters of Archbishop Ullathorne*, op. cit. pp. 511–12, letter dated 18 August 1887.

words, and it is not surprising that Manning was accused of being a Socialist and a Utilitarian. His fellow-bishops of the bench suspected the Millite doctrine of 'the greatest happiness of the greatest number' in his words and he was accused of pandering for popularity.* His intimacy with Gladstone was cited as the origin of these ideas and the profound distrust of Gladstone in Catholic circles was plain to see. The most progressive of Manning's original suffragan bishops—Dr. Ullathorne—wrote: 'Gladstone is a man I can by no means admire, who in my mind is revolutionizing the country.'[72] The same bishop was later in 1888 to write that he told Lord Llandaff (Henry Matthews), the Home Secretary of the day, 'that the last Reform Act had prepared the ruin of England'.[73] Purcell describes Gladstone as the man who would 'attempt to wreck the unity of the Empire'.[74] On these matters Manning held views diametrically opposite.

Nowhere is Manning more outspoken than when he discusses the questions of the rights and duties of Labour. 'There is no justice, mercy or compassion in the Plutocracy. There is my creed', he wrote.[75] His was a lone voice that cried in 1874 at the Leeds Mechanics' Institute: 'I claim for Labour, and the skill which is always acquired by Labour, the rights of Capital. It is Capital in its truest sense.'† No other voice from the Roman Catholic bench of bishops or the leading laity rose in unison with his until the advent of Bishop Bagshawe of Nottingham; most bishops complained that he talked only of rights and not of duties. Ullathorne, for example, resolutely refused to meet Bright although he lived in Birmingham.

Compare Manning's prescient policy with that advocated by Vaughan, his successor, one year after Manning's death. Vaughan was speaking at the Catholic Conference of 1893 held in November of that year, and he had this to say on the condition of the poor and the working classes:

We need to make an appeal in these days to the laity, to men and women who have *leisure* and education, who have sympathy with the wants and sufferings of the *lower orders*. They must be brought into organization, and so into contact with the suffering portion of humanity in such a way

* 'Manning's contempt for public opinion in his Ultramontane battles should absolve him from the charge of mere popularity-hunting in his fight for the poor' (Lunn, A., *Roman Converts* (1924), p. 122).

† Lecture to Leeds Mechanics' Institute, later published as a pamphlet, *Rights of Labour* (1874).

as will, in the first instance, give them a clear knowledge of the wants and sufferings of the people. It is for the *rich* to show them that they are their true, hearty, and *sincere friends.*[76]

Although such condescending language is far removed from Manning's blunt speech, yet it is obvious that the latter's influence had achieved something. He had made the Hierarchy realize that the 'condition of the people' required amelioration (even though Vaughan still misguidedly thought this could be done to satisfaction by private benevolence). Private charity Manning had held to be inadequate—the poor had a right to expect help from the State. This idea was fully appreciated by more prescient Catholics than Vaughan. A writer in the *Dublin Review*, commenting on Vaughan's speech, wrote:

Men in power and authority wax eloquent when debating upon the necessity of charity to the distressed and sympathy with the sons of toil; they are even ready and anxious to loosen the purse-strings of the philanthropic and to lessen actual pressure by timely doles. This is all very well in its way, but it is no solution to the social question. The masses want justice rather than intermittent charity, and they will never be satisfied till they get it.[77]

Manning's lesson had certainly been learnt.

Manning was never a member, as such, of the 'Christian Socialist' movement. He was on friendly terms with F. D. Maurice, but not with Kingsley. He had travelled his own path of social reform because he was convinced that only such a policy could save society from destruction. The idea that society was on the verge of some terrible disaster was an idea that always haunted him—in a way that was almost pathological; it crops up again and again in his letters. If a certain course of action is not pursued, then 'I fear the worst', he would say. Writing to Gladstone, 22 September 1867, he cried: 'you know how heartily and largely my politics, if I have any, go for the people, but they go first and above all for the Christian Society of the World without which I believe the people would relapse into materialism and moral disorders of the world without God, as S. Paul has described it'.[78] Things must indeed have looked threatening to him in 1867, with the Peace Congresses, Garibaldi, the Reform League, Fenianism and Ireland looming large in his eyes.

Christianity, to Manning, was not a code of belief as much as a code of action: an intensely practical rule of life, not an intellectual proposition: it was something that had to infuse itself into all a person's actions. The clearest evidence of this belief can be seen in the matter to which he first concentrated his energy at the outset of his episcopal career—the problem of education.

Chapter II

THE SCHOOLS

★

IN any study of the social policy of a great English ecclesiastic of the second half of the nineteenth century 'the education question' must be dealt with at length. For this is the period that saw an increasing belief in the civilizing value of education, which was to result in the Education Act of 1870 and the development of state education. Cardinal Manning's policy in reference to education can be conveniently divided into three sections. The first section concerns his policy prior to the passage of the 1870 Act and, chiefly, the matter of the provision of schools. In the second section it will be seen how Manning attempted to influence the framers of the Act itself and how his attitude differed from that of many of his co-religionists in that he realized the necessity of the State's entering the field of education. There will also be traced in this section how the aftermath of the Act affected his policy, culminating in his membership of the Cross Commission. The third and final section will deal with the Archbishop's attitude towards the Universities of Oxford, Cambridge and London and with his own attempt to provide a Roman Catholic university at Kensington.

The problem in the second half of the eighteenth century and the first half of the nineteenth century caused by the rapid industrialization of England was one which came to be viewed increasingly in educational terms. More basic education was required for the new trades. In particular a knowledge of accountancy and of foreign languages became desirable and the pursuit of scientific research became a recognized characteristic of the change. It is true that this increased interest in education was one which rested largely on a utilitarian basis. Education was desired either because it enabled the following of a new trade which would carry with it increased social status, or because it was desired to undercut a rival manufacturer by the discovery of a new technique in production. The stimulus, therefore, more often than not came from the realms of industry and there was a consequent concentration on 'the useful' and more mechanical aspects of knowledge.

26

But the impetus was by no means entirely utilitarian; more often it was moral and philanthropic. When in 1802 Sir Robert Peel passed the first Factory Act—the 'Health and Morals of Apprentices Act'—he did so largely from moral and philanthropic motives. The Act was not a great success because it did not contain any clauses for enforcement. From 1802 to 1878 there was a steady stream of acts designed to protect children in factories. The 1819 Act contained no provision for enforcement, but the Act of 1833 was enforced. This latter is important because it was the first attempt at compulsion by the Government on behalf of the moral and material welfare of the population. The Factory Acts, however, with their regulations made it impossible for domestic industry, which depended so much on child labour, to continue and thus they accelerated the process of industrialization. (Marx contended that the Factory Acts created the mill-owners as the 'nouveaux riches'.)

The working-classes wanted the ability to talk, to argue, to get into politics. For proof of this assertion we have only to see the rapidity of the growth of the Mechanics' Institutes all over England —a growth stimulated by the Nonconformist Academies and one which kept apace with the industrialization process. This desire became more urgent with the passing of the Second Reform Bill by Disraeli in 1867 which gave votes to all householders in the towns and, consequently, to many working men, and with the passage of the Third Reform Bill in 1884 by Gladstone which extended the franchise to all householders in country districts.

The extension of the franchise concentrated the attention of the politicians on the fact that the electorate must be educated in order to use their vote sensibly and to be able to appreciate and understand political policies. 'We must educate our masters', declared Robert Lowe.

In addition to these moral, philanthropic, industrial and political reasons for the sudden increase of interest in education in the 1840's and 50's, it is possible to discern certain philosophic influences at work. This is particularly recognizable in Jeremy Bentham and his disciples—Chadwick, James Mill and John Stuart Mill. The Utilitarian philosophy of the greatest happiness of the greatest number and the search for this happiness (the hedonistic calculus) led increasingly to the belief that happiness was only to be obtained through the medium of education. To be happy, it was contended, it was necessary to work for the improvement of one's social position—but to obtain this one must obtain a higher form of employment, to obtain which in its turn education was necessary. Education, therefore, became the gateway to a better and easier life and to happiness. The philosophy found practical exposition in 1869 with the publication of Bain's *Education as a Science*.

But in addition to Benthamite philosophy, the Idealist movement stimulated the existing trends. The inspiration was taken from von Humboldt who influenced Matthew Arnold. The greatest Idealist was T. H. Green and after the publication of Arnold's *Culture and Anarchy* in 1869 the movement gained many converts. To the Idealist the State was the great educator whose duty it was to provide education for the people. On the other hand, the Utilitarian believed in the individual search for knowledge with the least interference from the State. In the conflict between the Utilitarian and Idealist philosophies we see foreshadowed the struggles of the 1870 Act between the individualist and family-rights group and that which asserted it was both the right and the duty of the State to provide adequate educational facilities for the masses.

During the nineteenth century it became increasingly obvious that the historical significance of education had begun to be appreciated. The historians of the period saw in education a means whereby 'the silent social revolution' was accomplished and society renewed itself. It was regarded as creating an escape-hatch or a safety valve for society. It created a middle class which prevented the poor and the rich from coming into open conflict. The poor man by dint of education and hard work might eventually gain access for his children into the middle class and a middle-class, wealthy man might marry his daughter to an impoverished aristocrat and thus make sure his grand-children were to grow up in the top stratum of society. Thus revolutionary conflict was avoided and society continually renewed itself. The nineteenth-century historian contended that revolutions only occurred (as in France in 1789) where the class boundaries were too rigid and where it was almost impossible to gain admission to a more privileged level of society. Education was to be the antidote to revolution. T. B. Macaulay was perhaps the first historian to notice this connexion. He was vitally interested in the problem of education and during the years 1834-8 had largely devoted himself to the task of organizing Indian education. J. R. Green followed this lead and pointed the way to a real study of the historical significance of education. Carlyle saw the connexion, but to him history was 'the essence of innumerable biographies'; but for Buckle the environment, and education in itself, was the dominant historical lesson. This central idea is perhaps most clearly discernible in the writings of Henry Hallam, the noted Whig historian. His *Constitutional History of England from the Accession of Henry VII to the Death of George II* (1st edn. 1827) was highly popular. Hallam condemned Queen Anne because her 'understanding and fitness for government were below mediocrity'—she lacked education. He argued whether 'a thoroughly . . . enlightened man' would have enlisted on the Royal or the Parliamentary side in the Civil War. Throughout his work is the implication that education is necessary for the work of government and hence for stability and for making just and right decisions. As the century wore on the connexion between education and a stable society came to be more deeply appreciated and understood.

The Churches were caught up in the tide of the Industrial Revolution and they soon found (especially the Established Church) that they could not keep pace with the new towns. In 1808 the British and Foreign Schools Society was founded, in which Joseph Lancaster applied the principles of factory organization to schools and which was characterized by a bitter hatred of the Establishment, and in 1811 the Church of England retaliated by founding the National Society, which employed the Monitorial System of the Rev. Andrew Bell. These two societies largely monopolized elementary education down to 1870. The Roman Catholics entered the field of elementary education much later. Cardinal Wiseman in 1851 formed the Catholic Poor Schools Society on the principles of the other two societies. This society dealt directly with the Government on the education question and had at its head Charles Langdale and later the convert Thomas Allies. Wilfrid Ward declares that between 1848 and 1863 the Catholic schools, through the medium of this committee, received £239,757 in all. In addition it won the right to have Catholic school inspectors paid by the Government and to set up Reformatories and Industrial Schools.

Since 1833 the National Society and the British and Foreign Schools Society had received grants from the Treasury, and from 1839 the Roman Catholics became eligible for the grants of the Committee of the Privy Council on Education, set up in that year. The teaching in the Catholic schools was copied from the system of Bell and Lancaster 'as modified by the Christian Brothers of France and Ireland'.[1] The provision of education was perhaps more urgent for the Catholics than for the other two societies. This was largely because of the tens of thousands of Irish immigrants swelling the ranks of the poor Catholics in England. The chief problem was that of finance. The Irish famine of the forties filled the workhouses with both orphaned and deserted children and they received little instruction. It was, therefore, incumbent on Wiseman to make some provision for this great influx of destitute and pauper children. It would be untrue to say that he did not make a start on the problem. The Catholic Poor Schools Committee was set up in 1851, as we have seen, to receive Privy Council grants, and in 1855 Wiseman opened the first Catholic Reformatory for boys at Hammersmith and the first Industrial School for boys at Walthamstow. Both received Home Office certification. A Training College for men teachers was opened at Hammersmith in 1850 (and existed until 1947). Wiseman's chief problem was to make sure of an equitable share of the Privy Council grants.

This was the situation inherited by Manning in 1865 when he succeeded to the direction of the Roman Catholic Church in England. But he also inherited a different intellectual atmosphere. During his first five years as Archbishop a notable philosophical change in tone and temper began to take place in England. The philosophy of Utilitarianism was changing into Positivism. They both stimulated the scientific movement, a movement whose impact on the Churches in general was revolutionary, and on Manning's educational policy paramount, and in a sense they were both expressions of that movement. Both Utilitarianism and Positivism accepted the methods of science as the correct approach to speculative thought. Positivism, however, differed from Utilitarianism in that Comte attempted to preserve Christianity as an emotional religion while rejecting its dogmas. God was no longer to be worshipped, but Humanity. The nineteenth century was the age of the great positivists—Richard Congreve, Harriet Martineau, George Henry Lewes, George Eliot and Frederick Harrison. Their worship of Humanity resulted in a desire for social reform, the organization of labour (and, later, the English Labour Party was to owe more to them than to Karl Marx).*

* See J. Martineau's *Types of Ethical Theory* (1885) and his *Study of Religion* (1888).

There is little doubt that Manning was influenced by Positivism—in so far as its social implications were concerned. He found it more attractive than Utilitarianism; it was less negative and self-seeking and called for heroic qualities. He had, of course, no sympathy with its theological implications.

In 1830-3, Sir Charles Lyell published his *Principles of Geology*, a work which not only created geology as a science but which hit at the very roots of Evangelical theology. The impact of this blow was driven home with Darwin's *Origin of Species* and, in 1863, his *Antiquity of Man*, and again by Spencer ruthlessly applying the theory of evolution to history and politics. Even Newman's *Development of Christian Doctrine* (1845) implied the evolutionary theory. The extraordinary ferment which these discoveries caused in society resulted in terms of abuse—Rationalist, Atheist, Agnostic —being hurled at anyone and everyone who did not conform to rigid orthodoxy in religion. These scientific theories came into vogue at a time, as we have seen, when the Industrial Revolution had created a thirst (and a market) for scientific discovery.

Manning's reign began, therefore, in a period of great excitement and a great thirst for knowledge and discovery, in a period when the churches were thrown upon the defensive and when they were in great danger of losing their hold upon the new middle class that was arising. He at once recognized the magnitude of the problem and began by turning his attention to the work of providing schools and orphanages, first for the poor, and then for the middle class.*

At the outset of Manning's career as Archbishop, certain 'Old Catholics' (in particular Sir Charles Clifford) approached him to say that they had collected a large sum of money for the building of a cathedral in memory of the late Cardinal Wiseman.[3] They asked Manning to preside at a public meeting when the money would be handed to him. This meeting was held at Willis's Rooms and to the surprise of Lord Petre, the Earl of Gainsborough, and Clifford, Manning devoted most of his speech to the subject of the

---

*A. C. F. Beales contends that as early as 1847 (presumably while a priest at Bayswater) Manning founded the first Catholic orphanage.[2] This is an erroneous date; Manning did not become a Roman Catholic until 6 April 1851. He took up residence at Bayswater in 1857, so presumably Mr. Beales intends to refer to that date. The fact remains, however, that he did establish the first Catholic orphanage and from this beginning the problem of education was to prove ever foremost in his mind.

uneducated poor Catholic children of London (estimated by him at twenty thousand). He talked of them as 'destitute, uncared for, untaught, running wild in the streets, without knowledge of the faith, a prey to apostasy or immorality'.* Sir Charles Clifford immediately called Manning to order and remarked that the meeting had been arranged to consider the projected cathedral. 'The education of the children was beside the mark.'⁴ £16,000 was handed in as a first instalment Despite the rebuke from Clifford it was soon evident that Archbishop Manning did not intend to pursue the building of a cathedral. He wrote in his Journal:

One idea has governed me. I believe, in fact, I learned it from Carlyle. I mean that mechanism without dynamics is dead. . . . I bought the land . . . and some thousands are given and others left for the building. But could I leave 20,000 children without education, and drain my friends and my flock to pile up stones and bricks? . . . My successor may begin to build a cathedral.⁵

Knowing that he was about to give offence to the 'Old Catholic' families, Manning deliberately set aside their pet scheme in favour of the children of the despised Irish poor. To many Manning's action appeared plainly dishonest.

It is significant for his future policy that when Manning issued his first Pastoral Letter only two weeks after his consecration,† it dealt with education in his diocese. He wrote in this: 'Help us in gathering from the streets of this great wilderness of men the tens of thousands of poor Catholic children who are without instruction or training. It is our first appeal to you. But it will not be our last.'‡ He was later to claim that the poor people responded magnificently; the 'Old Catholics' remained unconcerned. After commenting on the magnificent efforts the Jews were making in the East End of London, he asked what certain Catholics were doing, adding sarcastically: 'Oh, I forgot; they are examining their consciences or praying.'⁶

Approximately four months after issuing his first episcopal letter Manning sent out a second one on the same subject, in which he said that on his visit to Rome to receive the Pallium from Pius IX he had obtained the Pope's special blessing and admonition for his work for the education of poor children.

---

* Purcell, op. cit. II, p. 353. It is interesting to observe that Manning advocated education as a cure for 'immorality' and crime.

† 8 June 1865.   ‡ Pastoral preserved in the Bayswater collection.

His most notable Pastoral Letter, however, was issued on 8 June 1866, the first anniversary of his consecration. This caused much controversy among Catholics and Protestants alike and Manning was handled roughly by the Press. It will be necessary to quote at some length from this Pastoral in order to understand the question at issue and the reasons for the controversy:[7]

Every Diocese has local and particular duties and works which press their full weight upon it, and such as can be discharged by no central body whatsoever. The multiplication and maintenance of the local and parochial or Mission Schools must rest upon each Mission and each Diocese. The Poor School Committee assists according to its power in such local needs; but obviously it is unable to do more than give in a proportion hardly appreciable. . . . It is therefore to create a Central Diocesan Fund, from which the Missions may be assisted, that you are invited to attend a public meeting of which notice has been already given, for the 14th of June next.

It is not necessary at this time to enter into the details of this subject. It will be enough to say that a Trust will be created for the receiving, holding and transmitting of funds, and a Council to advise us in the application of the same.

It may be safely affirmed that thousands of Catholic children in London are without education. Two very careful and guarded calculations have been lately made of the number who may be said to be practically without education. One of these estimates them at twelve thousand, the other at seven thousand.

If in any one place a thousand Catholic children without education were to be seen together, we should be horrified. But though scattered, they exist, and they are destitute as if they were all congregated in one of our maze of courts.

There is also a second class of our children for whom we must provide, namely, those who fall under the operation of Law for offences, or are committed as friendless and abandoned.

But, lastly, there is a class of our poor children of which we hardly know how to speak. It is believed that more than a thousand of our Catholic children are detained in the workhouses and workhouse schools of London. . . . The education is exclusively Protestant.

Time compels us to pass over all other topics. The agony and bitterness of Catholic fathers and mothers, who had rather see their children in a parish coffin than in a Poor Law School . . .—all this and much beside we must pass over.

It will be seen from the above that Manning's work for poor children was to be divided into three specific categories: the

4

provision of schools for the uneducated; the provision of reformatories, industrial schools, and orphanages; and, thirdly, the 'rescuing'
of Roman Catholic children from the workhouses. Only in the last
category did the question of religious proselytism enter, and it was
this that aroused the ire of the Press and notably *The Times* which
was always hostile to Manning—as we shall see when we deal with
Ireland. *The Times* of 12 June 1866 spoke very favourably about
the Pastoral in so far as it dealt with (*a*) the education of the Catholic
poor children and (*b*) the proposed provision for those children
who came under the law or the police. When it came to the third
category, it had this to say:

> It is when we come to a third class of poor children that Dr. Manning
> suddenly . . . leaves the region of facts and common sense and friendly
> co-operation and plunges into a haze where nothing can be distinctly
> recognized. There are, he says, or rather says it is believed—by whom,
> he says not—more than a thousand Roman Catholic children in the London
> workhouses and workhouse schools . . . where they are brought up with
> exclusively Protestant books, catechisms, prayers, teachers, and worship.
> This he describes as a denial of right . . . . What the Pastoral comes to . . .
> is simply this, that there are good Protestant philanthropists ready to
> take in hand young Catholic vagrants and delinquents unable to find a
> shelter in their own communion, and that, in one way or another, nobody
> can say how, a thousand children of Roman Catholic parents, many of
> them mere babes, are in Protestant schools and workhouses. What is the
> grievance? . . . It is the great rule of this country that people must help
> themselves and take care of themselves, both individually and in classes
> and sects. . . . The weak will always go to the wall, unless they have friends
> to watch over them, and do something for them. Dr. Manning and
> his friends appear not to lack either activity or business habits. Let
> them organize a system of protection for the poor, to see either that
> they are kept out of the workhouses, or that, once in, they are not
> compelled to change their faith. The British public has not over-much
> confidence in those dismal institutions, and if the Roman Catholic
> Hierarchy will insist on letting the daylight into them, they will be well
> backed.[8]

This article undoubtedly irritated by its smugness but at the
same time stung by its truth. There was little use in lamenting the
numbers of Catholic children in the workhouse schools if the
Catholics themselves were unable to supply any alternative provision. Manning at once saw the justice of the article and on 14
June 1866, at the public meeting which he had called for in his

Pastoral in order to establish the Westminster Diocesan Education Fund, he referred to *The Times* article. He pointed out that the solution was not so simple as *The Times* suggested. How could the Catholics be sure that if they provided the alternative institutions, the children would be transferred to them? To prove this point he mentioned the fact that the Catholics had already in existence industrial schools at North Hyde and Norwood but that great difficulty had been experienced in obtaining the transfer of children. He declared:

> In the year 1859 Mr. Stokes, Government Inspector of Public Schools, but then Secretary of the Poor Schools, by the direction of my predecessor, entered into correspondence with the Marylebone Board of Guardians, with the view of getting them to send the Catholic children in the workhouse to North Hyde or Norwood. . . . He offered to take all the children from the workhouse upon the payment of a certain sum per head from the Guardians; but the answer which he received was that the Guardians had no legal power to comply with his request. It was admitted that there were at the time forty-six Catholic children in the establishment. Mr. Stokes wrote again requesting to be referred to the Act of Parliament under which the Guardians were legally incapable of delivering up the children, and the reply which he received was that they had no further answers to return. I ought to mention that an offer was made that the education of the children should be under the inspection of whoever the Guardians might appoint to the office, but, notwithstanding that, the application was not entertained.[9]

This attitude of the Guardians, it was later to become evident, was by no means an uncommon one. The bigotry and religious rivalry of so many of the Boards was one of the reasons why Manning was later to doubt the wisdom of the Government setting up School Boards under the 1870 Act. He was afraid they would be merely an excuse for sectarian squabbles.

In the same speech, Manning went on to illustrate this attitude further:

> An Act was obtained by Mr. Lyall (in 1864) by which schools might be certified as Industrial Schools under the Poor Law. Immediately that the Act came into operation, our schools at North Hyde and Norwood were certified as schools in connection with the Poor Laws, and application was made to ten or twelve unions in London for the removal of the Catholic children to the institutions upon the payment of the capitation fee already mentioned, and subject to the inspection of the Poor Law authorities, but, as before, it ended in an absolute refusal.[10]

Referring more directly to the article in *The Times*, he continued: I admit that I am not able to give the names, ages and parents of the total number of Catholic children who are to be found in the workhouses; but then I do not know their names, I do not know where they are, I have no access to them, and I do not know where to find them, and as their Bishop, I cannot confirm them. Now, this is my grievance, I think it is a great grievance.[11]

The meeting was held in St. James's Hall on 14 June 1866, and after speaking of the case of the workhouse children Manning proposed more specific remedies. He said that there were approximately from seven thousand to twelve thousand Roman Catholic children in London who received no education whatsoever—a state of affairs which he ascribed to 'the poverty of the Catholic population'.[12] He estimated that a minimum of thirty-five new schools must be built in London. That was the first problem. Secondly, he said that at least two new reformatories and two additional industrial schools must be built in the Diocese to accommodate those falling under the law or into the hands of the police. He concluded: 'If as I have reason to expect, the justice of Englishmen, and the equity of Parliament will enable us to obtain from the workhouse schools the entire number of Catholic children, whether it be under or over one thousand, we ought to have doors open to receive them.'[13] In this latter case he was empowered by Bishop Grant of Southwark to act for his diocese as well.*

The outcome of the meeting was the foundation of the Westminster Diocesan Education Fund. Manning drew up the headings under which the Trustees were to make grants. They are interesting as illustrating the order of importance in which Manning placed his projects, viz.:[14]

1. Mission Schools;
2. Diocesan Schools;
3. Encouragement of Masters and Pupil Teachers;
4. Education of Destitute Children;
5. Miscellaneous Grants to Schools;
6. The Maintenance of the Diocesan Inspector and Secretary of the Fund.

Under *Mission Schools*, would be included all parish elementary

---

* Dr. Grant, after negotiations, was only too willing to make over to Manning the trouble and ill-will the workhouse campaign would entail.

schools, which would of course be eligible for Privy Council grants. *Diocesan Schools* would embrace all certified schools, such as industrial and Poor Law schools, reformatories, Rescue Homes, orphanages. The third category would refer to the financing of the Hammersmith Training College and grants to intending teachers. The fourth category is concerned with the workhouse children. These latter were 'practically received "in statu naturae", as the messenger who brought them from the workhouse took back with him the workhouse clothes in which the child had come'.

It can, therefore, be seen that those who would assert that Manning's educational work for poor children was influenced solely by the considerations of religious bigotry are misguided. The 'rescuing' of children from Protestant workhouses was placed fourth in his list. The provision of education for the uneducated occupied the first three places. The children in the workhouse schools were receiving some instruction; they could, therefore, wait until the children who were receiving no instruction whatsoever were first provided for. Naturally, this attitude aroused opposition among some Roman Catholic groups who felt that the Archbishop was placing the things of Caesar before the things of God. Although the Archbishop's policy was based on a sectarian core, it was not narrowly interpreted and possessed much wider social implications.

While Talbot was not in many ways typical of English Roman Catholic opinion, he did give expression to a belief widely held when he declared to Manning on this point: 'I have always taken the greatest interest in the poor of London, but always in order to save their souls, not merely to make them more respectable members of society. . . . It is putting this world before the next.'[15]

To Manning a human being was a *soul-body*, to be treated as a whole. He was wont to assert that a soul without a body was a spirit, whereas a body without a soul was a corpse. One cannot work for the improvement of one element and ignore the other. Talbot's distinction was to Manning merely the worst kind of hypocrisy and an excuse for doing nothing. Physical well-being was a first stepping-stone to spiritual well-being.

Manning soon collected £6,000 to form his Diocesan Fund. At the meeting we have described, he collected £1,200 and received postal donations of £2,200 and annual subscriptions promised a yearly total of £2,300. In addition collections were to be held

periodically in all churches of the Diocese for the fund. It is significant that Lord Petre, Stafford, and Edward Howard were the
only members of the aristocratic families that came forward to
Manning with offers of active help. The Cliffords were conspicuously
absent.*

Manning's administrative genius in centralizing diocesan efforts
was particularly happy. There is little doubt, however, that the
system would have been extended to the whole country and a
national fund established but for the opposition he knew it would
receive from certain members of the Hierarchy (notably Clifford,
Goss, and Brown of Newport) in their tenacity to keep under their
personal control all diocesan matters and their jealousy of supposed
infringements on their jurisdiction. Even the sensible Ullathorne
was small-minded in this respect.† Manning regarded it as a great
success that Grant of Southwark had allowed him to act for that
diocese as well as his own in the matter of the workhouse children—
and this had only been obtained after Manning had given the most
stringent promises of secrecy that the rest of the Hierarchy should
not learn of the arrangement. Under these conditions it is little
wonder that the Westminster fund never reached national proportions.
The consequence was, of course, that the Westminster Diocese was
leaps ahead of any others in the provision of education by Manning's
death. It was ten years after Manning's establishment of the
Westminster fund before a tentative beginning in grappling with
the problems of education in the Salford Diocese (under Bishop
Vaughan) occurred. Vaughan was a disciple of Manning and at this
time his devoted admirer and imitator. It was not until the death of
Manning that the Diocese of Liverpool became thoroughly awake
to its educational responsibilities.

Only one year after the setting up of the Westminster fund,
Manning was able to announce, in his first annual report, that
twenty day schools had been opened and that 1,100 extra children
were receiving education for the first time.

There is no written record to prove the effect Manning had on
the obtaining of the Reformatory and Industrial Schools Acts of

---

* See records of subscriptions of the Poor School Committee and the Westminster
Diocesan Education Fund at the H.Q. of the Catholic Education Council, Westminster,
and at Archbishop's House, Westminster: *passim*.

† See Butler, *The Life & Times of Bishop Ullathorne, 1806–1889* (B.O.W., 1926) II
pp. 145–6. (Refers to Croke-Robinson's appointment at Kensington.)

1866, but there is little doubt that the great publicity given by Manning both in the Press and in his Pastorals to the plight of Roman Catholic children in the workhouses and the great publicity which followed his successful organizing of the Westminster Diocesan Education Fund had a great impact on the minds of politicians. Manning had created an organized demand for equitable treatment for his co-religionists and had given, in public, palpable proof of the religious intolerance of many Boards of Guardians. His influence must have counted for much in obtaining this legislation. The Reformatory and Industrial Schools Acts of 1866 not only enjoined that delinquent and destitute children who were Roman Catholics should be brought up in Catholic denominational institutions, but also that the latter should be rate-aided. 'From then onwards the task—at times a most bitter struggle—was to persuade anti-Catholic Boards of Guardians to transfer Catholic children.'[16] Before 1870 Manning had established a large industrial school at Ilford in Essex, opened a large reformatory for boys, known as St. Edward's, East Ham, and commenced a third industrial school for boys at Hammersmith.* Reformatories were in existence at Liverpool and Bristol for girls and Manning thought it better to utilize these, rather than keep the girls in London. He seems to have been under the peculiar impression that Bristol and Liverpool were not as corrupt as London. Perhaps the finest reformatory in the country was that set up by the Cistercian monks of Mount St. Bernard Abbey at Charnwood Forest, near Leicester. These monks, at Manning's special request, undertook to take approximately a hundred boys of the worst type off Manning's hands and take care of them in the country, teaching them a trade. The system of training there became a model for the generation and received glowing tributes from Manning and occasional visits. It won the most enthusiastic praise from Charles Dickens, perhaps the shrewdest of observers and critics, who visited the Abbey on two occasions and who was greatly impressed, as the following extracts show. The reformatory had been in existence in Wiseman's time and Dickens's visits date from this earlier period. On his first visit in 1857 he wrote:

In going through these rooms as I consider the faces that pass before me, it seems unnatural to believe, although I know it for a fact, that all these lads are criminals in greater or lesser degree, and that many of

* One had been established at Walthamstow in Wiseman's time.

them have been in jail several times before being sent here—so open, fearless and honest do they look.[17]

And two years later, on a second visit, he wrote:

Games are going on as we enter [i.e. Dickens and Fr. Lawrence, O.C.R., his guide], and the large courtyard is ringing with merriment; but no sooner are we perceived than the game is broken up, and with loud shouts, all the players rush towards my companion, pressing round him, calling out his name, seizing his hand, literally striving to 'touch the hem of his garment'; never have I seen such enthusiasm and affection![18]

In addition to this outstanding testimony, the government inspector writing about Manning's own foundation—St. Nicholas's Industrial School at Ilford—said it was 'easily the best of the Industrial Schools'.[19]

The Reformatory and Industrial Schools Acts of 1866 did not remove the onus from the voluntary bodies for the foundation of such schools and thus a heavy financial burden was laid upon the voluntary societies. The situation was to become critical in 1870 when along with the School Boards came a corresponding increase in the candidates for this type of education. It was some little time after the passing of the 1866 Acts before the Roman Catholics were able to effect the transfer of children from the Poor Law authorities.

Manning, however, was shrewd enough to realize that the provision and staffing of all the Poor Law schools necessary for the diocese was well-nigh impossible because of the financial situation. The Catholics were poor and such schools could *not* be maintained on the pennies of the poor. The only solution from the *impasse* was, he thought, to get those Religious Orders of men and women who were interested in the poor to open such schools at their own cost, maintain them—with a little help from the Westminster fund— and staff them with members of their own Communities. The latter, holding a vow of poverty, would not require wages and thus an immense saving in finance would be accomplished. He therefore set about systematically to lure such Orders into his diocese. From 1865 to Manning's death in 1892, a galaxy of these Religious Orders made their appearance in the diocese. The outstanding work was done by the Sisters of Charity who soon had built a school at Mill Hill, London, which accommodated two hundred boys and which did not cost Manning a penny, and they rapidly set to work in a similar school at Leytonstone. The Sisters of Mercy agreed to begin an industrial school for girls at Eltham (again without financial help from the diocese), and before 1870, industrial schools for girls had been set up at Finchley and Isleworth and Poor Law schools for girls at Hammersmith, Totteridge, Homerton, Portobello Road and Hampstead—all of which were staffed by nuns.* The Poor Servants of the Mother of God established an industrial school for girls at Tower Hill. Similar educational work was undertaken by the Poor School Sisters of Notre Dame at Southend and Woolwich, by the Servites at Stamford Hill, London, and by the Daughters of the Cross of Liège at Chelsea. It can be seen, therefore, that Manning's policy in this respect was an outstanding success. The influx of Religious Congregations of nuns posed difficulties at first and many English Catholics objected to the rapidity of their expansion. Another source of complaint was that so many of the nuns were foreign, and especially French. The arrival of French nuns developed into a steady stream after the enactment of the anti-clerical laws of the French Republican, Jules Ferry,† and the closing down of convents and monasteries. But it is certain that without Manning's encouragement of these women it would have been financially impossible to carry out his educational policy. It was a far-sighted policy and one which yielded rich fruits.

The work for boys was not neglected, either. In addition to those schools already mentioned, Manning took over the Orphanage of the Brothers of Charity of St. Vincent de Paul at Hammersmith in 1875, an institution which owed much to the indefatigable energy of St. George Mivart, and the Rev. Lord Archibald Douglas was placed in charge. It was moved to the Harrow Road and Manning later placed it under the control of the Oblates of St. Charles, the Congregation of which he himself had been a member. Over seven hundred boys passed through this house before 1875. Meanwhile the Cardinal placed Father William Barry, a distinguished theologian and a secular priest of his diocese, on full-time work for orphans. He opened a Home in the East End in 1889 and later four others, including one at Stepney and one at Enfield.

This work assumes heroic proportions when we consider that, in

* See Peter F. Anson, *The Religious Orders and Congregations of Great Britain and Ireland* (Worcester, 1949), *passim*; and F. M. Steele, *The Convents of Great Britain* (1925), *passim*.

† Ferry became Prime Minister of France in September 1880 and fell in 1885.

spite of the agreement with Dr. Grant of Southwark, that prelate had defaulted on his part of the bargain and had neither built schools nor made any attempt to provide funds to aid Manning in the 'rescue' of Southwark children. When Grant died in Rome in 1870, his successor James Danell proved even more awkward and, although he promised to contribute his fair share of the building programme, in fact never did so. On Danell's death in 1881 Manning succeeded in getting his great personal friend, Father Robert A. Coffin, C.SS.R., appointed but, although he began to remedy the defections of his predecessors, he died a year and a half later. It was, therefore, left to Bishop Butt to carry out the agreement. It was only with his accession in 1885 that the Diocese of Southwark assumed responsibility for its children and tackled the problem in earnest. It was a great help to Manning, now that he was at long last able to get financial help for the children of the area south of the Thames. Butt in 1887 set up the Southwark Catholic Rescue Society.

Manning tried to galvanize the rest of his suffragan sees into action, but on the whole (with the exceptions of Leeds, Nottingham and Salford) was not very successful. Wherever he saw signs that a bishop was willing to undertake this kind of social work, he was always ready with his advice and help. An example of this can be found in Liverpool. The Bishop of Liverpool had allowed the Brothers of the Christian Schools to open an industrial school in Liverpool in 1866. The Government Inspector, the Rev. Sydney Turner, refused to give a certificate to the school because it was run by a Religious Order. Bishop Goss did not know what action to take and (through Fr. Nugent) brought the matter to the notice of Manning for his advice and help. Manning at once sought a personal interview with Mr. Turner. At first the latter was adamant, but he had an equally adamant opponent. Manning won the day and the school got into its stride armed with a certificate—although Mr. Turner said that this was not to be regarded as a precedent for the future.* This is only one example of Manning's willingness to help, beyond the confines of his own diocese.

We come now to the policy of the 'rescuing' of the Catholic children in the workhouses. The struggle went on unabated for seventeen years after Manning issued his famous Pastoral Letter in June 1866. Manning's Pastoral had undoubtedly aroused public

---

* For the whole incident in detail see Bennett, op. cit. p. 565 et seq.

interest, especially when *The Times* had devoted much space to it
and when Manning later replied to that newspaper's argument.
The Poor Law Amendment Act of 1866 stated that

any parent, step-parent, nearest adult relative, or next of kin of a child
not belonging to the Established Church relieved in a Workhouse or
District School . . . (or failing these) then the God-parent of such a child
may make application to the said Board (Poor Law Board) in such behalf,
and the Board may, if they think fit, order that such child shall be sent
to some school established for the reception, maintenance, and education of children of the religion to which such child shall be proved to
belong.

This was, it is tempting to think, a direct outcome of Manning's
great agitation. The Guardians were to pay such charges as the Poor
Law Board ordered. But even so the Act was a dead letter, as each
case would have had to be investigated separately and Manning
had shown that the Guardians were reluctant to deliver the children,
even going so far as to assert that they had changed their religion.

Perhaps the most outstanding factor in Manning's opposition to
the kind of education given to Catholic children in the Protestant
Workhouse and District Schools was his deep belief in the absolute
irreconcilability of a non-Catholic and a Catholic education. In view
of the later troubles in 1870, it might be of use to examine in what
Manning considered this irreconcilability to consist. In other words,
what was the distinctive feature of a Roman Catholic education,
in order to obtain which Manning thought so many sacrifices were
worth while? Was it concerned solely with sectarian advantage?
There is no doubt that the most obvious reason for his advocacy
of a Roman Catholic education *was* sectarian—namely that it was
intended to produce good and knowledgeable Roman Catholics,
understanding and practising their religion. But if we probe deeper
than the surface we find what is still talked of as 'a Roman Catholic
attitude towards education'—in other words, we discover a philosophical reason. The eighteenth century had been the century of the
Utilitarian philosophy of life—a philosophy we examined at the
beginning of this chapter. It persisted well into the nineteenth
century, until it gave birth to the idea of secular education. *Secular*
education implied a certain view of the *purpose* of education.
Education meant to both the Utilitarian and the Secularist a training
for *life*; a means of bettering one's social position, of obtaining a
more satisfying employment, a mechanism whereby one could

reduce the number of pains and increase the number of pleasures. On the other hand, to a Roman Catholic like Manning, education meant a training for *death*. As Mr. H. O. Evennett of Trinity College, Cambridge, has expressed it: 'Death and original sin are the constants in the light of which the Catholic Church surveys humanity.'[20] This life was but a preparation for the life to come, therefore the values of the future life were of primary importance, the values of this life of secondary importance. 'If education is what remains after we have forgotten all we learnt at school, the quintessential left by a Catholic education is a lasting consciousness of the fact and the meaning of death.'[21] Death was not 'some unhappy, inexplicable fatality which blots the fair cosmic landscape, and the mention of which embarrasses their [the children's] elders, but the appointed gateway to the next life, through which all must pass at some moment not of their own choosing'.[22] In fact, character, moral virtues and intellectual abilities were all fostered in a Roman Catholic education with *death* as the end in view, they were the means which the individual must employ in accordance with Christian law in order to attain 'self-realization in and through the Beatific Vision in an eternal happiness'.[23] In other words, a Roman Catholic education was permeated by a peculiar philosophical and religious atmosphere, which was missing elsewhere.

From this brief consideration, it can be seen how truly irreconcilable would be the Roman Catholic concept of education in Manning's mind with that of the Utilitarian or Secularist or non-Catholic attitude. Both dealt with different values and both were working for different ends. Manning's attitude towards the workhouse children, as well as towards the role of the State in education, was coloured by these views. Unless they are understood and appreciated, his policy appears meaningless and narrow. A Roman Catholic child not educated in a Roman Catholic school was, to Manning, likely to misunderstand the meaning and purpose of life and to organize his life in reference to a set of secondary and basically unimportant values. This attitude of his was later to crystallize into the two demands of the right of the parent to have his child educated according to his conscience and secondly that his education should not cost him more than his neighbour who sent his child to a State (or Secularist) school. Before the intervention of the State in 1870, however, Manning's fight was against bigotry and indolence—and after 1870 against 'State-ism'.

Manning's continued campaign and agitation led on 5 February 1867 to a demand in Parliament for a return to be made 'of the number of Roman Catholic children received into the Workhouses of the Metropolitan District during the last seven years, specifying whether they had been retained in the same, or discharged, or transferred to District Schools; together with the names of these schools'.[24] The returns proved to be a shock for Manning, in that there were considerably more children than he expected. At least 1,708 Catholic children were in the schools and this number did not include the children retained by those Boards of Guardians who had failed (contrary to the law) to keep Creed Registers. Of all these children only four had been transferred to Catholic schools on request. The state of affairs which this return showed led to Parliament strengthening the powers of the Local Government Board as set out in the 1866 Act quoted. The Board was now given the power to *compel* the Guardians to transfer a child from the Poor Law school to a Catholic school, should the parent, or next of kin, or God-parent of the child request it. What is more, the Guardians were to be ordered to pay 6s. a week towards the maintenance of such a child in the Catholic school. As Manning let it be known that he was willing to accept less than the 6s. fee (in some cases 5s. and in rare cases 4s.) the Guardians were desirous of transferring the child before application was made by the next of kin to the Local Government Board (because they would then have to pay 6s. a week). Transfer was therefore facilitated. Even so, one or two Boards of Guardians would not yield until forced.

That Manning was able to exert great influence in making sure that the Poor Law Bill of 1868 was passed can be shown by a study of his letters to Gladstone covering this period. Manning was able to influence the action of the Liberals (who were in opposition) through Gladstone, in order to prevent them from opposing the Government on this Bill. He wrote to Gladstone on 15 March 1868, saying: 'When the Poor Law Bill comes to you I will send you a memorandum.'[25] He was as good as his word and wrote again to Gladstone three months later:

I am not anxious about it (the Poor Law Bill). Nothing is more sensibly felt by the Catholics of England than the treatment of our poor children in the Workhouse Schools.

I would therefore ask of you, and of all you can influence to support the clauses in the Bill which affect us. They are the clauses of Mr. Villiers'

Report in 1864: and therefore your own. I know how kindly you acted last year in this, and I ask the same again.[26]

He concluded this letter by asking for an interview in order that he might specify the exact points at stake. He wrote again on the same subject on 3 July 1868.[27] As we have seen, his efforts bore fruit and Gladstone gave all the support he could. This latter is clear from the letter Manning wrote on 29 July 1868 when he said: 'I write one word to thank you for your kindness in watching and supporting the Poor Law Bill.'[28]

Manning always devoted his Lenten Pastoral Letter to the poor children and continued to preside at the annual meeting of the Westminster Diocesan Education Fund in St. James's Hall. *The Times*, however, launched a severe attack on Manning in 1873 and at the success of his policy in organizing a whole new system of education in London and especially on his policy in regard to the workhouse children. It declared (27 February 1873):

> This being a Protestant country, we are bound to assume that the welfare of the child will be at least as much insured by her being brought up as a Protestant Christian as a Roman Catholic Christian.[29]

On this argument it based its attack.

Manning replied the following day[30] in a letter which is worth while quoting in full as it sets out his aims. His arguments are interesting when studied in conjunction with his attitude to the Education Act of 1870.* The letter is as follows:

Sir,
   . . . The Statute Law of England requires that Roman Catholic children in Workhouses shall either be duly educated in their religion within the walls of Schools under the Poor Law, or shall be transferred to Schools of their own religion.

   I deny that either one or the other of these obligations is at this moment justly and adequately fulfilled. . . .

   I beg to clear away at once the assertion—which well expresses the misapprehension studiously propagated at this time—that Roman Catholics deem nothing gained unless the whole control of education is handed over to them.

   To this I reply:

   I. That, if the Guardians of the Poor shall elect, of the two Statutory obligations imposed upon them, to provide a *bona fide* Roman

---

* See Chapter III.

Catholic education for the children of that religion in their existing schools, and shall, in the judgment of the Local Government Board, *bone fide* fulfil that engagement, I ask no control whatsoever over them, or the public money entrusted to their administration. . . .

II. Secondly . . . that the attempt to form a double education, Protestant and Catholic, within the walls of the same school, would be most unwise, most inexpedient, and highly injurious to both classes of children, as well as embarrassing to the unity of the general administration. . . .

III. Being, therefore, convinced that such combined education is not only impossible, but hurtful to Protestants and Catholics alike, and that it must always involve the Guardians in embarrassing and displeasing questions, I have believed the most peaceful and effectual course was to elect the other branch of the alternative given by statute law, namely the transfer of Roman Catholic children from Poor Law Schools to Certified Schools of their own religion. . . . Our schools are open to the double inspection of the Local Government Board, and of all the Boards of Guardians who have transferred children to our care. . . .

I studiously refrain, Sir, from all comment on a multitude of other points in which your article seems to me to be vulnerable. I will only remind you that the warmth which you seem to perceive in the last letter you had the courtesy to publish for me, was not kindled, as you say, by an impeachment of 'bigotry', but of graver matter.

In the confidence that you will oblige me by publishing this letter tomorrow,

I am Sir,
Your faithful servant,
HENRY EDWARD,
Archbishop.

From 1866 to 1888, the Westminster Diocesan Education Fund had been largely concerned with the provision of schools and school-places. But in 1888, Manning's Lenten Pastoral Letter touched on a new evil which the Fund was to help to remedy in the future. This was the provision of 'Homes for Destitute Boys'. Boys were sent to work at an early age and had nowhere to live and often no parents or friends. They were living in rat-infested cellars and sleeping under tarpaulins on the Thames embankment. Manning was determined to do something for them to prevent their moral degeneracy and criminal tendencies. The foundation of Homes, therefore, where these boys could live, sleep, wash and be fed (in return for a meagre sum deducted from the boys' wages) became a further item devolving on the Westminster fund (in 1888). No boy was to be turned away because he had no work or money; religion was not to be made a condition of help. Similar Homes for destitute girls were not required, because of the numerous convents which offered provision for this work. Numerous Homes for boys sprang up all over the city, most of them lay-managed, but a few run by Religious Communities.[31] A further way in which Manning attempted to provide for these boys was by emigration, especially to Canada. In May, 1886, Manning became a member of the Association for Promoting State-directed Colonization. Both before and after this date we find that children were sent to Canada in the care of the Cardinal's secretary, Father Seddon. The resident clergy in Quebec looked after the children's welfare until the Government agent at Montreal found jobs for the older boys. There was plenty of work and a dearth of labour. Boys who were too young to work were adopted by Roman Catholic families; a small number of these, however, remained in Catholic Homes in Canada. Manning's emigration policy eased the financial strain on his diocese and at the same time proved more beneficial, for the boys were able to start life anew in a young country where opportunity was free and work plentiful. In 1880 hostels were opened in Ottawa and Liverpool to deal with the emigration and reception of the children.

Before leaving the question of the education of the poor, some mention must be made of Manning's relationship with Dr. Barnardo. The latter had done great work in the Metropolis in the provision for destitute children. He accepted any destitute child and in 1887 it was estimated that one-fifth of the children in his Homes were Roman Catholics. This posed the same sort of problem for Manning as did the workhouse children. He found, however, that Barnardo was reluctant to hand over to himself the Catholic children and expensive litigation had to be started each time it was desired to effect the transfer of a Catholic child. Canon St. John relates how he tried on behalf of the Cardinal Archbishop to reach some agreement with Dr. Barnardo, in order to prevent the necessity of appealing to law. 'Dr. Barnardo began', he relates, 'by telling me that he wanted to be quite frank with me, and then stated, not unpleasantly, that he hated the Catholic Religion and everything to do with it, but owing to his inability to deal with the vast number of children and youths that were applying to him for assistance, he would rather see Catholic children go to Catholic Homes rather than that they should be left in degraded surroundings.' However, during Manning's lifetime relations were always uneasy and lawsuits common. Cardinal Vaughan, in 1899, managed to reach some agreement with Barnardo.

With regard to the training of Roman Catholic teachers to staff his schools, Manning made full use of the training college for men opened by Wiseman at Hammersmith in 1850 and he himself opened one for women at Wandsworth. In 1861, however (four years before Manning became Archbishop), the Revised Code came into operation with its refusal to make curriculum-grants to anything but the three R's. The natural consequence of this was 'no straining after higher classes, as the grant will not depend on them'.[32] Because of the Revised Code and the tendency not to concentrate on anything but the three R's, entry into the teaching profession was greatly discouraged. To Manning, this meant the ruin of the structure he was laboriously building up. He attempted to solve the problem by making the training of teachers eligible for aid from the Westminster Diocesan Education Fund. We have seen how in 1866 he made this the third item on his list for help—after the Mission and Diocesan Schools. He made financial grants to intending teachers and to pupil-teachers, in addition to supporting the training colleges. He made an all-out drive for teacher recruitment, stressing the vocational as opposed to the pecuniary aspects, and was to an extent successful.

In 1869 Manning joined the Metaphysical Society, indeed 'Archbishop Manning and Mr. Ward were among the first before whom the proposal to co-operate in its formation was laid, and they readily undertook to do so'.[33] Wilfrid Ward relates how 'Archbishop Manning, Mr. Ward, Mr. Tennyson met at Mr. Knowles's* house, and discussed the claims of the various thinkers of the day to be invited to join and forthwith arranged among themselves who should communicate with whom'.[34] There, in the Society's meetings, he met and associated with scientists like Huxley and Tyndall, agnostics like John Morley and Leslie Stephen, and a galaxy of men of letters of all beliefs and none—Tennyson, Browning, J. A. Froude, R. H. Hutton, Mark Pattison, Ruskin, Sidgwick, Dean Stanley, F. D. Maurice, Martineau, Gladstone, Lord Selborne and the Duke of Argyll. Manning joined the Society because he realized that

* James Knowles, later editor of *The Nineteenth Century*.

5

nothing was to be gained from the scientists and the clergy remaining in two mutually hostile and suspicious camps. He felt that some effort ought to be made to bridge the gap and that scientists and churchmen ought to get together to talk over these interesting modern speculations. He, himself, wrote of the attitude the Roman Catholic Church in England should take towards these discoveries:

We do not live in an exhausted receiver. The Middle Ages are past. There is no zone of calms for us. We are in the modern world—in the trade-winds of the nineteenth century—and we must brace ourselves to lay hold of the world as it grapples with us, and to meet it, intellect to intellect, culture to culture, science to science.[35]

There was no salvation in hiding and none in aloofness. The more progressive Catholics rallied to Manning's lead. On 10 December 1872 it is recorded that W. G. Ward,* the noted convert and sometime lecturer at St. Edmund's College, Ware, was to read a paper at the Metaphysical Society entitled: 'Can Experience prove the Uniformity of Nature?' And Ward was soon followed by another Catholic, Professor Mivart, and then by Dr. Gasquet and Father Dalgairns. Newman was amazed at Manning's consorting with agnostics and atheists and highly disapproved of this method.†
'Newman's experience, sympathies, and mind were narrow. A certain unreality often reflects his ignorance of the world of ordinary men and women.'[36] Newman had received an invitation to join the Society but declined saying: 'I am not a ready man, and should spoil a good cause. And then, I am so dreadfully shy, that I never show to advantage, and feel it myself acutely all the time.'[37] But Manning persisted and he read five papers (not four, as stated by Purcell[38]) before the Society. These were: 'What is the Relation of the Will to Thought?' (11 January 1871); 'That Legitimate Authority is an Evidence of Truth' (14 May 1872); 'A Diagnosis and Prescription' (10 June 1872); 'The Soul before and after Death' (13 February 1877); and 'What is Philosophy?' (25 November 1879). He listened to Huxley read a paper on the Resurrection and

* Pius IX, when he heard of the objections to Ward (a married man) teaching theology, said: 'It is a novel objection to the fitness of a man to do God's work that he has received a Sacrament of Holy Church which neither you nor I have received (Ward, *Life of Wiseman*, I, p. 74).

† Apparently Newman was unable to prevent Fr. Dalgairns, a fellow-Oratorian, from taking part. See Newman's letter to Dean Church of 1876 expressing disapproval of Manning's action in Ward's *Life of Newman* (ed. 1913), II, p. 333.

entered into discussions about whether or not a frog possessed a soul. In these ways Manning attempted to ally the Church with the New Learning and to indicate to his followers that religion was not incompatible with progress and science.* Purcell claims that Manning was 'a moral martyr' when he took part in the meetings of the Metaphysical Society and 'whether he knew it or not, was out of his depth'. This may well have been true, although Wilfrid Ward in his *Life of Newman* does not comment on any such deficiency.[39] In fact, Maisie Ward in *The Wilfrid Wards and the Transition* quotes her father as rather inclining to the opposite viewpoint regarding Manning's intellectual capabilities. He claimed that the Archbishop had ' a perfect gift of expression in speaking "extempore" '[40] and that he could deliver himself of facts 'in such perfection of order and effect as it would be difficult to surpass in the most carefully revised writing'. From Wilfrid Ward's words it seems as though Manning would have acquitted himself satisfactorily at the Metaphysical Society, even though his contributions may not have been distinguished by great originality of thought. Manning frequently lectured in Mechanics' Institutes and set up Catholic Academies in all the large towns modelled on them. This aspect of the Cardinal's policy we shall deal with in more detail in the chapter on Higher Education.

This policy he continued when he developed the provision for middle-class education in his diocese. The Industrial Revolution with its prospects of increasing prosperity for those with initiative, genius or scientific training gave rise to a fairly prosperous middle class, owing their livelihood to industry or trade or both. Consequently a demand for an education, which was advanced, scientific, and devoid of the dead weight of the classical tradition provided by so many of the upper-class boarding schools of the time, arose.

Writing in the *Dublin Review* in 1863 on the 'Work and Wants of the Catholic Church in England', Manning placed second in his list 'an adequate system of education for the poor and middle classes.'[41] We have seen how he provided for the poor; he began by entrusting middle-class education to the Oblates of St. Charles. His nephew, Monsignor William Manning, an Oblate, was persuaded

---

* Disraeli in *Lothair* makes Appollonia refer to the knowledge that the Cardinal is giving some lectures on science in this amusing way: 'It is remorse. Their clever men can never forget that unfortunate affair of Galileo, and think they can divert the imagination of the nineteenth century by mock zeal about red sandstone or the origin of the species.'

to undertake the foundation of a school to provide middle-class education in London. St. Charles's College was opened in 1874 with that intention and replaced an existing dame-school, which Manning had started two years before he became Archbishop. The following account of the College, as it was opened in St. Charles's Square, Kensington, quoted from the *Westminster Gazette*,* will illustrate how advanced were Manning's educational ideas and how accurately he had conceived the purpose of such a school. The College had cost £40,000, and was

a fine building of noble dimensions being 300 feet in extent. . . . It stands in its own grounds of . . . eleven acres in extent. . . . On the cricket-field, the play-ground, the gymnastic yard, and the gardens, £1,300 have been well laid out. Beyond its walls an open landscape stretches as far as eye can reach.[42]

The reporter continues with his eye-witness account:

All the modern appliances, carefully considered by the architect, Mr. F. W. Tasker, have been introduced, and special care is bestowed on ventilation. The class rooms on the ground floor are lofty and large, and the dormitories are of equally good dimensions.† The principal corridor is about 200 feet in length. The students are provided with a good billiard room, and with a library well stocked with light and amusing literature. There is also to be found the latest of fashions—an asphalt skating rink. The bath rooms and day lavatories are large and well arranged, and there is, I may add, in case of sickness, an excellently appointed infirmary.

Referring to the academic side of the school he went on:

Of the high standard attained in the studies of this college it is unnecessary to speak, as the Cardinal Manning himself had justly attributed this success to the action of the Prefect of Studies, the Rev. Henry A. Rawes, D.D. To Mathematics, I may mention, especial attention is paid, and with highly satisfactory results, by a distinguished Professor, member of the Mathematical Society, and late Fellow of New College, Oxford.‡

Such a remarkable foundation enjoyed great prestige in its day. From the great attention to health and sanitary provision it will be seen that Manning had been influenced by Kingsley and the Hygienic Movement. The increased attention to games as part of the curriculum which this movement enhanced—and evidence of which

---

* A paper of which Purcell became editor.
† The school took a number of boarders.
‡ All efforts to identify with certainty the 'distinguished Professor' have failed but it may possibly be Dr. R. F. Clarke, a distinguished scientist who later headed the College after the failure of the University venture. See Ward's *Life of Newman* (II, p. 198, n. 1).

can be seen in Manning's College—came later to be much over-done.

St. Charles's College was one of the reasons why Manning would never allow the Society of Jesus to open a Grammar School in London. He could not afford that his magnificent enterprise at Kensington should be ruined by the Society's attracting the best pupils. In addition Lord Petre had invested much money in St. Charles's College and it was Manning's duty to see that his confidence had not been misplaced. St. Charles's College existed until 1905 when it became a training college for women teachers. Part of the proceeds of the sale went to found the Cardinal Vaughan Grammar School. During the 1939–45 War the training college moved to Roehampton, because of bomb damage. Today the Cardinal Manning Secondary Modern School for Boys exists on the site and a similar girls' school is to be opened there shortly. The old chapel of the College is today the Church of St. Pius X, Kensington.

St. Charles's College, however, did not by itself provide sufficiently for middle-class Roman Catholic education in London. Manning decided to secure the help of the de la Salle Brothers in founding a similar school. Here the trouble began. The Jesuits had for long been trying to open a school in London for the well-to-do. Every effort was prevented by Manning. This may appear an incongruous attitude in Manning's policy. Unfortunately, the Society of Jesus tended to have a large following among the 'Old Catholic' families, and this was soon discovered by the Cardinal. He knew that the Jesuits had actively worked for the appointment of Clifford to Westminster[43] when Wiseman died and he remembered that they only of all the Religious Orders did not congratulate him on his appointment. Even as an Anglican Manning had profoundly distrusted the Jesuits. In Manning's diary for 1848 we find an entry under 5 December, which reads: 'Broechi told me that the Jesuits are able and excellent in their duties as priests, but that their politics are most mischievous; that if a collision should come with the people the effect would be terrible; that they stick to the aristocracy . . . the people call them "Oscuri, Oscurantisti".'[44] How much Manning's antagonism to the Society owes to views he acquired in his visit to Rome in 1848 and how much to later experience we cannot say, but from his various writings concerning the Jesuits it seems not unlikely that much of his opposition arose from a corrupt reading of history—namely Tierney's edition of *Dodd's Church History of England*.* The latter concerned itself largely with the age-old quarrel between Seculars and Regulars and as the authors were Secular priests it adopted a somewhat partisan attitude. In any case, the work—and in particular, Vol. V on the reign of James I—was a severe condemnation of the Society of Jesus, whom it attacked as political intriguers and power-seekers. The following statement in one of Manning's autobiographical notes illustrates without a doubt that the Archbishop had read Tierney-Dodd:

> The exclusive, narrow, military, aristocratic character of the Society shown in the time of James I with the arch-priest figment and the continual thwarting of the English clergy down to good Father Lythgoe, whom I just remember, seems to me to be a mysterious permission of God for the chastisement of England.[45]

The views related here are very reminiscent of Tierney-Dodd in Vol. V, Chapter I.

His opposition to the Jesuits opening a school in London was also based on a fear that they would seize all the promising youths who wished to be priests for their order and leave mediocre material for the diocese. A number of secular priests from the diocese had joined the Society, including Father John Morris, the Cardinal's Secretary. It was his constant fear, and hence he felt that the Society of Jesus was the cause of the depression of the pastoral clergy. They took only the intellectual cream of aspirants to the priesthood. What is more, any school staffed by the Society would be exempt from episcopal jurisdiction. The Jesuits before 1870 already had a boarding school a few miles out of London—Beaumont College, in addition to Stonyhurst and Mount St. Mary's College—for the wealthy and ennobled. Their men were trained in the classical tradition, in order to teach in these schools. Consequently, Manning's real objection to a Jesuit school in London was that he felt they were not competent to give the kind of scientific-commercial education for the middle classes that he desired. It was no use teaching classics in such a school and ignoring science (as it was ignored at Stonyhurst); pupils from the middle classes would not attend. The impact of the Great Exhibition of 1851 and of the Paris Exhibition of 1867 with their educational implications were not lost upon him. The Jesuits, however, became the big stick whereby

---

* *Dodd's Church History of England* by Rev. M. A. Tierney, F.R.S., F.S.A. (London, Dolman, 1843), especially Vol. V.

the 'Old Catholics' were to attempt to beat Manning. As soon as it was learnt that Manning intended to open a new middle-class school in London, a mysterious latter appeared in the *Daily Telegraph* saying 'the Jesuits would be prepared to launch £100,000 into such a scheme' and they had 'resources practically inexhaustible of ability and cultured intellect'.[46] From the outset it was obvious that a quarrel on who should staff the school was likely. Manning soon discovered that the writer in the *Daily Telegraph* was Mgr. Capel, the man whose ill-administration had ruined the University venture at Kensington and who had much reason to try to revenge himself on the Archbishop. The latter wrote to Bishop Vaughan on 20 October 1880:

My dear Herbert,

The enclosed is Mgr. Capel's 2nd letter in the D. Telegraph. He is endeavouring to make capital out of our Middle Class movement; and as you see to bring in the Jesuits and a St. F. Xavier's School into London.

I have tonight a second meeting of Middle-class men at the house. We have tested the exaggerated statements as to middle class boys in non-Catholic schools, and find them extravagant. The number cannot be more than 150 scattered over 15 miles by 9—2 here and three there.

And we have room for them all in our middle class schools if the Parents will send them. I have said that one more central school shall be founded for the middle and East of London.

I will keep you informed for I look for trouble from Mgr. C. and S. F. This is building with one hand and fighting with the other.

HENRY EDWARD.[47]

Manning was as good as his word, for on 25 October 1880 he contacted the Superior of the de la Salle Brothers, who had already set up a secondary school at Clapham in the Diocese of Southwark. This school had a decidedly technical and scientific bent and it was probably this that first attracted Manning to the Brothers. Brother Potamian wrote to his Superior at Paris about the Cardinal's proposal. 'His Eminence specified the subjects which he wished us to undertake', he wrote, 'viz. the higher mathematics, physics and chemistry.'[48] Brother Potamian himself was well-qualified to undertake such an establishment: he held the degrees of B.Sc. and D.Sc. of the recently established University of London and was eminent in his field of study.

Manning wrote to Vaughan on 31 October, 1880:

You will see by the enclosed that I have taken the Bull by the horns. After this no talking will do.

And if any boys are found to need schools we will have them. The Oratorians are opening a middle school and the French Xian. Brothers have consented to come into the E. Centre of London.

My chief work will be for the higher efficiency of teaching.

I have many good schoolmen, Classical, English and Mathematicians if only I can get them together and support them—but the poverty of our middle class is incredible. They cannot pay on an average £4 a year for a boy.

Mgr. Capel is beginning some movement—and talking of an English Jury. He will ruin himself beyond remedy.[49]

Before writing the above letter and after seeing Brother Potamian, Manning had written to the Brother General of the de la Salle Congregation and elicited a promise that the Order would undertake the venture. But Potamian, himself, was afraid of the 'Old Catholic' influence which was working for the Jesuits, and he misunderstood Manning's motives. He wrote to his Superior:

The Cardinal will not have the Jesuits, so he has pitched upon us as a substitute. There is much ill-feeling on account of the Cardinal's hostility to the Jesuits, and did we rush into their place, we would not by any means meet the support we would want from the laity in order to make our venture a success.

Dr. Battersby adds:

It was fast becoming clear that the whole scheme of the Central School was a subtle snare to entrap the Cardinal. It was, in fact, closely connected with the dispute going on at this time between the English Bishops and the Regulars, particularly the Jesuits.[50]

The 'Old Catholic' elements considered that the Cardinal was too deeply implicated to go back on his scheme and they were determined that it should be a financial failure if the Jesuits did not run it. Letters were appearing in the Press* demanding that the Jesuits should run it—and what is far more significant, the corollary of these demands, for a 'liberal-classical' as well as a scientific education. In other words, it was developing into the old demand for a Jesuit Grammar/Public School for the upper classes in

* In a letter to Vaughan 8.11.80, Manning referred to 'anonymous writers in the D. Telegraph' (M.P., Bayswater).

London. The situation was becoming serious for Manning. A certain section of the pro-Jesuit faction worked hard behind the scenes to get the de la Salle Brothers to withdraw, in order to leave the field clear for the Jesuits. Two gentlemen* approached Brother Potamian and threatened him: 'The Brothers are not the men we want; they are the teachers of the poor; we want the school to have such an *éclat* that the boys may take it as an honour to belong to it.'† 'I would advise the Brothers', one of them declared, 'to look carefully before they commit themselves to such a risky enterprise'. This kind of pressure had its effect and the de la Salle Brothers withdrew their offer. The Society of Jesus itself was probably not cognizant of such intrigue; it was the means wherewith to checkmate the Cardinal for certain Catholic families and cliques. The outcome was a compromise; Manning would not give way and the Brothers promised to assist him by arranging transport to their school at Clapham for boys in the Westminster area. The Oratorians helped the Cardinal in every way they could and opened a splendid middle-class school for him. It was, perhaps, in this aspect of the Arch-bishop's policy rather than in any other that he betrayed that tenacity of purpose, so closely allied to the narrow-minded.

Manning felt bitter about the collapse of his scheme and ascribed the blame for it to the Jesuits. He wrote to Vaughan on 8 November 1880: 'The other Orders would be in peace and charity but for the example and misleading of a body which has from its outset been a cause of internal evil to Priests and people.'[51]

Manning's efforts for middle-class education were not exhausted, however, with all this. By the time of his death (1892) he had over a dozen middle-class schools in London, a number of them staffed by Marist Brothers. In these foundations he frequently used his own initiative and it proved a success.

Once again, it can be shown that he did not confine himself to his own diocese in encouraging the educational provision for a growing middle class and in encouraging competent scientific instruction. For example, because of the close friendship between the Cardinal and Fr. Nicholas Rigby, parish priest of Ugthorpe in Yorkshire from 1827 to 1886, the latter opened a new middle-class Boarding School 'to accommodate 84 boarders in the large three storey building which he built adjoining the Church'.[52] Manning showed his interest by journeying all the way to Yorkshire to bless

---

* A Mr. Dalton and a Mr. Conolly.   † Battersby, *Brother Potamian*, p. 57.

and open it in 1868. One of its alumni became a bishop. In all these ways by his dynamic enthusiasm and inspiring example Manning encouraged the forward movement in education in his day.

In regard to education for the wealthy, Manning did little. They were already well provided for by the existing colleges and public schools: Stonyhurst, Mount St. Mary's and Beaumont (Jesuit); Ampleforth and Downside (Benedictine); Hinckley (Dominican); Old Hall Green, Ushaw and St. Mary's, Woolhampton (Secular); Ratcliffe (Rosminian); the Oratory School (Newman); and the seminary-colleges of Oscott, St. Edward's, Liverpool, and Prior Park. He did, however, provide in London St. Aloysius' College, Highgate (1879) and St. John's, Islington (1881) for a more 'refined' education. It is interesting to observe how science was neglected in the public schools. Latin, Greek, History,* Geography, Arithmetic and Philosophy was the composition of the Stonyhurst curriculum throughout Manning's episcopate.[53] Apparently the recommendations of the Taunton Commission of 1864 (or the Clarendon Commission of 1861) had made little difference to them.

We must conclude this discussion of Manning's policy in the provision of schools and education for his co-religionists with a review of his work for the education of girls. In the field of elementary education girls had approximately the same advantages as boys—but this was not the case in respect of higher education. It would, however, be incorrect to say, as Dr. Battersby does, that there were 'no Public Schools for girls and few endowed schools', in England. There were a number of private schools[54]; and Queen's College, London, was founded in 1848 and Bedford College in 1849 to supply the need of qualified teachers for these schools. The real improvement came, however, in 1878, when women were admitted to degrees and examinations in the University of London and other universities were to follow suit. In 1875, the London School of Medicine for Women had been founded and henceforth a new field of endeavour was opened to them. The Schools Enquiry Commission which sat from 1864 to 1867 commented on the extremely poor provision of secondary education for girls and the dearth of adequately educated female teachers. As a result Girton College and Newnham College were admitted to the examinations of Cambridge University and Somerville College and Lady Margaret Hall were established at Oxford in 1881. This higher education for women

* Probably ecclesiastical history, combined with some ancient history.

became more firmly established when the Victoria University, established in 1880, admitted women and the Scottish universities admitted them in 1892. In the nineteenth century, three main objections against the higher education of women were usually advanced, namely that they were intellectually incapable of profiting by such an education, that they were physically incapable of undertaking it, and that such an education would somehow unfit them for motherhood. The last objection was the one which bore most weight with churchmen of all denominations. Manning, although he held the current view that woman's place was in the home as wife and mother and although he would have nothing to do with 'the shrieking sisterhood' and 'rights for women', at the same time did not take a narrow stand on the question of higher education. He was fortunate in the foundation of boarding schools and secondary day schools for girls in that he did not suffer from the normal dearth of competent women teachers. Nuns flocked to this country from abroad (especially from France) and the Oxford Movement had resulted in many wealthy and educated women converts joining the older-established congregations of nuns, whose subjects were mainly English in nationality. Many of these convents were strictly enclosed and catered for the wealthy—for example those at New Hall and Hammersmith. It was not in these old-established convents that Manning was interested. He again felt that the well-to-do and the poor girls were well catered for, not so the girls of the middle classes. His policy was, therefore, to encourage new Congregations to come to England or to encourage new native Congregations which would be more flexible and not strictly enclosed, to undertake this work. These nuns organized themselves from a centre and consequently were more supple and more adaptable to changing circumstances. The Poor School Sisters of Notre Dame did heroic pioneering work at Southend and Woolwich and other Orders opened schools at Chelsea, Stamford Hill, London, Brentford, Finchley and Isleworth. The La Retraite nuns undertook education for middle-class girls at Clapham (1880), the Dames of Nazareth at Ealing (1880), the Most Holy Sacrament nuns at Golden Square (1874).[55] The outstanding success of Manning's efforts to attract these nuns to his diocese becomes plain when we read the comments of the final report of the Cross Commission in 1888, the commission on which the Cardinal had himself served. 'It is admitted and proved very conclusively', it declared, 'by the remarkable results of the labours of members of religious communities in Roman Catholic schools, that the employment of women of superior social position and general culture has a refining and excellent effect upon the schools in which they teach.'*

Towards the end of Manning's life the Hygienic Movement had at last borne fruit in the Government's decision to separate unhealthy children from healthy ones in school and here Manning was destined to be the pioneer. The Cardinal on learning of the new policy at once contacted Bishop Butt of Southwark and asked him to build a special school for handicapped children, and he, for his part, would build two. Manning made the Diocese responsible for financing the building of two ophthalmic schools and staffed them with nuns, and Butt built a school for children suffering from scalp diseases and staffed it with Sisters of Mercy. The Local Government Board gave financial help.

The nineteenth century is perhaps outstanding chiefly for its advances in the field of education and, as has been seen, Manning was in the vanguard in this progress. In the matter of State education he was to prove equally enlightened and show at the same time his greatness as a fighter when he considered the claims of conscience were at stake.

* *Report*, p. 80.

Chapter III

THE ACT OF 1870 AND ITS CONSEQUENCES

*

WE have already examined the reasons why education became such a prominent question in the mid-nineteenth century and we have seen how Cardinal Manning attempted to keep pace with the modern developments in the provision of schools and in the kind of education those schools gave. But 'the fear that technical instruction on the continent was superior to our own, and would lead to a serious challenge to our industrial economy focused attention on the education of the intelligent artisan, who was acknowledged to be the backbone of our industrial supremacy'.[1]

This fear accelerated the demands for schooling, and Manning in common with the other religious advocates of denominational schools found himself unable to cope with the problem. By 1867 it had become obvious that the State would have to intervene in the field of elementary education. 'Many . . . called it "madness" to introduce the beginnings of a democratic franchise without taking steps at once to create a national system of elementary instruction.'[2] Manning had been Archbishop of Westminster for only two years before the 1867 Reform Act enfranchised a million new voters. Illiteracy was still rampant and the voluntary bodies were unable to educate the new electorate; the State would have to intervene if the country was to have a literate electorate. The attitude of Manning towards State entry into the field of education has been widely misunderstood. Purcell declares that owing to Manning's absence from England during the year 1870, when he was a leading champion of the Opportunist cause at the Vatican Council, 'no organized attempt was made by Catholics, in Parliament or in the country to resist the introduction of the godless principle into the National system of education'.[3] He also states as a fact that 'Manning did allude on one occasion to the Education Bill' in a letter to Gladstone in 1870—thereby implying that this was the only occasion when he did mention the matter to Gladstone. Mr. Christopher Howard goes

61

even further than Purcell when he asserts: 'When the expected education bill was introduced in the House of Commons on 17 February 1870, Manning, together with the entire hierarchy, was in Rome attending the Vatican Council. It passed through all its stages without his taking any step to protect the Catholic schools whose vital interests were so closely affected.'[4] Dr. McEntee is more misleading when she states that Manning waged 'unceasing warfare on the principle of secular education which was first incorporated in English law in 1870'[5] and when she asserts that on his return from Rome he began 'a rather tardy reversal of policy'. Leslie contends that all Manning did was to meet the Bill of 1870 with 'a divided episcopacy and an epigram, calling it "the endowment of the party of disendowment" '.[6]

Forster's Bill did not, however, take Manning by surprise; he was well prepared for it, accepted it as inevitable and confidently attempted to exert his influence 'behind the scenes' over Gladstone. As early as 11 February 1868, Manning knew that the State would have to make provision for educating the illiterate population. He wrote to Gladstone on that date: 'I am afraid of the educational question. Unless the denominational system is maintained in all its integrity . . . there will be a split with those whose support is now with you.'[7] That simple statement indicated his views at the outset, that in any reform of education denominationalism must be retained. On 11 March of the same year he wrote again, arguing for the retention of 'a true, full, unimpeded, Catholic education'.[8] It is, therefore, clear that Manning, fully two years before the passing of Forster's Act, was well aware of the 'dangers' of a secular educational system being set up, and that from this time he envisaged what, in fact, came to pass, the establishment of the 'dual system'. His attitude, unlike that of most of his co-religionists of the day and of the foremost ecclesiastics of the Established Church, was not adverse to the entry of the State into the field of education at all. He knew the State *must* provide. As he himself said: 'putting away all ecclesiastical questions, it cannot be denied that the State is justified in providing for the education of its people. It has a right to protect itself from dangers arising from ignorance and vice, which breed crime and turbulence.'[9] His only anxiety was to ensure that the State would leave alone without interference the existing denominational organization—in fact, that the State system should be what Forster tried to make it, one which merely 'filled up the gaps' in the existing provision. The two systems, he felt, could exist side by side without friction provided that they were financially on the same basis. Together they would form a truly national system of education—national and uniform even in their diversity. His anxieties were very real, for as early as 1867 Joseph Chamberlain had been laying the basic principles of Nonconformist agitation, principles which attacked the very roots of Anglican and Roman Catholic educational theory. These basic principles were three and were largely adopted later by Secularist agitators. Chamberlain declared:

1. That it is as much the duty of the State to see that the children are educated as to see that they are fed.
2. That the right to education ought not to be restricted by any Religious Tests.
3. That the enjoyment of this right ought not to depend on the caprice of charity or the will of parents.[10]

Manning would have agreed with the first of these principles but the other two ran counter to his fundamental convictions— denominational education and the right of the parents to determine the circumstances of their children's education. It was clear that there could be no via media between such opposing philosophies.

In order to press his views upon the attention of Gladstone, Manning wrote to him in 1869 in reference to Mr. Forster's Endowed Schools Bill. The letter is important because it disproves the statements of Purcell and others that Manning did nothing to make the views of the Roman Catholic Church felt at parliamentary level on the education question.

The Hierarchy at their Lenten meeting in London had expressed concern at Forster's Endowed Schools Bill. Forster's Bill for liberalizing these schools was a natural corollary to the report of the Taunton Commission. This latter had shown the chaos still existing in the matter of endowments and how ill-adjusted school curricula were to modern conditions. The Bill originally proposed the setting up of a State examining body, the permitting of secondary education to receive grants from the rates, the integration of the Local Authorities into the financing and determining of the scheme, and powers to review all existing endowments.* Many Roman

* For a clear account of the Royal Commissions and Forster's Endowed Schools Act see R. L. Archer, *Secondary Education in the Nineteenth Century* (C.U.P., 1921), p. 170 et seq.

Catholic schools would thus be affected—especially those run by Religious Communities and the boarding schools. Manning, as we have seen, was particularly interested in the poor and middle-class education and he had been caught up in the scientific movement. He was firmly on the side of the Government in this matter of examining the endowments and modernizing the content of education. It was, however, obvious that his suffragan bishops were to a man against the measure and they requested him to write to the Government and explain their views. As their Metropolitan he was bound to comply but he makes it clear in the letter that he is merely acting as the spokesman of the bishops and not expressing a personal view. The letter is as follows:

April 10th., 1869

My dear Gladstone,

Though most unwilling to write to you I feel compelled to do so.

This week the Catholic Bishops of England and Scotland have assembled in London, and have carefully examined the Scotch Schools Bill, and the Endowed Schools Bill.

On both we have the greatest objections to urge. You will remember perhaps that about last July at this house I expressed my fear that the subject of education would bring on a serious contest. I fear the beginnings of it are already come. . . . But I do not enter now into the subject. I only desire to ask that I may know to whom and when I may state what I have to say. To do it in writing would be laborious and I am heavily taxed already. You know me well enough to know that I am sincerely desirous to view all public questions from your position: and to render difficult matters as little difficult as possible. But there are some things in education in which we have no choice, but duties only . . .

H. E.
Archbishop.[11]

Unfortunately when Forster's Bill reached the Statute Book, it was seen that he had had to forego the State examining body, the desire to use the local rates for secondary education and the participation of the Local Authorities. Manning, himself, would have been dubious about this last clause because he felt that, like the Boards of Guardians they would be bitterly sectarian if they had any share in educational policy. The Bill, however, did establish three commissioners who were given powers to examine and reconstitute schools whose endowments were more than fifty years old. They soon established schemes for over two hundred schools, introduced modern languages, modern history, and science into the secondary schools, and created governing bodies, where necessary. Some provision was made for the education of girls. The only part of this work which Manning was likely to criticize was that no adequate provision for technical training was made. But even more startling was the Bill's interest in religion! It empowered a parent to write to the school in order to withdraw his child from the religious instruction of that school, if he thought fit. A prohibition was also included in the Act against a teacher orientating his non-religious teaching around a sectarian topic. These interferences in religious matters were ominous for the future and Manning did not view them with amity. However, the episode connected with the Endowed Schools Bill does show that the Hierarchy, headed by Manning, was fully aware of the questions at issue. The Bishops would have been blind, indeed, if they had not seen in them a portent for the future.

The greatest opponent of government action in the field of education, among the ranks of the Roman Catholic Hierarchy, was Dr. William Bernard Ullathorne, the Benedictine monk who ruled the Church of Birmingham for thirty-eight years. Concerning Forster's measure of 1869 and his proposed future policy, Ullathorne called together a large Roman Catholic meeting—on his own initiative—in the Birmingham Town Hall, at which he spoke and was adamant against any State 'interference' with education. He was particularly critical of the projected School Boards. His action is more significant when we consider that Birmingham was the centre of Chamberlain's activity.

When Forster's Bill of 1870 was about to be introduced Manning, who was in Rome for the Vatican Council, at once wrote to Gladstone:

I am anxiously waiting for a copy of Mr. Forster's Bill. From the Report I have both hopes and fears. The one year is too short a time; and the local management may become very dangerous, and oppressive to us. But till I see the Bill I will not risk more.[12]

Forster's original proposals were five in number and bitterly disappointed Chamberlain and his Nonconformists. He proposed dividing the country into school districts which would then be examined for educational deficiencies. When the latter had been ascertained, the denominations were to be given twelve months' grace to remedy the deficiencies, after which time locally elected School Boards would be formed with a mandate to open schools where necessary. These Boards were to have the power to compel attendance at school and could provide for religious instruction subject to a conscience clause.

These proposals were gall indeed to the Nonconformists. The Anglican schools were 'to be buttressed' and an obnoxious 'dualism' established. Their concept of a national system of education had been rejected.

It must have been very encouraging therefore to Gladstone to hear from a prelate who had *hopes*, as well as fears or dislikes, in connexion with the 1870 Bill. It can be seen from the letter that Manning's old fear of local management had cropped up again and this fear was aggravated by Ullathorne's constant pulpit denunciations. Manning was especially vulnerable on this point, having had so much experience of the Boards of Guardians and their bigotry. He was afraid that the new School Boards which the Act proposed to establish would follow the same policies. When he had seen the Bill in draft, Manning wrote again to Gladstone from Rome in May 1870. He declared:

As to the Education, I am very anxious. I see the Bill is conservative, and provides for the moment. But I fear the lean kine will eat up the fat kine. I would earnestly press on Government that the Catholics of the three Kingdoms need, and ought to be treated as a whole. The need of denominational education for them is admitted for Ireland in the late Report. It exists in England and Scotland now. And ought not to be withdrawn.

The integrity of our Schools as to (I) Doctrine, (II) Religious management, and the responsibility of the Bishops in these respects cannot be touched without opening a multitude of contentions and vexations.

In America the Bishops have formed their own Schools to avoid the Common School System. We in our poverty should be forced to do the same.

I cannot but repeat what I wrote to Lord De Grey. The Reformatory Schools Act gives a basis on which we can unite with Government. It secures our teaching and management: It gives full guarantee to Govt. in the secular part of education.

If this be secured we should be able to act fully upon the conscience clause: and co-operate heartily with Govt.

What I chiefly deprecate is local Board Administration. We will forego the School Rate to be still under the Privy Council.[13]

Here we have Manning's early programme. At this point he does not lay great stress upon the suggestion that the Voluntary Schools should be assisted out of the rates—in fact, he voluntarily agrees to give up the School Rate if they receive special treatment. The suggestion that the Voluntary Schools should be assisted out of the rates had been in Forster's first draft Bill. This clause, however, was to raise such a furore among the Nonconformists that it had to be dropped. Even the year's grace, which Manning had objected to as being too short a period, had to be cut to six months before the measure reached the Statute Book. Forster had refused, however, to countenance the full proposals of the Birmingham Radicals for secular schools. Manning desired to retain control of his own schools and the right to teach doctrinal religion in them, as well as the right to appoint his own teachers. It is obvious that he relied on Gladstone to achieve these ends. For the latter

on education and related questions . . . was profoundly a Churchman . . . He did not for a moment . . . dream of weakening the position of Church schools, much less of closing the future against them.

Shortly said, on this issue, the Prime Minister's mind was the negation of Nonconformity. No man had less appetite for unsectarian Board Schools.[14]

And Manning knew his man! It was through this knowledge that the Archbishop hoped to save his schools.*

On 25 March Manning wrote to Gladstone to clarify his demands still further:

My object now is to speak of the education Bill, I look with the greatest anxiety on many points but above all on two.

*Purcell quotes only *one* letter from Manning to Gladstone on the whole of the education question.[15] It is true that Manning did write to Gladstone on the date Purcell appends to his letter, 6 April 1870. The letter is in the Gladstone Papers at the British Museum. But this letter deals only with the influence Manning considered Lord Acton was exerting on Gladstone and not with education. The letter Purcell quotes is strangely reminiscent of (*a*) Manning's letter to Gladstone of 7 March 1870 in its reference to the fact that the American bishops had formed their own schools and that English Catholics might be forced to do likewise and (*b*) to the letter of 25 September 1887 from Manning to Gladstone in which he refers to the fact that the Birmingham League had made use of the Minister. The letter quoted by Purcell is not in the Bayswater archives.

1. First the shortness of the time granted us for forming new schools of our own.

In the past three years we have opened in London 30 new schools and have gathered out of the street 3,000 (additional) children.

Give me time, and just proportionate help, and there will not be one of our children without a school. But if at the end of a year* you cease to help, and even cease to give us fair law to do a vast work you will both paralyse our powers, and subject us to the dangers, and grievances of local boards, and mixed schools. The time ought to be largely extended and ought to be not *dial* time but *moral* time.

2. The other point is the Local School Boards. They will be either Poor Law Guardians or Middlesex Magistrates, or Education Pedants, and from these three we pray you to deliver us. The only hope of Justice for us is to be under the Privy Council. I cannot but add that though I fully see the conservative character of the Bill, I fear it will end in undoing the existing schools.

My belief is that you are strong enough already to do what you will.

And with the union of the Anglicans and the Catholics you have a great accession of strength.

I do not see why the School Rate should not be granted in proportion to private efforts by *enactment* of Parliament. If left to the will of the Local Boards I have no hope for our Schools. . . .[16]

If the granting of the School Rate could be achieved without the media of School Boards, Manning would be happy. He dreaded the latter and was particularly anxious that Gladstone should discover some way of obviating their necessity. He knew that he thought alike with Gladstone on the religious question. Gladstone had already 'praised the harmony of voluntary exertion and state aid, but if it was necessary to rely on one of these, he preferred the former "through which you get heart and love and moral influence"'.[17] Gladstone had also referred to what he termed 'the popular imposture of undenominational instruction'.[18] But even he was forced along on the tide of the extreme wing of his supporters and the Nonconformists. It was as much as he could do to guarantee *the existence* of the Voluntary Schools. If he could but cling to that he would ensure the establishment of the dual system. To do more, Gladstone was powerless.

* The year's grace in the final Bill was reduced to six months.

Unfortunately at this time there was the political irritation of the Vatican Council. Lord Acton* was in Rome as a self-appointed observer throughout the proceedings; he was a member of the 'Old Catholic set' and thoroughly disliked and distrusted the ultramontanism of Manning. He filled Gladstone's ears with much adverse comment. Manning cultivated a friendship with Odo Russell, the British diplomatic resident at the Vatican, and the latter by his letters to Lord Clarendon and various Government Ministers was able to rectify many wrong impressions created by Acton's influence. It was chiefly owing to Russell's protestations that the British Government held a neutral policy throughout this difficult year. Gladstone had been in favour of inviting the Powers of Europe to intervene and break up the Council—but Lord Clarendon, amply supplied with information by Manning through Russell, resisted the proposal and carried the Cabinet against Gladstone.[19] Gladstone's later bitter attacks and pamphlets on Infallibility and Vaticanism led to a severe rupture in his intercourse with Manning. Manning had warned Gladstone against paying too much attention to Acton in his letters, declaring:

Let me speak freely. I know that Acton corresponds either with you, or with those who are in contact with you. I believe both. You will of course sympathise with him rather than with me. But I pray you to see that you are hearing only one side, and that from a partisan of the most hostile animus. For the sake of us all, for your own sake, for your future, for the peace of our country, do not allow yourself to be warped, or impelled into words or acts hostile to the Council. If you desire to do good to Ireland, and therefore to the empire, do not render it impossible by touching a religious question.[20]

The matter of the Vatican Council, and the frustration of his efforts to secure foreign intervention, made Gladstone antipathetic to the Roman Catholic position in reference to Forster's Bill. He admitted as much himself, when he replied to Manning's letter of 25 March 1870. 'I need not say', he declared, 'that the R.C. position to all such demands (in education) is much damaged by the impression here of what is going on at Rome.'[21] In the same letter, he replied more specifically to Manning's proposals:

* For a very informative and readable account of Acton's character and career—especially in this connexion—see the excellent article by the late Dr. R. A. L. Smith in *The New Statesman and Nation* for 27 May 1944.

As to the year's interval, and the maintenance of the system of Privy Council grants, nothing has occurred to shake the intimations of the Government that to *hold* their ground on these points will probably require all their strength.

What would be easy . . . would be to escape from present difficulty by [postponing] the subject for another year. But this you would not recommend and it is a thing far from our duties and views. Whatever demands are left *now* open from the quarter I have indicated, will come up with compound interest at a high rate.[22]

Gladstone informed Manning, in other words, that the existing Bill was as much as he could hope for. The Nonconformist and Radical pressure within the Liberal Party was increasing in intensity until in April 1870 Gladstone was writing to the Archbishop, lamenting that 'the question of National Education is passing I fear into great complications'.[23] 'To avoid a damaging division', in the Second Reading, 'Gladstone pledged himself to make some amendments.'[24]

But with the final draft of the Education Bill and its establishment of what Manning had always advocated—the dual system— the Archbishop declared himself to be content. 'The education Bill is decidedly improved', he wrote; 'I still believe the doctrinaire faction prevailed beyond its power . . . over the real desire of the country.'[25]

Manning, however, found it very hard to convince his suffragans —and especially the redoubtable Ullathorne—that the measure was 'decidedly improved'. Ullathorne wrote to him as late as 14 September 1870: 'As I shall stop in London on Friday evening, I propose calling upon you, should you be at home and disengaged. I should like to have a talk upon the education question.'[26] Whether this interview took place or not we do not know but three days later Manning wrote to Ullathorne to explain why he advocated cooperating with the Government:

'It seems to me', he wrote, 'that our best course is to co-operate to the utmost of our power, and thereby to obtain a share in the treatment of questions which may affect us. If they should offer to include our clergy in any Boards, I think we ought to accept it. We can but retire, if in conscience bound.'[27]

This seems to have upset Ullathorne a little: he declared:

'Allow me to say that I cannot myself understand the policy of beginning by joining the education boards and that members of the Poor School Committee have expressed to me their perplexity as to this proposition. . . . It seems to me that by such a step we give up the contest for denominational schools.'[28] And yet Liberal feeling in the country was enraged at the Bill, which it considered 'enormously favourable to minorities', and Garvin holds it was 'conceded to Church and Catholic feeling'.[29]

On the same day that Ullathorne wrote to the Archbishop (7 Oct. 1870) Manning replied to a previous letter from the Bishop of Birmingham in strong words, declaring,

I am much obliged by your letter of yesterday on the importance of joint action among the Bishops on the subject of education.

In this, I fully consent. It was this conviction which induced me on Feb. 7 1868 to invite the Bishops to joint counsel and action to prepare ourselves against what has come upon us. That invitation was not followed up . . .

Again in Oct. 1869 I circulated among the Bishops the heads of the subject for treatment with Government that we might act in common.[30]

Ullathorne's letter of 7 October drew from Manning a full explanation of why he thought they should co-operate with the Boards. He declared:

The Boards may destroy our lesser schools by reporting them to be insufficient or inefficient. The effect of this in London would be to destroy one half of our schools. By opening negotiations with the Boards, as I have done with the Privy Council, I hope to save these. By standing aloof from the Boards we should be exposed to the danger of their hostility.[31]

In the long run perhaps Manning's view was the more statesmanlike. To have held aloof from the scheme and refused all intercourse with the Boards would have led to competition on a vicious scale with the Board Schools. The Roman Catholics would have been bound to lose in such a struggle because the Board Schools were backed by public money and could easily outstrip competition. This becomes clear when we look at the financial provision made for the School Boards in the Act itself. The latter declared:

The expenses of the board are to be paid from a fund called the school fund, constituted primarily by the fees of the children, moneys provided by Parliament, or raised by loan, or received in any other way, and supplemented by the rates, to be levied by the rating authority. In providing buildings etc., the board may borrow money so as to spread the payment over several years, not exceeding fifty.*

What is more the Boards themselves would have been hostile if Manning had held aloof and would have sought any opportunity to get rid of the Catholic schools. Gladstone had already indicated, as we have seen, to Manning that separate treatment for Catholic schools was impossible because of the sectarian feeling over the Vatican Council.

Manning was bitterly attacked for participating with the School Boards. A typical example of this attitude came from a Father Formby of Hinckley, Leicestershire, when he described Manning's policy in a letter to a friend as 'simply anti-Christian'. He continued:

His first act . . . is to open the gate of the citadel and to let the enemy have free ingress. He concedes that the Civil Power has the right to be the Schoolmaster of its subjects. But to concede this right is the denial of the Parental right under the first law of creation, and the right of the Sacerdotal order to be freely chosen by the parents as those in whom they have confidence, and . . . of their just autonomy.[32]

The first serious difficulty in regard to the new Act in Manning's mind was the 'Cowper-Temple' clause. As early as October 1869, Forster had declared his policy in regard to denominational instruction and its place in a scheme of national education. 'It would not be fair', he said, 'to tax a Roman Catholic to teach Methodism . . . [but] it would not be unfair to levy a rate on a Roman Catholic for the *secular* education of a Methodist.'[33] The implication was there at the outset, that denominational education would not be permitted in publicly-financed schools. The question of the impossibility of denominational teaching being paid for out of the rates poses an interesting problem. The Reformatory and Industrial Schools Acts of 1866 had made it incumbent on the State to discover the religion of a child and to permit it to be sent to a school of its own religion—and it was to be given 6s. a week for maintenance. Was that not 'religion on the rates'? Similarly the 1893 Act for Deaf and Dumb Schools and the Act passed in 1899 for Defective and Epileptic Children were to follow the same principle. No objections were raised at a later date over the paying of State salaries to denominational prison chaplains or military chaplains. It is, however, true that the public conscience is not awakened unless it perceives

* From the text of the Act. Section relating to School Boards.

some national application of principles used previously only on a minor scale. The same attitude can be discerned in the struggle for female suffrage. The prohibition of 1870 can largely be ascribed to Nonconformist jealousy of Anglican supremacy.

The Cowper-Temple clause was an attempt to find a 'via media' between the extreme Radical point of view of 'secular schools' and that of the denominationalists. It forbade the use of 'religious catechism or religious formulary distinctive of any particular denomination', in the Board Schools. The clauses embodying the ideas of Cowper-Temple-ism are to be discovered in the regulations in Section 7 of the Act. These state:

1. It shall not be required, as a condition of any child being admitted into, or continuing in the school, that he shall attend or abstain from attending any Sunday School, or any place of religious worship, or that he shall attend any religious observance or any instruction in religious subjects, in the school or elsewhere, from which observance or instruction he may be withdrawn by his parents, or that he shall, if withdrawn by his parents, attend the school on any day set apart for religious observance by the religious body to which his parent belongs.

2. Time for religious observance or instruction in the school must be at the beginning or end of school meeting, and must be shown in a time-table conspicuously posted in the school.

3. School must be open to inspection, except that the inspector is not to inquire into religious knowledge.

4. School must be conducted in accordance with the conditions required to obtain a parliamentary grant.*

These clauses were acceptable to Gladstone only as the lesser evil compared with secular education; he himself referred to what he termed 'the popular imposture' of undenominational instruction. In fact, as Mr. A. C. F. Beales remarks, what the clauses did were 'to render impossible any relations between the Voluntary Schools and the Board Schools—thereby wrecking Gladstone's original plan'.[34]

Manning wrote to Gladstone to clarify the issues at stake in 'Cowper-Temple-ism':

The maximum of prohibition in the Text of the Act is, I hope, Section 14—'(3) No religious Catechism, or religious formulary which is distinctive of any particular denomination shall be taught in the School.'

* Act of 1870, Section 7.

I hope this means.

1. The *school hours*.
2. Not before or after.
3. By School Board Teachers *as such*: not alia veste.
4. But before or after they may teach as the Parents, or denomination requires if they will.
5. That when the Bible is read and interpreted they must follow Huxley's reductio ad absurdum.[35]

Such a synopsis of the clauses illustrates how Manning intended to circumvent its unpleasant aspects. He would provide denominational teaching in the Board Schools after school hours by Roman Catholic teachers willing to give their time voluntarily. Manning warned Gladstone, however, that if the scheme did not work out in practice he would find in him a formidable opponent, writing: 'We are willing to recognise both Parliament and Government: but we must not be asked to accept the legislation of Atheists.'[36] The Cowper-Temple clause was described by Disraeli as creating the teachers into a 'new sacerdotal caste'. On the other hand Gladstone himself, speaking in Committee on the Education Bill in June 1870, in reference to this clause, had said:

It is our wish that the exposition of the Bible in schools should take its natural course, that it should be confined to the simple and devout method of handling which is adapted to the understanding and characters of children; but we do not admit that that simple and devout character of teaching can be secured by an attempt to exclude all reference to tenets and doctrines.[37]

If that was true, who was to make the 'reference to tenets and doctrines' but the teacher and would not his references be coloured by whether he accepted those tenets and doctrines as true or false? Disraeli's criticism was all too palpably just. Gladstone's remark was in fact conceding the whole of Disraeli's and Manning's fears. By uttering it he thought to deal the death blow to undenominationalism when in fact he was simply adding fuel to the flame of sectarian bitterness. It was now 'nobody's religion, taught by anyone, at everybody's expense'.[38]

It was evident that Roman Catholic children could not be allowed to attend such schools unless there was absolutely no alternative. To a Roman Catholic a Roman Catholic education with a Roman Catholic atmosphere was essential. Dogmatic instruction after school hours was no adequate substitute. As G. K. Chesterton was later to describe it: 'Every part of education has a connection with every other part. If it does not all combine to convey some general view of life, it is not education at all.'[39] In other words, to a Roman Catholic, the integrating factor in the curriculum was religion. In the School Board system this was jettisoned and a vacuum created. Even today educational theorists are still seeking to fill that void. Huxley, Chamberlain, and their associates failed to grasp this viewpoint. 'They had a vague idea that it meant that a child could only do a simple addition sum when surrounded by a smell of incense.'[40] In fact, as Athelstan Riley was to declare fifty years after the passing of the Act, 'to herd together children of every denomination to be taught by teachers of any religion and no religion *must* be repulsive to every man, considering the matter dispassionately, who values religion'.[41] The system of undenominationalism ensured the continuation of the Voluntary School and set the seal upon the dual system of education.

The Bill of 1870 was adopted at a time when France and Paris were in a state of chaos: the time of the Paris Commune. The latter considerably alarmed Manning, especially when England seemed to be about to adopt a 'secular' system of education. He wrote to Gladstone:

I believe the State of France and of Paris to be traceable in chief to a godless education. The education of England is still Christian. The tradition is unbroken. The mass of the people desire to bring up their children as Christians. We are tormented and harassed by a clique of doctrinaires who believing nothing, trumpet secular education. My friend Huxley is at the head of them. I am very glad to see Mr. Forster attacked as 'playing into the hands of the clergy'. If government will be firm and outspoken the country will support it, in affirming that the education of the English people is Christian; and that though the Government grants public money only to the secular element, it desires to see the religious element vigorously and adequately supplied by the free action of the people. The worst disaster that could befall us would be an 'Imperial Education'. It must be godless. It would paralyse all voluntary religious effort, and in a generation the whole Christian order of England would be undermined, if not overthrown.

Stimulate by all agencies in your power the voluntary religious energies of the three Kingdoms. This may yet save us. . . .[42]

It might be useful at this point to sum up the final provisions of the Education Act of 1870, as it reached the Statute Book, in its bearing on the denominational schools. The short period of six months was allowed to the Voluntary Schools to make provision for the education of hitherto unprovided or inadequately provided areas. After this date the areas would be assessed and Board Schools built where necessary. A conscience clause meant that parents could withdraw their children from religious instruction in the Voluntary and State Schools by request; the Cowper-Temple clause severed the connexion between secular and doctrinal instruction in the Board Schools. The Guardians were authorized to pay the school fees of the children of indigent parents who wished to attend a Voluntary School if they so desired and if they had received an application for this relief from the parents. Rate-aid was not granted to the Voluntary Schools and building grants were to end at the close of the year. Hence the result was a dual system of education, consisting of the denominational schools aided by Privy Council grants and voluntary subscriptions and the undenominational schools completely maintained by public funds.

It is not possible, however, to attain to a complete understanding of the complicated negotiations between Manning and the Government of 1870 unless we also take into account the attitude of the Roman Catholic laity and its press towards state intervention.

Public opinion in general in 1870 was divided into four different sections. First, there was the National Education Union which represented Anglican opinion; there were the Nonconformists under the leadership of Dr. Henry Allen who, to a large extent, shared the same views as the N.E.U. and supported a retention of the Voluntary System, aided by the rates; there were the Roman Catholics who can be said, on the whole, to have wanted to retain the Voluntary System, together with rate-aid; finally, there was the frankly secular National Education League. How serious the educational problem was for the Roman Catholics can be seen when we consider that some 44 per cent. of Catholic children were still without education in 1870. These children would probably be compelled to attend Board Schools. Development in Manning's diocese in the provision of Catholic schools was well advanced but the other bishops had nothing comparable to the Westminster Diocesan Education Fund and hence they would be more seriously affected.

The Catholic press was certainly alive to the issue. As early as

1868 the *Dublin Review*—which can be regarded as Manning's own literary organ—was able to sum up the situation accurately:

> We may here briefly state for the sake of clearness what are broadly the constituent members of these hostile armies. To the 'secular' school system belong the Unitarians, the Congregationalists, Deists and Atheists, and practically the organization known as the British and Foreign Schools Society of which Lord Russell is the president. It is a large and increasing party. In support of the 'denominational' system are ranked, on the whole, the Church of England, especially its National Society for Education, the Wesleyans and Baptists, and, prominently, the Catholic Church.[43]

The same article went on to forecast the dangers of the idea of State intervention in the field of education:

> We believe the national consequences would be
> (1) . . . to sign the national apostasy from Christianity . . .
> (2) it would be the formal return of the nation, through an act of its Legislature, to an unmythological Paganism.
> (3) It would be the destruction of the National Church . . .
> (4) it would be the beginning . . . of the break-up of our Empire.

The article ends with a plea for the co-operation of all forces against the proposed intervention—thus foreshadowing Manning's later policy of taking 'Christian education as the *genus* and denominational as the *species*'.

But, on the other hand, certain elements among the Roman Catholic laity 'like the Dissenters looked to State intervention for the improvement of their position. Their hopes were not so great, since they were very much of a minority faith and subject to suspicion of being un-English and vaguely disloyal to the traditional English way of life.'[44]

While Gladstone was writing to Manning in 1871 that 'all you say would lead me to believe that you and the Government are on the same lines with respect to this important matter',[45] the Catholic laity were organizing themselves in opposition to the Government.

Mr. Howard is mistaken when he states that 'the entire hierarchy was in Rome' during 1870, as Manning had decided to leave one bishop at home to be in charge as *locum tenens*. This bishop was Dr. Brown, the Benedictine Bishop of Newport, and an Inopportunist of the most militant kind. Brown, a distinguished scholar, was fully empowered and eminently qualified to take the initiative. He had been a bishop for thirty years and at seventy-two years of age was vigorous and competent. However, he thought fit to remain in Wales throughout the year and was somewhat out of touch with events. Consequently, the direction of affairs at home passed into the hands of one or two wealthy Catholic magnates— and especially into those of Lord Howard of Glossop. (These magnates disliked Brown for his constant suspicions of the orthodoxy of Newman.) The *Tablet* of 25 February 1870 declared: 'The Catholic Community does not look with favour upon the Bill. It must be amended to become even tolerable. . . . In the absence of the Bishops, who will be of course communicated with, Catholics are not left without heads to watch and care for them.'[46] It goes on to record that 'a meeting in the rooms of the Poor School Committee has been sitting for three long days this week, under the Presidency of Lord Howard of Glossop, and has minutely examined the Bill in all its bearings'.

A month prior to this Lord Howard himself had written to the *Catholic Times* to state:

My object in writing this *letter* as I suppose I should call it, but *urgent appeal and personal application* as I elect to call it, is to put before the dioceses a position in which matters are—a position of which none can individually be unaware, however little they are collectively alive to it, judging from any published acts.[47]

As Manning himself was the head of the Hierarchy and as he alone could take the initiative in getting the Hierarchy to act collectively, the last part of Howard's letter was a veiled criticism of the Archbishop. Howard was unaware that the latter was working 'behind the scenes', trying to influence Gladstone in favour of a dual system of education.

Howard of Glossop's letter, however, stung the Archbishop by its innuendo and in February 1870 he did issue a directive on education: 'A pastoral letter by His Grace the Archbishop of Westminster was read on Sunday (last) at the different Churches in his diocese. Dr. Manning, with considerable force, urges his flock to multiply our Schools till not one Catholic child shall lack a sound Catholic education.'[48] It must have been a shock for Howard and his fellow 'Old Catholics' to find that all Manning advised was the utilization of the period of grace that the Bill proposed to the best of their ability in building new schools, and that he did not specifically condemn the policy of government intervention in the field of education. It almost looked as if His Grace wished them to co-operate with the Government. At the same time as Manning was issuing his pastoral, one was promulgated in the Beverley Diocese by his friend, Dr. Cornthwaite. The latter astounded Howard and his friends by ignoring the question of education altogether and devoting his letter to the Fenian problem. It was obvious that Cornthwaite had agreed to leave the field clear for Manning, so as not to prejudice his policy by any premature denunciation or comment. When the other bishops issued pastorals at this time they concentrated on the Vatican Council.

The newspaper that was most widely read by the great mass of the working men who were Roman Catholics was *The Northern Press and Catholic Times* or *The Catholic Times* as it was called for short. It was a home-rule organ and had pronounced pro-Irish and pro-Manning sympathies. Early in 1870 its policy had been unmistakably clear. 'The time has surely come', it had declared in January, 'when Catholics ought to make known definitely their views upon the education question. Parliament meets a month hence and we may take it for granted that during the approaching session education will be next, at least, to the Irish Land question in importance.'

By September 1870 it was obvious that Howard had got the laity organized to oppose Manning's policy—and wittingly or unwittingly the Press had helped him. It was reported that

a Committee of some of the most influential Catholics of the town has been formed and has had several meetings to consider the best means of meeting the present crisis in Catholic Education. From enquiries instituted, the deficiency in school accommodation, so far as the returns received go, show that to provide schools for the Roman Catholic children, liable otherwise to be driven into the rate-aided schools, will require an expenditure of twenty-two thousand pounds.[49]

Howard had been joined by the Marquis of Bute and the Duke of Norfolk, both of whom addressed meetings in London on the education question in October.

While the 1870 Bill was before the House 'the Catholic Poor School Committee met nine times, petitioned the Commons, and interviewed the Catholic M.P.'s and the Government four times'.[50]

Before going to Rome, Manning had agreed to give up the right to a Catholic Inspector of Schools but in spite of this clear indication that it was the Archbishop's desire to co-operate with the Government as far as possible, Howard organized national subscriptions to provide a bulk sum of capital to help those schools refusing to accept the terms of the Government. By 1871, when Manning returned to London, the organizers of this fund handed him £40,000 for these schools. They hoped to trap the Archbishop; they had presented him with a *fait accompli* and they thought that he would thus have to follow their lead. Their surprise must have been complete when, after accepting the money, Manning insisted on it 'being given to those schools only which had accepted the Government's terms, thus compelling hundreds of schools', declares Purcell, 'to come under a yoke which their managers hoped to escape'.[51]

Before proceeding to discuss Manning's policy in reference to the practical working of the 1870 Act, it is necessary to comment on a statement made by Purcell to the effect that Manning called a meeting of bishops at Rome, some time during 1870, to consider Mr. Forster's Bill.[52] It is very unlikely that such a meeting took place. If it did do so it would certainly have been informal and no written record of it exists.* Perhaps the subject may have been touched upon at lunch one day when the bishops were present but no formal meeting was convened. Purcell gives no reference for his statement.

The School Boards were the first public authorities on which the working man got an opportunity of labouring. The Act stated in this connexion that the School Board was to be elected 'by the burgesses in a borough, and by the ratepayers in a parish, each voter having a number of votes equal to the number of vacancies, having the right to give all or any number of such votes to any one candidate, and to distribute them as he pleases'. The outcome was that many working men were elected by the votes of their *confrères*. The *Catholic Times* commented on this phenomenon in its issue of 5 November 1870, stating: 'Two interesting matters connected with these Boards which are beginning to attract considerable attention are the nomination of working men and of ladies, as candidates for election.'

At first Manning and the bishops were elated with the results of the elections to the new School Boards. 'Helped by the cumulative

*The writer has been assured by the historian and former archivist at the English College, Rome, the Rev. Henry G. Rope, M.A., that no such formal meeting took place.

vote, the Church party and the Catholics almost everywhere topped and swept the polls.'[53] Even Birmingham, the centre of Radical agitation, returned nine denominationalists out of a total of fifteen at the first election. Of the six secularists, Chamberlain only just managed to obtain the last place. Such resounding success for the Churchmen, however, was only likely to consolidate the ranks of the secularists and this became especially noticeable when the new Boards began to make full use of Clause 25 in the Act. This latter declared:

The School Board may, if they think fit, from time to time, for a renewable period not exceeding six months, pay the whole or any part of the School fees payable at any Public Elementary School by any child resident in their district whose parent is in their opinion unable through poverty to pay the same; but no such payment shall be made or refused on condition of the child attending any Public Elementary School other than such as may be selected by the parent, and such payment shall not be deemed to be parochial relief given to such parent.

As Garvin points out, 'the application, however limited, of Clause 25, meant payments out of rates to sectarian schools under private managers'[54] and hence challenged the secularists and Nonconformists on one of their basic principles. It was not surprising, therefore, to find the latter exerting all their energy to gain control of the Boards and agitating for a reform of the Act.

Manning's own attitude hardened when the secularists became more adamant and loud in their demands and increased their efforts to get control of the new Boards. Huxley came prominently into the field in November 1870, as a candidate for the London School Board. An article appeared in the *Catholic Times* under the heading 'Huxley on Education' on 12 November. 'Huxley, the great materialistic philosopher of infidelity, has spoken!' it declared, and went on: 'As a candidate for election on the London School Board, he has told us his views; and most singularly, this chosen champion of secular education confirms the words and deeds of the opponents of that system by admitting that if we expected by secular education to obtain "honest men, decent men, or thoughtful or religious men" we expected to get out of the Education Act that which had not been put into it; "what right had we to expect to find grapes on thorns, or figs on thistles?"—"something else must be added to mere intellectual training". The professor's "something" is really wonderful—gymnastics.'

It was thus only when the secularists came more militantly into the open contest that Manning prepared to do battle. By the early 1880's sufficient time had elapsed to be able to take stock of the new measure and its practical effect. Since 1871 Chamberlain was conducting a vigorous campaign in the country for 'free schools'. This proposal was 'taken to mean that fees would be abolished in the Board Schools only'.[55] This was a subtle move on the part of the secularists, for it meant that the Voluntary Schools would have to do the same or cease to function. They could not hope to compete on the same basis as schools financed by public funds. The policy, if adopted, would force the Voluntary Schools to close down or submit to the Board's authority.

In addition, Manning's early fears of the School Boards had by this time been justified. 'In these little cliques all the evils of a clique —factiousness, jobbery and waste—were felt. . . . Details of intimidation, misrepresentation, and unscrupulous influence employed to maintain sectarian supremacy.'[56]

It had become evident that where Board Schools and Voluntary Schools existed in the same town, the latter were at a great disadvantage. It was not only that the Board Schools were able to draw on public taxation to keep their schools going, but also that every penny that a person paid in taxation represented a penny less that he was able to contribute to his Voluntary School. This situation also meant that the person who sent his child to a Voluntary School was paying roughly twice as much as his neighbour who sent his child to a Board School. Usually lower fees were charged in the latter than in the Voluntary School. But the Board School received 17s. per child from the rates, whereas the Voluntary School could only count on 6s. 10d. from charity. This resulted in poverty in salaries, equipment and buildings. What is more the Church School was assessed for the rate to support the Board School. The Government's grant to the Voluntary School in areas where there was no Board School was in proportion to the amount of charity received by the school and consequently meant that the charity must be kept to a high level to earn a tolerable grant. The latter never exceeded 17s. 6d. in any case. But should the local School Board state that it had room for all the children in its own school or schools, then the Voluntary School received no grant at all. Parents who could not afford the Voluntary School fees were forced to ask the Guardians for relief in the daytime and this was a great grievance, for it meant that a man would lose wages and possibly his job, if he did so. The extraordinary thing was that 'in this unequal setting the Voluntary Schools population, nevertheless, increased to over two millions in 14 years, whilst that of the Board Schools reached less than a million. Academically the products were best, moreover, in the Catholic Schools, whose record of "complete passes" each year, till 1875, was the highest of all (72.14%).'[57]

Manning's remedies for all these troubles were

(1) Let a school rate be levied over the whole population as a part of the general taxation of the country,[58]

and

(2) Let all schools, with or without religious teaching, partake in the school rate, as they partake now of the grants of the Consolidated Fund under all the conditions of the Statute law and of the minutes and codes of the Committee of Privy Council.

He argued:

the exclusive enjoyment and control of the education is given only one form of opinion, and that form which is repugnant to the majority of the people of the United Kingdom, namely, that such schools should be only secular, to the exclusion of religion. . . . If the Government may tax the whole people for education *the whole people have a right to share in the beneficial use of such taxation.*

In 1884 Manning decided to marshal all the forces in opposition to the Birmingham Radicals and he founded the Voluntary Schools Association for the purpose. It is unhistorical of Snead-Cox to state that 'Cardinal Manning . . . had no organisation to his hand fitted to make a direct appeal to the constituencies . . . the Catholic body had no programme'.[59] The first meeting of the V.S.A. was held at his house and had for its programme (*a*) a re-opening of the 1870 settlement by appointing a Royal Commission to enquire into the grievances, and (*b*) a demand for a share of the school rate.

A General Election was due in November 1885, and it would be conducted on a further-widened franchise. Education and 'free schools' were bound to be major issues at the polls. Chamberlain was actively engaged in addressing meetings all over the country. ' "Give us your children, they shall cost you nothing; and we shall stamp them with our trade mark" '[60] was how Manning described the Radical programme, and he declared that 'Chamberlain and the aggressive Liberals will try to make it a final destruction of the Voluntary Schools'.[61]

Before the election Manning issued instructions to Roman Catholic voters—an unprecedented action. Two questions were to be put to candidates for election:

(1) Will you do your utmost to place voluntary schools on an equal with board schools?

(2) Will you do your utmost to obtain a Royal Commission to review the present state of education in England and Wales, and especially the Act of 1870 and its administration by the School Boards?

Catholics were to vote as they answered in the positive or the negative to these questions. Dr. McEntee is nearer the truth than Mr. C. H. D. Howard when she states that in 1885 'on the question of education, he (Manning) supported the Conservative candidates'.[62] Although Manning did not actually give this advice in so many words, he knew that the practical outcome of the questions he directed to be put to parliamentary candidates would achieve this result. But Howard, in his article in the *English Historical Review* on this matter, has ignored a most vital reason for Manning's action.[63] During this very year Gladstone's Government had been attempting to secure the appointment of a pro-English bishop to the vacant Roman Catholic See of Dublin and had carried out a merciless vendetta against the popular candidate, Dr. Walsh of Maynooth. We shall deal in detail with this episode in the chapter entitled 'Ireland', but suffice it to say here that the Government had stationed at Rome an 'unofficial' agent—Mr. Errington, an 'Old Catholic'. From the evidence to be presented later, it will be seen that it was not unlikely that Manning wished to teach the Liberals a lesson and to prevent this kind of political interference in a purely ecclesiastical matter for the future. Gladstone had to be taught that he was not yet strong enough to ignore the value of the Irish vote.

The action that Manning pursued at this election was one in accordance with his Irish policy of keeping closely in line with the Irish Parliamentary Party, and Parnell refused to support Gladstone.[64] In fact for the interests of both Manning's Irish policy and his educational policy it was incumbent on him to support the Conservative candidates. It is extremely difficult to assess exactly Manning's influence in returning Salisbury to power. Certainly the Irish vote played a large part in that result, but how far the Irish were influenced by Manning and how far by Parnell's Manifesto of 21 November 1885 it is impossible to say with certainty. But both Parnell and Manning were aiming for the same outcome, namely, that the Irish members should hold the balance of power, and between them they obtained the desired result. Salisbury was returned, but without an adequate majority.

After Salisbury's victory, Manning wrote to his fellow-Oblate, Bishop Vaughan of Salford, as follows:

What strikes me is this:

1. The Parliament of 1869 [sic] gave to the Liberals and the Nonconformists a complete supremacy. The Act of 1870 was founded upon the secular and Nonconformist basis. It has established and endowed the Nonconformist education.

2. The Parliament and Government of 1885 is the first reaction against 1870, and the Christian schools have a chance.

3. The Act of 1870 will not be repealed: and the Board-Schools cannot be broken up.

4. But an Act may be framed which will check the profuse expenditure and multiplication of Board Schools, and restore to Christian Schools their freedom of multiplication.

5. What more can be done? If we were asked what should we say?

6. What we need is a permanent settlement and protection against Chamberlain and Jules Ferry.[65]

Alas! Manning was not to get all that he desired—but he did secure from Salisbury's short-lived ministry the second plank in his electoral platform. Before Gladstone returned to power in February 1886, Salisbury had set up the Cross Commission (under the chairmanship of Sir Richard Cross) to enquire into the working of the 1870 Act. Manning was appointed a member, and soon became the dominating figure. In 1888 the Commission reported. It issued a majority and a minority report (thereby giving the Government an excuse for not implementing it in full). Only eight of the twenty-three commissioners signed the minority report. Manning signed the one issued by the majority and it declared:

183. That there is no reason why the principle of Voluntary Schools receiving annual aid from the rates should not be extended, and rate aid, in respect of their secular efficiency, should not be given to Voluntary Schools (as it is now to Industrial and Reformatory Schools), without the imposition of the Cowper-Temple clause, which, under the Act of

1870, affects those schools only which are provided and supported entirely by rates. . . .

We should regard any separation of the teacher from religion as injurious to the morals and secular training of the scholars.

The only implementation of the Cross Commission's findings occurred in 1891 when Salisbury, back in office, carried a proposal to accord all aided schools 10s. per child to replace the fees which were abolished. Payment by results was finished. This made education free in all schools, whether Board or Voluntary. Thus one year before his death, Manning was able to witness this great change for the better. In 1886, writing to Gladstone, Manning had declared his belief that:

it will be possible to find a scheme which will combine the Voluntary System and the Board Schools giving equal legal recognition, and free development to both. We should then have one system of National Education conforming itself to the needs and desires of the people instead of a Departmental System in constant friction and collision with both.[66]

Later he had declared: 'I used to tell Forster that the Birmingham League had made use of him.'[67] And later still: 'Though my judgment of the Board School System is unfavourable, I see the improbability of reversing the work of 1870.'[68] His beliefs and struggles were to reach fruition in the episcopate of his successor. In 1902, by the Act of that year, Vaughan was to see the Voluntary Schools 'put on the rates', for the new Local Education Authorities were compelled to maintain them financially. Thus the whole of Manning's programme had been achieved and his policy vindicated by time. The fight after 1902 was only to be for complete equality, not for survival.

It is clear, therefore, that the statements quoted at the beginning of this chapter, and which assert that Manning had no policy towards the Act of 1870 and the development of national education, are untenable. He originally supported the idea of State intervention; the actual system of the School Boards, although he always feared and deprecated it, he actively opposed only when he found it prejudicial in practice. It is difficult to see what other policy could have been adopted with success under the circumstances, for to have remained entirely aloof would have been a suicidal policy for Roman Catholic schools.

Chapter IV

HIGHER EDUCATION

*

WHEN we consider Manning's attitude towards the higher education of the laity and of the clergy, we encounter what appears to be, at first sight, a contradiction in aims and policy. We have seen how Manning was in the vanguard in the provision of education for children at both the elementary and secondary levels and how he encouraged the 'scientific' movement in education. We have discovered that his main aim in this was to enable the Roman Catholic layman to play his part once more on the stage of public affairs and to bring the Roman Catholic Church into the main current of English life and thought. In this way it would cease, in the eyes of Englishmen, to be foreign and subversive and its aims would be made manifest to all. To achieve this policy completely, however, it was necessary to have a Roman Catholic laity educated to the same level and as far as possible in the same way as their non-Catholic counterparts. The contradiction appears to exist at the outset—why did Manning, while holding these views, oppose and prohibit the attendance of his clergy and laity at the national universities of Oxford and Cambridge?

Manning's opposition to the kind of education acquired at Oxford and Cambridge had its roots in his Anglican days. When he was Archdeacon of Chichester he had written in July 1846 his views of the inadequacy and unsoundness of the education acquired there.

He declared:

It is remarkable that in the three last centuries, during which the population has multiplied four-fold, the scientific character of England—I may even say science itself—has spread itself abroad, and multiplied its branches, even in a still greater proportion. All forms of pure and of applied science, ranges of intellectual labour unknown to our forefathers, have become the habitual employment of a countless multitude of minds. These later centuries are characteristically centuries of science. We date the exact method of scientific investigation within the last three hundred years; and it is specially observable, that while the popular intellect has taken so strong a course in the direction of professional and abstract science, our Universities, and especially one of them,* have become comparatively unscientific. . . . The very defence set up for the Universities by some†—namely, that they educate what is universal in man, that is, man as man, and not professions as professions—(good as it is in their behalf as great lay schools of popular education)—is a direct inversion of the true order and even name of an University, which is a system professing to teach all faculties as such. The defence proves the indictment.[1]

In this passage we discover Manning's foremost objection to the type of education provided by Oxford and Cambridge; we need not look far for the second.

Our Universities [he declared], are not the schools of the poor, nor of the middle classes, but of what I may call the titular and natural aristocracy of the country. . . . There is the great middle class, for whom in the Universities a new and distinct provision is required.

Writing in the *Dublin Review* in 1863 on 'The Works and Wants of the Catholic Church in England', Manning recorded 'another great want is that of a higher, literary and scientific education for our laymen'. In this article he marshals the pros and cons of the case for allowing Catholics to attend Oxford and Cambridge. The chief of the reasons for attendance there, he lists under nine headings. The first two deal with the argument that since the repeal of the Penal Laws Catholics must take their part in public affairs and that they must be educated accordingly. In the third place, it is argued that 'it is safer for Catholics to study there than in Paris, in Pisa, or other continental cities'. The remaining arguments are all grouped around the statement that 'Inasmuch as Catholics must be mixed up with Protestants in every walk and state of life, and that more and more as the religious animosities of the past are mitigated by the gradual fusion and blending of families and classes, there cannot be any special danger in their beginning early to learn how to carry themselves towards their Protestant fellow citizens.' Place a Catholic student 'in a hall or college founded for Catholics only, under the government of a Catholic president and fellows, with Catholic discipline and instruction, and all the helps of the spiritual life (and) . . . such a youth would be sustained and raised above himself, and a Catholic public opinion would be created within the walls.'

---

* Oxford.

† Later by Newman in *Discourses on the Scope and Nature of a University Education*.

Although the arguments for the case are stated honestly and boldly in this way, we soon discover that Manning is not influenced by them. In his argument against Catholics being permitted to attend Oxford and Cambridge, it is with considerable irony that he quotes Newman to support his view. He declares

the whole argument so elaborately and eloquently developed by Dr. Newman, in his Lectures on University Education, applies with direct force to this subject. . . . Not only would all history and philosophy be anti-Catholic as delivered from the Chairs of Anglican professors, but that it would not be worthy of the name of history or philosophy if withdrawn from the light and guidance of Catholic theology. Count de Maistre said that history since the Reformation has been in conspiracy against the Catholic Church. We may say that philosophy since Descartes has to a wider extent than is suspected joined in the conspiracy. And yet these are essentially the history and philosophy delivered at the English Universities.

He concluded on a pessimistic note:

We are firmly convinced that in twenty years Rationalism will inundate England. . . . And we cannot doubt that every year this unbelief will more widely spread, and that the two Universities will be thoroughly pervaded by it. Instead, therefore, of implicating ourselves in a sinking wreck, it is the prudence of common sense, as well as the obligation of Catholic duty, to keep ourselves free, not only from all entanglements with it, but as far as possible from the vortex which it makes in going down.

This article contains strong views pronounced by a man who had two years more to wait before he wore the mitre at Westminster. It is interesting and enlightening for it shows that Purcell was quite wrong in ascribing to Manning the fear that the universities might 'protestantize' the Roman Catholic youths who went there.[2] His fears were two-fold. On the one hand he was apprehensive lest that Germanic liberalism, free-thought and agnosticism which he perceived were affecting Oxford and Cambridge would infect the Catholic laity and give rise to 'an unsound school of thought and principle among our laymen'.[3] On the other hand, he believed Oxford and Cambridge to be socially unrepresentative of the country and unwilling to cater for the middle classes' intellectual needs. Grounds for his fears on both these counts undoubtedly existed. Germanic thought had struck at Oxford, long before Manning was writing in the *Dublin Review*. We know that in 1860 'Jowett was attempting to construct a "via media" between Atheism and Athanasianism',[4] and that he was declaring that 'the Bible must be interpreted like any other book'. The University itself was in a furore and ardent Anglicans were attacking the leaders of the new liberalism. Manning declared that

the modern spirit of cultivated unbelief, in the form of criticism and philosophy, has not only entered but established itself, so as to be the predominant intellectual tendency of the more studious members of the Universities. The Protestant Bishops of Winchester and London have confessed what Dr. Colenso has repeated—that the graduates of Oxford and Cambridge are turning away from Anglican Orders.[5]

Thomas Arnold* and A. P. Stanley had popularized the idea of Biblical criticism and the reasons for the adoption of this approach can be found in the stimulus given by the scientific discovery of the century—especially that of the new science of geology. Sedgwick, one-time secretary to the Prince Consort, and a veritable German-izer, had popularized the science of geology within the walls of the ancient universities and together with Prince Albert's influence had perhaps done more than any other single man to advance its claims and the influence of Germanic thought. A deeper study of geology and biology had brought into question the whole field of existing Biblical cosmogony. The principles of scientific examin-ation were applied to the Bible and Biblical scholarship, as they were to every other branch of knowledge at this time, and as a consequence Oxford and Cambridge became whirlpools of rational-ism and speculative thought.

When a movement of this kind—nigh cosmic in its extent—is in its early stages it is frequently carried to excess. So it was in this case, and the line between 'theory' and 'fact' was but faintly drawn. The outcome was scepticism. This attitude becomes vividly clear when we read what an undergraduate wrote to Dr. Vaughan con-cerning the atmosphere at Oxford under the impact of these changes. He considerably influenced the attitude of that prelate when he wrote:

You have no idea how irreligious the atmosphere, especially the in-tellectual atmosphere, is here at Oxford. And it is not that men scoff or sneer at religion. What strikes me is that the number of men, both pro-fessors and undergraduates, who simply discard the supernatural in religion altogether, who believe in nothing but what is material, and believe in

---

* His younger son Thomas had become a Roman Catholic.

no-one but themselves. There are others, on the other hand, who are too afraid to declare they have no religion but who look upon religion as being simply a social conventionality, by the non-observance of which you scandalise your neighbour.[6]

The attitude of mind to which the undergraduate refers was amusingly parodied in the mock examination of the Head of an Oxford College by an Inspector in 'The University Commission or Lord John Russell's Post Bag of 27th April, 1850'—

> Law, grammar, music, dialectics,
> Optics, with swimming, and aesthetics.
> Gymnastics, surg'ry and conchology
> And *The*—no—no I mean *Ge*ology
> Colonization, economics,
> Brewing, baking, and mnemonics
> With rhetoric, and the art vehicular
> And history general and particular,
> Algebra, skating, and astronomy,
> With metaphysics and gastronomy,
> Give me an outline of pneumatics;
> Explain how you would cure rheumatics;
> Define rent, wages and mahogany
> What's the last theory of cosmogony?[7]

Among all the welter of new sciences, the implication of the stanza is that theology is a thing not to be spoken about—geology is an adequate substitute.

Mr. H. O. Evennett sums up the total effect of the change in the intellectual temper at Oxford and Cambridge by saying that 'scepticism and rationalism *were added to* Protestantism'.[8] It was this condition that activated Manning's opposition to the old universities. Catholic youth, he conceived, would receive advanced training in numerous university disciplines, but their faith and religion would remain in the juvenile stages that they occupied after leaving school. Advanced knowledge would be gained in secular subjects but not in the divine. Could the latter hold ground in these circumstances and in the conditions prevailing at Oxford and Cambridge? For Manning, the question did not need an answer—obviously they could not. It is interesting to observe how closely allied, basically, were the ideas of Manning and Newman on the essential qualities of a university education. Newman's *Discourses on the Scope and Nature of a University Education*, and especially *Discourse II*, are devoted to an extensive eulogy of 'oneness', 'wholeness' and 'unity' in education. In *Discourse II*, Newman claims that all education must be treated as 'a whole' and that to be worthy of the name it must develop the whole man. If it neglected any part of his nature, it was not true education at all. This was, also, Manning's belief; the education given at Oxford and Cambridge, he considered, neglected the spiritual side of a man's nature and ignored the vocational aspect of education, *ergo* it was not a true education. Manning believed passionately in this quality of 'unity' in education at all levels. Writing in 1849, he had declared that the school was

one living system, in which every part is so united and penetrated by one common spirit, that no separation can be made. Instruction relates only to the *matter* that is taught. The school includes the whole *conduct* and *discipline*—the taught and the teacher, and all the circumstantial habits and influences which perpetually, for good or ill, determine the character and working of the school. The whole *tone* of the school is a part of education, and capable of a good or an evil, a religious or an irreligious direction. There is in a school nothing, however slight and unobserved, which may not leave its effect upon the moral nature of children.[9]

If we apply this paragraph to higher education, substituting the words 'university' for 'school' and 'students' for 'children' we shall have a clear conception of Manning's belief in the kind of education a university should provide. If 'the whole tone' of the university is a part of education, how far-reaching is an education going to be whose '*tone*' is one of rationalism and scepticism?

Dr. Gordon Albion asserts that Manning was responsible for the papal prohibition against Roman Catholics going to Oxford and Cambridge and characterizes his whole policy in this regard as being 'adamant' in the face of opposition.[10] The issue had come to a head, however, in Wiseman's episcopate and the entire Hierarchy agreed with the policy of prohibition. This policy was in existence under Cardinal Wiseman, and Manning continued the arrangement. Manning was not the originator of the policy—although along with Ward he had supported it completely—and he makes this clear in a letter to Mgr. Talbot in 1864: 'The bishops decided', he declared, referring to the Low Week meeting of the Hierarchy, 'against the Protestant Universities in all ways; but that a Catholic University is not possible. To this I cannot agree. And I trust that they will be encouraged to attempt, or to let others attempt something to meet the needs of our laity. It will not do to prohibit, and to provide nothing. Many will go to Oxford and Cambridge; and the precedent will be set, and all hope of anything higher will be lost.'[11]

This letter illustrates how Provost Manning conceived the basic problem and it is important in proving that he had long thought about the establishment of a Catholic university before he made the experiment at Kensington ten years later, in 1874. Prior to the Low Week meeting of the Hierarchy described in the letter to Mgr. Talbot,* Cardinal Barnabo had written from Rome to Bishop Ullathorne to express the view that Rome did not look with favour on Catholic colleges at Protestant universities.† Ullathorne acquiesced in this view. At the Low Week meeting in 1864, therefore, the idea of a Catholic college at Oxford or Cambridge was negatived. Shortly before Manning received the mitre, however, Newman wrote to Bishop Ullathorne about a proposal he had conceived of opening a house of the Oratory at Oxford. The letter contained the following points:

1. I consider that there is considerable danger to the souls of Catholic youth who go to the Protestant Colleges in Oxford.

2. I consider there is comparatively little danger in their going to a Catholic College there.

3. The former of these is the actual state of the case.

4. When I thought of our going to Oxford, it was with a view of meeting this actually existing danger.

5. If that danger ceased, I should not feel any special reason for our going there. . . .[12]

Manning understood from the outset that Newman's proposed Oratory was intended as the nucleus of a Catholic college at Oxford. He felt completely opposed to the scheme; to him it would solve nothing. If the only danger to Catholic youth was that they might be 'protestantized', then Newman's college might be a satisfactory means of offsetting this. But Manning objected not to possible proselytism, but to the prevailing philosophy—he objected to an 'atmosphere' which he considered pagan and materialistic. You cannot lock an idea or a philosophy outside closed doors and trust that it will not seep in through the cracks. Oxford, Manning held, was charged with the new liberalism and no building, even though

---

* Also a convert.

† Butler, *Life and Times of Bishop Ullathorne*, II, pp. 2 et seq. Oxford was in Ullathorne's diocese.

it contained a personality so distinguished as Newman, would be immune from it. W. G. Ward was perhaps the greatest opponent of the Oxford scheme. He felt that 'the rising generation, the future representatives of the Church in England, would be at Oxford during the most plastic years in which their views were being formed and their characters moulded, surrounded by the indifferent atmosphere of a University in which some of the ablest thought was now agnostic in its tendency'.[13] In the *Dublin Review* he opposed the policy 'with all the zeal of a Crusader'. Manning was considerably influenced by Ward and he felt that Newman's presence at Oxford would attract many pupils and disciples from Catholic homes. Such a college as Newman proposed would not be adequate to cater for the added influx attracted by his name. The most remarkable thing about Newman's proposition, however, is that he made it at a time when he was fully conscious of the Roman and hierarchical prohibition against the Universities and against the establishment of Catholic Colleges at them. Newman felt, and those who thought like him, that

the absence of Oxford life might conceivably do much more harm than its presence could do. For many, the alternative was Woolwich or Sandhurst—places fraught with far greater dangers than Oxford to those whose trials were moral rather than intellectual.[14]

If we probe deeper into the motives of Newman, we discover that his opposition to Manning on this issue arose from perhaps a more fundamental cause. Newman never really appreciated the danger to organized religion constituted by the new Germanic liberalism. He sympathized with the German school of thought and certainly with Dr. Döllinger and he felt sympathy for the more liberal schools of French thought. In fact Wilfrid Ward asserts that Newman had 'from the first largely sympathized with the policy of moderate liberal Catholics',[15] but cites Lacordaire and Montalembert as examples of the latter. Arnold Lunn when writing of this attitude is perhaps too savagely discerning when he declares

Newman is rather like a man who believes in the divine right of kings to dispense with Parliament and to over-ride law, and then grumbles because the king takes him at his word and threatens with death any citizen who does not wear side whiskers. The logical course is not to proclaim the divine right to shave, but to resist the divine right to rule.[16]

It was Newman's German friends that made him an Inopportunist over Papal Infallibility.

Manning, on the other hand, adhered to the opposite philosophical schools and was the reverse in temperament. He was 'out of harmony with the German',[17] although it is true that he sympathized with the French liberal party, whose desire to conciliate the claims of the Church and modern democracy strongly appealed to him. Unlike Newman, he felt that the Church would gain much from such a conciliation. On his appointment as Archbishop, Manning made a ten days' Retreat at the Highgate Passionist monastery, and among his notes and resolutions made at that time occurs the following which explains so much of Manning's basic attitudes as Archbishop.

I desire to be in the most perfect conformity to the Dogma of Faith, to the Theology of the Schools in its approved and pious opinions, to the traditions, instincts and spirit of the Holy See. I desire to speak in its accents and to act upon its precedents. I desire always to derive my guidance and counsel immediately from Rome. . . . I desire to hold inviolate the doctrines and laws of the Church without compromise.*

Opposition to Catholic youth attending Oxford and Cambridge was not, however, confined to Manning, Ward and those of a like mind. Bishop Hedley writing in the *Ampleforth Journal* in July 1896 about the reasons for the prohibition makes this clear. Referring to the year 1871, when he declares opinions were asked concerning the policy, he writes:

Several university men (converts) of high standing declared that to send young men to Oxford would be to shake the very foundations of their belief. One well-known convert thought that 'Those Catholics who are now being educated at Oxford would be among the most violent aggressors on the Church's interests, through the violently un-Catholic tendency of their intellectual training and habits.' A priest, who had been more than two years on the Oxford Mission, said that a very large proportion of the Catholic undergraduates give up by degrees the practice of their religion. The Headmaster of a school from which several boys had passed to Oxford, said that one and all of them suffered something from the deficient provision for carrying on their religious instruction. A convert clergyman residing in Oxford stated that the worldliness of the place and its un-Catholic and anti-Catholic life had the effect of making

* *Dublin Review*, CLXVI (Jan. 1920), fifth day, pp. 13–14.

Catholic undergraduates neglect their religion. The Superiors of Ushaw expressed their conviction that the general result, even of a Catholic college there, would be a coldness and indifference to the Faith, a critical and even contemptuous tone of mind in relation to things Catholic and to ecclesiastical authority, and plenty of that spurious liberalism which stands aloof from every object with which Catholics naturally sympathize.

It is clear from this quotation that the Oxford prohibition was not imposed simply by the narrowness of ecclesiastical opinion but that it possessed considerable lay support.

Another meeting of the Hierarchy was held on 13 December 1864, to consider Newman's idea of going to Oxford to establish an Oratory, and it is indicative of the minds of the bishops, and of how they regarded this scheme of Newman's as being but a prelude to the establishment of a Catholic college there, that they *unanimously* petitioned Rome to condemn the attendance of Catholics at the Protestant universities *and to forbid the setting up of Catholic colleges at them*.* Butler records that 'as a result of the meeting Newman abandoned the project of the Oxford Oratory and sold the land'.[18] Why did he do this, if he had not thought of the Oxford Oratory as merely a nucleus, for the establishment later of a Catholic college? The bishops had not forbidden Newman to establish a house of his Congregation—provided it was to be nothing more. There is no doubt that in his own mind he could not see himself there as a parish priest, but as a tutor. Mr. Evennett has scant grounds for his assertion that Newman 'was willing to agree "not to take part in University education" '.[19] As we have seen, Newman himself declared that if this was not to be so 'I should not feel any special reason for our going there',[20] and he had made this statement only ten weeks before the bishops' decision.

Writing to Sister Imelda Poole of Stone two weeks after this meeting of the bishops, Newman revealed that he clearly understood the implications of the decision, and also his original intention in going there. He declared:

If Propaganda brings out any letter of disapproval of young Catholics going to Oxford, (and people think it is certain to do so) my going there is either superfluous, or undutiful—superfluous if there are no Catholics there—undutiful if my going is an inducement to them, or an excuse and shelter for their going there.[21]

---

* They 'passed resolutions in favour of an absolute prohibition of Oxford'—Ward's *Newman*, op. cit. II, p. 65.

In 1864 Newman had issued a circular concerning his proposed Oratory at Oxford, and in it we find the sentence: 'Some such establishment has been for some time required in behalf of Catholic youth, whom the University, according to the provision of a recent Act of Parliament, admits to matriculation.'[22] The circular is given in full in Purcell (II, pp. 296 sqq.) and the extract quoted was enough in itself to arouse the suspicions of the bishops. If Newman was only interested in the parish at Oxford, why was he talking about University regulations and Catholic students? Bishop Ullathorne, Newman's greatest supporter among the bishops, was under the impression that the circular would be construed as favourable to the education of Catholics at Oxford. Although the circular was never published at large it had been read at the meeting of bishops and deemed to be inexpedient.

It is of vital importance to remember that all these events occurred before Manning became Archbishop of Westminster. He was not in control of the Hierarchy although he exerted a growing influence over Wiseman, and the bishops had no reason to expect his succession to Westminster.

Robert A. Coffin, one of the most distinguished of the Oxford converts, who originally joined Newman as an Oratorian and disciple but later left the Oratory to become a Redemptorist, was a firm opponent of Catholics' going to Oxford. After being English Provincial of the Redemptorist Congregation, in June 1882 he became third Bishop of Southwark. At the Southwark Diocesan Synod, Coffin vigorously opposed the views of those favourable to Oxford and declared:

I cannot conceive how the religious and moral conditions of a young Catholic man could be improved or that his faith, piety and moral feeling would be increased, even with the helps and safeguards proposed by the advocates of a Catholic College in a Protestant University, by a three years residence in the midst of Protestants and in an intensely Protestant and worldly atmosphere. . . . The result of three years residence of our young men in an English Protestant University would be an addition year by year to the numbers of worldly, disloyal half-hearted Catholics; who cause sorrow to the Holy See and who would perpetuate that want of simple and hearty obedience to and respect for Ecclesiastical Authority from which the Holy Church in this country has at this present moment, in my humble opinion, far more to fear than from all her open and declared enemies from without.[23]

8

Coffin went on to object in particular to the influence of Professor Jowett and Dean Stanley and declared his conviction

that this present urge for University Education arises in reality from the false impression that a young man who has not been at Oxford or Cambridge will not be able to take his proper place in Society or to mix easily with his equals in after life.

It was not long, however, after Manning's consecration before Newman decided to make another effort to establish himself in Oxford. The new régime might be more sympathetically disposed to Newman personally. He again bought land for an Oratory there, and gave out in public and in private (without reference to Manning) that the sole purpose of the establishment would be to staff the mission for Bishop Ullathorne.[24] In thus making the question a purely diocesan matter, both Ullathorne and Newman sought to evade the jurisdiction of Manning and the Hierarchy. Meanwhile Newman had cultivated powerful friendships. He had 'a considerable measure of agreement and support from Bishop Ullathorne, Bishop Clifford, and others. The English Jesuits . . . were ever his good friends.'[25] Propaganda raised no objection to his apparently harmless move. Manning was personally opposed because he felt that if Newman made his Oxford pulpit as attractive as in his Tractarian days, he would be an added inducement to Catholic youths wishing to flout the Hierarchy's prohibition; Manning's alarm was increased, however, when he learnt that Newman was actually preparing boys for Oxford in defiance of the papal ruling. Father Herbert Vaughan, O.S.C., later Bishop of Salford and successor to Manning, wrote from Rome to Manning on 29 March 1867, as follows:

I have come across the parent of a boy at Edgbaston. He told me that he is dumb on the question of education at Oxford but either St. John or Caswell* said that he (St. John or Caswell) looked upon an Oxford Oratory as the first step to a Catholic College there. If this be true and if they represent Newman, one could hardly feel a scruple at removing him from Oxford soon with a pitchfork. Is it possible that he has been deceiving his bishop and acting surreptitiously?[26]

A month before Manning received this letter, he himself had written to Mgr. Talbot: 'Dr. Newman is preparing Mr. John Townsley's son for Oxford, and my belief is that many of the boys

* St. John and Caswell were two Fathers at the Birmingham Oratory.

at Edgbaston will go there. We are slipping sideways into the whole mischief.'[27] Could such a man be trusted not to take boys into his proposed Oratory at Oxford?

Meanwhile Herbert Vaughan was still in Rome and before he left he was granted a private audience with Pius IX. This was in April 1867, and they discussed the visit to England the previous year of Cardinal Reisach. While in England Reisach had visited Oxford and had seen the plot of land that Newman had purchased for his project. Newman complained bitterly against Manning for what he considered a slight to himself in that he was not asked to meet the distinguished visitor. The truth, however, can be gleaned from the Bayswater archives. Manning wrote to Newman's bishop asking him to inform Newman of Cardinal Reisach's visit and invite him to meet the visitor. Ullathorne wrote in reply 'Dr. Newman is absent from Birmingham'[28] and gave that as the excuse why he had failed to invite him. However, Herbert Vaughan in his meeting with Pius discussed this affair and then went on to talk of the Oxford question. In giving an account of the audience he told Manning, in a letter dated 10 April 1867, that he made the following points to the Pope:

1. The imminent danger of (1) our losing control over our higher studies (2) of the formation of a liberal and an anti-roman school at Oxford.

2. The warning of which Trinity, Dublin, is giving examples.

3. That Newman's presence at Oxford has been publicly declared to be an encouragement to Catholics to go thither; that he is the representative of the liberal and national school of thought. . . .

4. The advantage of taking Trinity as a motive, as well as Oxford, to declare against the national universities a prohibition.

5. That we have all the elements of a University among ourselves.[29]

Vaughan concludes by recording that Pius IX said Newman was vain and that the Pope 'trusts his Archbishop, but not much his Bishops'.

The Prefect of Propaganda, Cardinal Barnabo, described to Vaughan 'in an absurd way the heavy weight he felt upon his stomach whenever Newman conversed with him. And he [said?] that Newman is disappointed in not getting a mitre, that such is human nature and we must all look after ourselves and Newman's anger, of which he is the object, has not much affected him, he considers it rather as a feather in his cap, if I may say so.'[30] There is little doubt that Vaughan's visit was followed by a hardening of anti-Newman prejudice at Rome.

Whatever influence Vaughan exerted in this visit, however, must be surmised; but the fact remains that Barnabo wrote direct to Ullathorne saying that an Oratory could be formed at Oxford, but that Newman was to remain at the Birmingham establishment.* This condition was the last straw! Newman had no interest—as Ullathorne knew—in founding an Oratory at Oxford if he was to remain in Birmingham, and the scheme collapsed. How far was Manning responsible for this *personal prohibition* of Newman?

Manning's defence is contained in a letter to Oakeley:

As to the question of the Oratory at Oxford, Newman will know that when it was proposed in the Cardinal's† time it was given up on the ground that it would have the effect of encouraging young Catholics to go to Oxford. . . . I never knew the facts until after the event, and had no part in them.

But since I have been here I have had part in the question and my part has been uniform and open.

I have opposed the sending young Catholics to Oxford as before. . . . As to the personal restraint of Newman's going to Oxford, I never heard or imagined such a thing until the Rescript had been for at least two months in England.‡

Newman was hyper-sensitive and from this date his attitude to Manning underwent the same course as it had done with Wiseman, Coffin and Faber, and he remained hostile.

Newman had formed a close alliance with the 'Old Catholic' families and this alliance was used by Manning's enemies to give him irritation and, if possible, to thwart his policies. This was particularly true concerning the Oxford question. The 'Old' families saw that the episcopal prohibition would cause serious damage to them socially and they were determined to resist. Manning always claimed that they did not care for higher studies; they wished 'to have latch-keys to Grosvenor Square'.[31] Mr. Evennett is hardly justified in asserting that Manning did not under-

* Ullathorne was surprisingly reticent in communicating this condition to either Newman or Manning and gave the former the idea that *he personally* would like Newman to give up the project.   † i.e. Wiseman's.

‡ Purcell, op. cit. II, pp. 371 et seq. Obviously Ullathorne had held back the Rescript from Manning for over two months. In Newman's letter to Rome giving up the idea of the Oxford Oratory he did not deny that he had been educating youths for Oxford (see M.P., Vaughan to Manning, 5.4.67).

stand the social disadvantages experienced by the rich, which were a direct result of his policy. He certainly understood them, but did not consider them of any value—to him it was simply snobbery and as such he smote it. Clearly Christopher Howard is also misled in asserting that Manning's attitude to the problem of university education 'revealed a failure to appreciate the attraction that the older English Universities had for young men of means'.[32] It was because of this attraction that he attempted to provide an alternative at Kensington. When the 'Old' families complained of *the laity* being prevented from competing with Protestants on an equal footing, they really meant only their *own circle*. It was an attitude of privilege that Manning had always resented, even before his conversion to Rome. He once declared: 'If the laity of the Church are to be invoked, it must be not the laity of wealth—the laity of any particular grade—not a class-laity, but the laity of the whole people of Christ.'[33] Ally this to his statement that 'Our Universities are not the schools of the poor, nor of the middle classes, but of what I may call the titular and natural aristocracy of the country',[34] and it is plain to see what little value he placed on the social aspirations of those Catholics who desired permission to send their sons to Oxford and Cambridge. He did not fail to understand those aspirations, but he considered them to be unworthy ones.

Mgr. Clifford, the Bishop of Clifton, was the chief representative of the ennobled and the well-to-do among the Hierarchy, and in 1871 he took it upon himself to make a lone petition to Rome for the removal of the ban, on the grounds that the repeal of the Tests had altered the situation. Propaganda's answer was to reiterate the ban and press for a Catholic university. As a matter of fact Clifford had never been very popular at the Roman Court. It was his custom when in the Eternal City to amuse himself among the English aristocracy there. Talbot once described to Manning how Clifford had 'hired a carriage by the month, and [went] out amongst the English every night, eating their good dinners, and gossiping at all their parties'.[35] He was considered to be Gallican in his ideas, as this extract from an unpublished letter from Fr. Edward Douglas, C.SS.R., to Fr. Coffin illustrates. On 1 August 1870, Douglas wrote:

The three aristocratic English bishops* ought to be really Roman and Papists, and especially Dr. Clifford who was educated I think by the Jesuits. But 'what ought to be' does not always follow.[36]

* Clifford, William Vaughan of Plymouth, Errington.

Clifford had been in 1870 the most truculent of the English Inopportunists and it was not likely that a few months later Rome would listen to such a stalwart of the opposition. (Clifford's correspondence with Newman betrays an enmity to Manning and his policies which is almost pathological in its intensity.)*

The Month supported Newman on the Oxford problem, while the *Dublin Review* was Manning's special defender. Ullathorne played a double role. Ostensibly he supported Manning's policy on Oxford and voted with the majority of the bishops in its favour, while secretly he was undermining that policy by his proposals to Newman concerning the foundation of an Oratory at Oxford and the entrusting of the parish there to him.†

In 1863 in the *Dublin Review*, Manning had recommended the establishment of a Catholic university and indicated that, with the co-operation of all interested in the subject of higher education, the scheme could be a great success.[37] We have seen how in 1864 in his letter to Talbot he again envisaged the foundation of such a university. The Holy See in 1867 informed the Hierarchy that the removal of religious tests at Oxford would not remove the prohibition against Catholics going there and it charged the bishops with the duty of providing alternative education. Once this idea was accepted by the bishops, Newman's hopes of returning to Oxford were doomed. For when in 1868, at the Low Week meeting, the bishops agreed to find some means of carrying out Propaganda's directions, it was obvious that the prohibition against Oxford and Cambridge must be retained and in a sense strengthened in order to ensure a reasonable chance of success for the new venture. Newman recognized this and expressly told Ullathorne so. He states in this letter: 'When I was in Dublin, I did my best . . . in getting a prohibition against Irish Catholics going to the English Universities, for I thought that the new Catholic University in Dublin would have no fair chance of success without such a prohibition.'[38] Newman, after 1868, could not in justice oppose Manning on this issue without being illogical. Yet that is precisely what he did!

In 1868 (after some initial opposition from Bishop Clifford who objected to a joint Pastoral as an infringement on his episcopal rights) the bishops had decided to set up a *personal* university—

---

* See the letters at St. Ambrose, Leigh Woods, Bristol 8. Much of this correspondence is outside the scope of this present work.

† The Jesuits eventually took over the parish.

which really amounted to a board of examiners which would examine pupils in the existing Catholic colleges at university level. It was a scheme not likely to have much success, although the Society of Jesus would have welcomed it as they were already running a department of advanced studies at Stonyhurst College.[39] It was, therefore, fortunate that the Vatican Council came on and it was impossible to pursue the scheme.

The whole matter was reviewed by the bishops in council in 1872. Following the meeting the prelates issued a joint pastoral letter to their several dioceses on the question of university education, and declared:

The late changes in the national Universities, in which all tests in religion have been abolished, caused us once more to seek the guidance of the Holy See. After reciting the decision of the Holy See, dated February 3rd, 1865, the answer runs in these words: 'The declaration then given was founded on the grave dangers which the said Universities presented: and the Catholics of England, both Clergy and Laity, complied with that declaration in the most edifying manner, although the state of the national Universities was far different then from what it has become since. . . . Not only does the Holy See perceive no reason why it should recede from the afore-mentioned decision of 1865, but in proportion as the reasons have increased in gravity, so much the more necessary does it appear that that decision should be maintained. (Letter of the Cardinal Prefect of Propaganda, September 19th, 1872.)[40]

It was clear that the prohibition had to stand; an alternative was urgently needed. The bishops were largely agreed in the policy of prohibition. This is well illustrated in the case of Charles Stourton, a well-known member of a Yorkshire 'Old Catholic' family, who had sent his son to Oxford in defiance of the ruling. Bishop Cornthwaite of Beverley threatened Stourton with ecclesiastical penalties if his son was not withdrawn. That this threat was effective is evident from the letter he wrote to the bishop: 'I will still venture to hope that your Lordship will not consider it necessary that my son should leave before the term ending at mid-summer year?'[41] The Hierarchy's injunctions were, on the whole, very well obeyed; in 1872 only eight Catholics were in residence at Oxford. But although so many of the bishops were enthusiastic about the prohibition, many had little interest in the alternative of providing a Catholic university. Throughout Manning's life as a Roman Catholic the idea of an English Catholic university seems to have attracted his attention. When Newman was encountering opposition in 1855 in Dublin to his plans for the university there, Manning suggested that he would do well to establish it on English soil instead of in Ireland. He wrote:

If you should find the national element in Ireland insuperable, would it not be well to re-consider the site of the University. All your arguments of centrality would apply to the West Coast of England as much as to the East Coast of Ireland. From the first I have rather acquiesced than assented to the present site: except as a balance to the Queen's Colleges. In the sense of your paper on Attica in the 2nd or 3rd Univ. Gazette, England is even more central to the Anglo-Saxon Race than Ireland.

The difficulty of contributions can be overcome by the motives which would satisfy the Holy See. This alternative would I hope be considered before that of your resignation.[42]

This letter had followed one in which Newman had requested Manning's help in persuading Aubrey de Vere to take the chair of Medieval History at Dublin. Manning was unable to persuade de Vere, who felt his talents lay more in the field of literature than history.

In 1873 the Hierarchy met in Synod and it was decided to go ahead with Manning's scheme for the establishment of a Catholic university college. When the matter had been discussed by the bishops in 1867, Bishop Clifford wrote to Manning a long and interesting letter giving his views as to how such a university should be formed. This unpublished letter is given here in full for it illustrates clearly the aims of the 'Old Catholics' and the reasons why the Kensington venture never met with their support. Clifford declares that he has thought much about the university scheme and he states that:

It seems to me that it would [be] better to treat these two questions separately.   1st. What plan could be agreed upon for the erection of a place for the Higher Studies, under the Hierarchy and with the concurrence of the Fathers of the Society.* 2ndly. Would it be advantageous to commence such an undertaking at Prior Park or elsewhere.

As regards the first point it seems to me that something of this sort might be proposed: 1. Let there be a house for the Jesuits where their professors and students can live in community: it would be strictly a religious house with the usual privileges and exemptions. The professors would be members of the University (or whatever name we give the

* Jesuits.

institution: for it would be better perhaps to avoid so high sounding a name at first), take part in the council, and government of the institution, and only come under the notice of the Hierarchy in regard to things which concern the university, not in any way as regards the management of their own house. These Jesuit professors would have to be named by their own Superiors and accepted by the council, whereas professors who are not religious would have to be appointed by the council. Moreover Jesuit professors could not be permanent, they would have to be movable by their superiors. The compact would be not between the Hierarchy and the individual professors, but between the Hierarchy and the Society, that the latter should supply say 3 or 4 competent professors for such and such subjects. These would be recognised and form part of the university staff. If the Jesuits in their own house wished to have more professors, or teach other matters beyond what the university at present required, they would be perfectly at liberty to do so as that would be a matter concerning not the university but their private arrangements.

Besides this house of Jesuits, I propose that there should be one or more houses of residence for students. In each of these should reside a head appointed by the Hierarchy—and also one or two professors might reside there. The rest of the house would be occupied by students. These houses would form the beginning of what in time might develop into separate colleges. One or two such houses might suffice to begin with supposing we began with 30 or 40 students. If these increased, more room would be required.

General rules of discipline would have to be laid down for these houses of residence and the head of each house would be responsible for the maintenance of such rules. Students ought to be required to reside in such houses, and houses of residence for students ought not to be allowed to be established except subject to the rules of the University.

The staff necessary to begin with would be 6 or seven professors, three or four of whom would be Jesuits. There would also have to be one or two heads of residences: and a President. Putting the salaries of these say at £100 a year and their keep and other expenses at £100 more, and taking into consideration the amount of accommodation required for so many persons, I do not think we could reckon the expenses at less than £2,000 a year. Then there would be the expense of furnishing at starting, and the expense of getting up some sort of apparatus of books etc. The question first to be considered is could some such scheme be made to work. The council of the University might consist of the professors and heads of houses or of some of them, the visitors, the Archbishop and two bishops chosen by the others—and these could decide the course of studies etc. which would have to be regulated in great measure by the requirements of the London University where the students would have to take their degrees—also all matters of discipline could be decided by such a council. But what about a President? That is the great difficulty. As you justly observe, if we undertake such a work the government must rest in the Hierarchy, and therefore who ever holds the supreme office must hold it under the Hierarchy.*

Now would it be necessary to have a permanent head, or would it be advisable to elect one from time to time? I have been thinking that we ought to look forward to making the professorships permanent and getting them endowed in time, as the best way to encourage learning and elevate the tone of the institution. In the case of religious the endowment would be for the body undertaking to supply a certain Chair. Supposing then that we looked upon the professors as forming a body permanently attached to the university, would it be preferable to appoint a permanent head, or would it be better to choose a president from time to time amongst the professors and heads of residences? So that the head should have the security of always remaining a member of the body, but not of always being the head?

If some such arrangement were thought advisable there might be less difficulty in appointing a religious from time to time. But the matter would have to be well weighed, before proposing it. I feel that we ought to avoid as much as possible from the beginning giving the establishment too much the air of a College of regulars.

Then comes the question of money. Could we get up £2,000 or £1,500 a year for the first five or ten years? I do not think congregational collections would do. To ask the poor to help in educating the rich would not be fair. Moreover we may judge from the Poor School Committee what amount we could have any chance of collecting; and to fail after begging in that form would throw the attempt into ridicule. Unless we could get a certain number to subscribe in sums of £100, £50, and £10, I fear there would be little chance of success.

If the modus operandi could be agreed upon between the Hierarchy and the Jesuits, then I think that the most advisable thing to do would be to draw up a sketch of what could be done, and send it round to the chief Catholics throughout England stating what sum would be requisite to begin and asking them to what amount they would contribute. I now come to the question about Prior Park, as a place for starting the University: or College for higher studies.

No doubt it would be difficult to find a place to begin, and perhaps Prior Park offers more advantages than could be found elsewhere for the

---

* Notice Clifford does not suggest Newman as President. Clifford as the leader of the 'Old Catholic' interests with which Newman had identified himself would most certainly have suggested the great Oratorian for the office of President if he had not been well aware that Newman would find it impossible to work under the directions of the bishops.

present. Still if the undertaking succeeds there is no doubt that more extensive buildings would be required whether at Prior Park or elsewhere. Now although it is advisable to rent a place at first, so that if the undertaking fails money may not have been thrown away in building; still before anything is begun even on a lease at Prior Park it ought to be considered whether in case the enterprise succeeded it could be continued at Prior Park. Because if from the very beginning it appeared that Prior Park would do for five or six years, but that it would not do when the enterprise succeeded, but that it would be necessary then in any case to move elsewhere, I should not like to upset existing arrangements for so short a period and with such uncertainty, and I am sure my clergy would not like it either. If on the other hand it were considered that Prior Park would ultimately suit the purpose, provided the institution was successful, then it might be well to rent it for a time on trial with a view of taking a longer lease afterwards or making such other arrangements as might suit.

I have written this much because I thought you might like to know something of my ideas before you spoke to Fr. Weld. Of course they are still of a very vague kind,

I remain my dear Lord Archbishop,
Your Servant in J.C.,
✠ WILLIAM CLIFFORD.[43]

If we examine this letter of Clifford we can see clearly what the 'Old Catholics' were trying to achieve:

1. The Jesuits would be in complete control. (Three or four professors were to be Jesuits out of an original total of six or seven. The Jesuits would be able to claim all exemption from episcopal jurisdiction and would be allowed to move their professors at will. Clifford was educated by the Jesuits.)

2. The college system was to prevail. (This would be based on the Oxford model, and all teaching in the hands of the Jesuits would be classical and cater for those likely to benefit from such a course—the children of the 'Old Catholic', aristocratic, families. Scientific instruction would be effectively excluded and with it the middle classes who were likely to benefit from it.)

3. The university was to be housed at Prior Park, Bath. (This was in Clifford's own diocese and he would be able to obtain a pincer grip on the new establishment to make sure that it developed along the lines he desired. The university would pay rent to the Diocese of Clifton for Prior Park.)

4. The Council of the university was to be a composite body, the majority of which would apparently be Jesuits, and Manning was to have two other bishops elected by the Hierarchy to be joined with him as Visitors. (One of the bishops elected would surely be Clifford, since the establishment would be housed in his diocese. This would mean that Manning's influence would be effectively negatived and that his guiding hand would be removed during the formative years. He would have only *a part* in the deliberations of the Council, not the final decision.)

5. Chairs were to be endowed. (The Jesuits would endow their own and so they would be in complete control of them. Clifford negatived the idea of parish collections and advocated the idea of subscriptions of £100, £50, £10. Thus the 'Old' families would have a permanent financial stake in the enterprise and their wishes and views could not, thus, easily be ignored.)

It was quite obvious that such an institution would in no way meet Manning's requirements, although it is curious to find that Manning discussed the question with the Jesuits and that the latter at first seemed to view the plan with approbation.[44] Father Weld, S.J., presumably with Manning's approbation, saw Newman; and the latter in a very revealing letter to Hope-Scott, dated 25 September 1867, indicated that he was searching for means to escape giving his name or co-operation. In this letter Newman declared 'I will have nothing to do with the plan, unless the Professors are lay'.[45] It is interesting to observe that when the University College was eventually founded at Kensington all the Professors (except one) were lay, and so Newman had to search for a new excuse to avoid working with Manning.

Manning's attempt to work with the Jesuits on this matter was doomed to failure partly because the Society seemed intent on turning the project into a recruiting ground for vocations to their own Order,* and hence ran completely counter to Manning's own ideas of the nature and scope of a university. In 1873 when the Hierarchy met in Synod, Manning therefore carried a proposal that the university be established in London, and under episcopal management. At once the 'Old Catholics' were up in arms, saying 'that it was contrary to the character and spirit of the ancient Universities to be simply Episcopal Institutions'.[46] But the

---

* See Newman's account of the conversation he had with Fr. Weld on this subject in Ward's *Life of Newman*, op. cit. II, pp. 197–8.

Archbishop knew that once the reactionary core of the titled and land-owning families gained control of the new institution, it would develop along the lines of an Oxford college and be rigidly classical, exclusive and narrow. He was determined that this should not occur. His fears were justified when, at the first meeting of the Senate of the new University College, 'Mr. Hardman rose and said that they should better discuss the subject in the absence of the bishops'.[47] In this insulting manner, the 'Old Catholics' sought to gain control of the College and to outwit Manning at the beginning. The price they paid was that Manning did not convene the Senate again. It was a drastic measure, but if the College was to develop upon national and modern principles it was obvious that the Archbishop's hand must be at the helm in the formative years. Much has been made of the supposed fact that Manning refused to employ the only two forces that could make the venture a success—Newman and the Jesuits. Dr. Gordon Albion states:

It must be confessed that the main cause of the failure (of the University College) was Manning's obstinately short-sighted and small-minded refusal to employ the two most powerful, indeed the only forces that could have ensured the success of such a scheme—Newman and the Jesuits.[48]

Purcell similarly claims that the two main errors resulting in the failure of what he terms 'the pretentious scheme' were 'the refusal of co-operation offered by the Jesuits' and the omission of Newman from the scheme.[49] He waxes indignant on the second of these points and declares:

A Catholic University in England without the co-operation of Newman must needs in the nature of things have little or no chance of success. It was like leaving Hamlet out of the Play. . . . There can be little or no doubt that had Newman been invited by the Catholics of England and by the bishops to lay the foundations of a future Catholic University, he would not have refused to make the attempt. . . . When an opportunity presented itself of enlisting Newman's special and splendid abilities in founding a Catholic University, rather than invite his aid, co-operation, or even advice, Archbishop Manning risked almost inevitable failure. . . . In a work so congenial to his heart as laying the foundations of a Catholic University in England, it is more than probable that Newman, with his unrivalled powers and gifts, would have succeeded, where, from the nature of things, Manning and Mgr. Capel were doomed to failure.

This picture of the inadequacy of Manning falls down on two points. Firstly, he *did* invite Newman to participate in the foundation of the College and take an active part in its management, and he even invited him to the Synod which established the College. Secondly, the Jesuits would not co-operate in an institution which they did not control. The history of the invitations to Newman is contained in letters which are in the archives of the Birmingham Oratory.

On 12 June 1873, Manning wrote to Newman about the approaching Synod. After declaring that 'at the meeting in Low Week the Bishops selected certain of the Clergy whose assistance at the Provincial Council they desired to invite', he went on: 'Our hope was that you would accept that invitation and I, therefore, write to convey it to you in our name. The Council will be held at St. Edmund's beginning on July 21. We shall do all we can to make you at home.'[50]

Newman's reply was curt and to the point:

My Dear Archbishop,

I feel the honour done me by the Episcopal Meeting of Low Week in asking me to be present at the Provincial Synod of next month.

I trust, however, that your Grace and the other Bishops will be so kind as to allow me to decline, as they did in [?].* I wrote to plead my age, and my total ignorance of synodal matters,

J. H. N.[51]

That was Manning's first attempt to enlist Newman's support, for at that Synod the Kensington scheme was scheduled for discussion and it was, in fact, set on foot. The next attempt came after the Synod had taken place, when Manning asked Newman to assist with the new foundation and be a member of the Senate. He wrote on 21 November 1873:

Your name was the first we all thought of in forming the inclosed list†: and in the name of all the Bishops I write to express our hope that you will give us your name as a pledge of good will and readiness to aid us by your experience and advice. We wish to begin unambitiously by meeting a need which is sensibly felt, and on the increase: leaving to the future the shape and extent such a humble beginning may henceforth assume.[52]

* The first Synod of Westminster under Wiseman. (Document faulty here.)
† Of names for the Senate of the College.

Three days later Newman replied to the invitation and threw cold water on the scheme. He refused to help, and the reasons he gives are interesting. He wrote:

My dear Archbishop,

I beg you will have the kindness to convey to the Bishops my most respectful and sincere thanks for the honour they have done me in thinking of me first. . . .

I have read the Prospectus which you sent me with great and careful interest: and I hope their Lordships will not deem it a presumption in me to say, that I feel an insurmountable difficulty in giving my name to it. I hope they will so far throw themselves into my history and my life-long opinions as to understand, that I could not without a great inconsistency take part in an Institution, which formally and 'especially' recognises the London University; a body which has been the beginning, and source, and symbol of all the Liberalism existing in the educated classes for the last forty years,

I am ever,
J. H. N.[53]

The charge, therefore, that Manning refused to seek co-operation from Newman for personal reasons is manifestly false. Newman was fighting against the new scientific liberalism that was symbolized by London University, whereas Manning was trying to ally it to the Church and thus Christianize it. The Archbishop clearly saw the forces which were shaping the future and he appreciated that if the Church was to remain a vital force and not a mere sentiment, it must not ignore the new liberal thought. It must try to leaven it with the civilizing influence of Christianity. The clock could not be put back. It is true, however, that the Kensington scheme was not particularly concerned with the university provision for the wealthier classes and its social benefits; it was aimed at providing a university training for the products of the middle classes and Manning's new middle-class schools. These boys would require a scientific and technical education at university level. It is undoubtedly a fact that Newman and Manning were poles apart, philosophically, on this question and if Newman had accepted the invitation to share in the Kensington venture there is ample evidence that he would have clashed with Manning on these basic principles.*

* One is tempted to wonder how much Newman's refusal to help Manning in his university was due to the fact that Manning had refused to become Newman's Vice-Rector in Dublin.

Newman regarded an association with London University as being far worse than allowing Catholic youths to attend Oxford and Cambridge. Manning expressed his attitude on this point in a succinct manner to Gladstone, when he wrote: 'We refuse Oxford and Cambridge as mixed and Godless. We accept the London University because we have no contact with it but for examination.'[54] A Catholic university college with the best Catholic lecturers and scientists producing men fully equipped with the highest qualifications in science, and with London degrees, was likely to make a far greater impact on the universities and on the country, than was a Catholic college at Oxford based on the traditional pattern and fully exposed to the Germanic influence in lectures, and in the confined and exclusive atmosphere of a university town.

The reason why Manning did not employ the Jesuits is clear. The Society of Jesus already ran advanced courses (on university lines) at Stonyhurst College and were planning similar establishments at Richmond in Yorkshire and at Reading.[55] These would be rigidly classical—we have seen in the last chapter how science was still not taught at Stonyhurst, and a modern curriculum despised—and would tend to cater for the needs of the wealthy and the 'Old Catholic' families. From the latter a large proportion of the Fathers of the Society was drawn. The Provincial, Father Weld, was of this stock and was a cousin of Bishop Clifford and of Bishop Vaughan of Salford, and he was completely out of touch with the true nature of the change in the condition of society. He never realized that the initiative in English life was slowly passing into the hands of the new middle classes, and Stonyhurst was to remain the privileged school of the Catholic aristocracy. The Jesuits were against the Kensington scheme from the start, and especially after their own scheme had been rejected. Father Purbrick, S.J., the Rector of Stonyhurst, was soon to become one of the protagonists in the movement for a Catholic college at Oxford. The Jesuits were the greatest opponents of London University. *The Month*, the official organ of the Society's views, published in October 1868 a scathing indictment of the kind of education London provided. The Society was particularly opposed to the site of Manning's University College, because it rightly realized that this would lead to a connexion with London University, where in philosophy 'a knowledge of Sir W. Hamilton's works would be almost useless'. The new institution would, also, attract students away from the philosophers' course at Stonyhurst, especially when it was rumoured that the distinguished scholar, Dr. Robert Clarke, had been appointed to the Chair of Philosophy. The Jesuits also felt that a university in London would be under Manning's personal direction and they had already had friction with the Archbishop on the question of their being allowed to open a grammar school in London. Manning consistently refused permission to the Society to establish a school in the Metropolis, and eventually the General of the Society took the matter up in Rome.[56] Manning stood his ground, however, and won the day.

Manning favoured the London University alliance chiefly for four reasons, in addition to those already mentioned: (a) before 1898 the University was simply an examining body; (b) college life was not *necessary*, and poorer boys would thus have a more equal opportunity; (c) there was no essential tutorial system; and (d) speculative philosophy did not play a dominant part. But the Jesuits attacked the scheme on the ground that an examining body was not a university at all. It is an error for Purcell to state that the Jesuits offered co-operation in the Kensington venture and were refused. The archives of the Society of Jesus yield no evidence of this.* Manning never invited them, and after the rejection of Clifford's proposed scheme they never offered to help. The Archbishop knew that if the proposed University College was placed in their hands, (a) it would assume the character of an Oxford college; (b) the course of studies would be adapted along traditional lines to the exclusion of science; (c) the middle classes would thus receive no encouragement to frequent it and it would hence become a preserve of the 'Old' families, achieving a narrow social function; and (d) the bishops would have no part in its functioning because the Society rejects all episcopal interference in their teaching establishments. It must also be remembered that the Society in England at this time did not possess any *eminent* men of science and certainly none of sufficient status to hold chairs in this discipline. It had a good assortment of teachers in its ranks and not a few popular writers, but it had no one sufficiently versed in and familiar with university work fit to be appointed to chairs. It is significant that all Manning's professors, as we shall see, were eminent in their

---

* There is no correspondence between the Society and Manning on this matter. The Rev. Leo Hicks, S.J., informed the writer that the archives of the Society contain no evidence of any relations between the Society and Manning.

9

fields; and the majority of them, being converts, had possessed teaching experience *within* the Universities of Oxford and Cambridge—or similar establishments abroad. Another significant feature is that with but one or two exceptions the chairs were held by laymen. An additional factor militating against the participation of the Society of Jesus in the Kensington scheme was the fact that at the Synod which established the College there was also discussed the bitter quarrel which had broken out between the Religious Orders and the Hierarchy in the country, and in particular the opposition of the Jesuits to the authority of Bishop Vaughan of Salford. The opposition was caused by the Society invoking alleged privileges and exemptions from episcopal authority in relation to their intention of opening a grammar school in Manchester and their desire to open one in London. Manning and the bishops appealed to Rome for a ruling and the Holy See found in favour of the bishops. By the Bull *Romanos Pontifices* the bishops were given the right, among others, to refuse permission to the Jesuits to open schools in their dioceses. These quarrels were not likely to sweeten relations between the Hierarchy and the Society of Jesus, and it is inconceivable that the former should place them in charge of the Kensington scheme at a time when the issue of the quarrel was still in doubt.

The Kensington University College opened in October 1874, after the bishops had issued a joint Pastoral (to which Clifford objected) on the matter and had agreed to provide Manning with £25,000. It is important for us at this point to analyse Manning's appointments to the chairs at the College in the light of his intentions, and to illustrate that they were of sufficient calibre to be successful as the nuclei of a new university undertaking.

Charles Seager, a distinguished orientalist, was appointed to the Chair of Hebrew and Comparative Philology. He had had a brilliant career, being in 1834 a scholar of Worcester College, Oxford, and two years later awarded a Kennicott Hebrew Scholarship. He graduated B.A. in 1836 and proceeded M.A. in 1839. He had studied under Dr. Pusey and became an assistant professor of Hebrew at Oxford. In Anglican Orders, he had been one of the first Roman converts of the Oxford Movement, being received into that Church at Oscott in 1843. He had been expelled from Oxford on his secession from the Establishment.

The appointment of Frederick Apthorp Paley to the Chair of

Classics was perhaps the most distinguished of Manning's nominations. He was an M.A. of Cambridge (1842) and had become famous as a Greek scholar with his edition of Aeschylus (1844-7), and had been one of the original members of the Cambridge Camden Society. From 1838 to 1846 he had been resident at his university, where he prepared pupils in classics and ecclesiastical architecture. In 1846 he had been suspected of converting a pupil* to Roman Catholicism and was expelled from the University, after which he became a Catholic himself. Until 1860 he was successively private tutor to the family of the Earl of Shrewsbury, to that of the Throckmortons and to the Kenelm Digby family. On his return to Cambridge in 1860 he became a private tutor and examiner in the classical tripos. In the meantime he had developed hobbies which were likely to have endeared him to Manning's heart: botany and geology. He published a book on the habits of earthworms and one on wheatears (1859), and the *Flora of Peterborough* in 1860. He produced an edition of the poems of Alfred, Lord Braye in 1881 and translated the Gospel of St. John verbatim from Vatican manuscripts. In the field of classics he was equally well known. He originated the theory that the *Iliad* and *Odyssey* were put together originally out of a stock of traditions and were not the work of one man. This theory created a school of thought in Germany. While Manning's Professor of Classics at Kensington, he was also Classical Examiner to London University and to the Civil Service Commission. Aberdeen University conferred on him the degree of LL.D. *honoris causa* in 1883.

When we look at the appointments to the science chairs we are able to appreciate clearly how hard Manning tried to get men of distinction to attract the pupils of the middle classes. The Chair of Biology was given to St. George Jackson Mivart and the Chair of Chemistry to Professor Barff. Mivart was educated at King's College, London, and was also a convert to Roman Catholicism. He had been called to the Bar at Lincoln's Inn in 1851 and was a member of the Royal Institution and a Fellow of the Zoological Society and the Linnean Society, of which latter he became Secretary and later Vice-President. In 1862 he had been appointed Lecturer in Comparative Anatomy at St. Mary's Hospital, London, and seven years later was elected a Fellow of the Royal Society. He was greatly influenced by Darwin, and Manning saw in his person that

* Thomas, the younger son of Thomas Arnold.

fusion which he so much desired to effect in England—the fusion of the scientific movement and Christianity. Mivart contributed to many learned journals and achieved fame in 1869 with his *Appendicular Skeleton of the Primates*. In 1879 he was to be president of the biological section of the British Association at Sheffield, and he was famous as an authority on Buffon. Honours were showered on him. In 1876 a Ph.D. was conferred on him by the Pope and in 1884 an M.D. by Louvain University. He was Professor of Natural History at Louvain from 1890 to 1893. Mivart was indefatigable in his efforts to reconcile Darwinism with Catholicism, and Manning showed his appreciation by editing and publishing for him his 'One Point in Controversy with the Agnostics' on this theme. A close friendship was established between the two and this was cemented at the meetings of the Metaphysical Society of which they were both members.

Barff was, perhaps, the apotheosis of the middle classes. He had achieved fame as an inventor and became renowned by the Barff process for protecting iron pipes from rusting, named after him. In this Barff discovered that if you blew steam over red-hot iron you covered it with a protective layer of ferroso-ferric oxide, which in turn prevented rusting.* This kind of practical discovery appealed irresistibly to the imagination and mind of the industrial classes. In Mr. Joshua C. Gregory's *A Short History of Atomism*,† page 91, the author refers to Barff's book *An Introduction to Scientific Chemistry* (1872). Barff regarded Dalton's Atomic Theory as a hypothesis likely to be superseded. Mr. Gregory wrote to the present writer that Barff 'records a statement by a clergyman who had been a pupil of Gay-Lussac. The French chemist always insisted on the distinction between facts, which were sure, and theories, which might pass. Gay-Lussac, the statement ran, never mentioned the Atomic Theory nor used a chemical formula till he had discussed the elements and their compounds fully.'‡ From this testimony it is clear that Barff was also, like Mivart and Manning, searching for a reconciliation between Christianity and the recent discoveries in science, he being especially insistent on the distinction between fact and theory.

* For a full description see Partington, *A Text-Book of Inorganic Chemistry* (Macmillan, 1933), p. 969.

† Published by A. & C. Black, 1931.

‡ Letter to the present writer from Mr. J. C. Gregory, B.SC., F.R.I.C., 16 March 1957.

The Chair of Modern History and Politics was awarded to Charles Stanton Devas. Devas was really an economist, and his appointment is significant. Manning desired someone to associate the Church with the new labour movements, with trade unionism, with the search for economic and social improvement. Devas was to prove particularly useful in this sphere—as can be judged from the titles of his published material. Such books as *Labour and Capital in England from the Catholic Point of View* (London, 1876), *Statistical Aspects of Wealth and Welfare* (1899), *Groundwork of Economics* (London, 1883) and *Key to the World's Progress* all indicate how closely allied to Manning's sympathies and views he was. When Manning appointed him to this chair, Devas was barely twenty-six years of age, but had had a distinctive career. An Old Etonian, he had been educated at Balliol College, Oxford, where he took Firsts in history and law. He too was a convert and he was to be an examiner in political economy to the Royal University of Ireland. He was a great social advocate and 'frequent contributor to learned journals on Socialism, its impact and economic consequences'.[57] Devas's son, the Rev. F. Devas, S.J., writing of him later declared: 'By treating political economy, both in books and lectures, from a definitely Catholic standpoint he was one of the earliest to oppose the current teaching which declined to consider history or ethics as relevant to the subject.' Devas frequently read papers for the British Asssociation and the Manchester Statistical Society, and was one of the leading progressive thinkers of his generation.

The careers of these professors illustrate how Manning's mind was working when he made his appointments. They were not the only distinguished professors employed in the Kensington scheme: Gordon Thompson was Professor of English Language and Literature; Dr. Robert Clarke, who was to be the English representative on the Biblical Commission of 1902, held the Chair of Philosophy, and the Rev. Croke Robinson the Chair of Ecclesiastical History in addition to being Vice-Rector. But the others were the chief instruments by means of which the Archbishop hoped to revolutionize the intellectual atmosphere of his flock.

It is, however, when we come to consider Manning's selection of the Rector for the new venture that we discover one of the reasons for its failure. His choice was Monsignor Thomas John Capel (1836–1911), and his selection has been widely criticized. Purcell claims that he had 'no claims to be regarded in any sense as a representative of higher studies' and adds that Manning made him Rector of the University College at Kensington with the view of pacifying him, as he was 'already a thorn in the Archbishop's side'.[58] This is hardly just. Manning would not have entrusted the success of his cherished project to a man whom he did not trust and whom he did not consider competent. Capel possessed qualities that attracted Manning. He was, first of all, an experienced administrator —and this quality is the most important one for a head of a University College. He had been Vice-Principal of St. Mary's Normal College, Hammersmith, for four years (1856–60), and in 1873 had founded a highly successful Catholic public school at Kensington. In the second place he was a well-known lecturer. For eight years (1860–8) he had lectured at Pau in the south of France and was an authority on the works of Bishop Colenso. He had been personally requested by Pius IX to lecture at Florence and at Rome and he had done so with great effect, being highly popular among the English and American residents. Later in life he was to lecture in Florence and California and to become a distinguished prelate in the United States, where he died. In London he was very popular with the aristocracy and was a preacher in great demand for society weddings and funerals. Disraeli portrayed him in *Lothair* as Mgr. Catesby, with a latch-key to most stately mansions. His friendship with the well-to-do was thought by Manning to be a sure way of attracting the sons of the aristocracy to study under his guidance, and his appointment was a sop to the 'Old Catholic' families. He was a cleric and Manning felt that he could influence policy through him. The choice was very unfortunate. Capel had little interest in the foundation; his real interest was in his Catholic public school at Kensington and he made the interests of the University College secondary to those of the school. 'The bishops stipulated that he should give up his school and take this work only',[59] declared Manning in an autobiographical note. He never did so. 'He evaded, and carried on the school, and involved himself deep in debt for it, and drew plans for a college of £50,000, and started a company to get the money; and as he stated to Lord Petre, the University College was as Leah, and the school as Rachel to him.' Capel proved unsympathetic to Manning's policies and ideals. The fact that things were not well even reached the public press, and grave scandal was caused. The *Manchester Guardian* commented on the strained relations not only between Capel and the bishops but between the former and his aristocratic friends. It declared in April 1879, 'It is currently stated here that grave differences have arisen between the Marquis of Bute and Monsignor Capel; and it is not improbable that the Marquis will leave the Roman Catholic Church.'[60] Manning himself recorded in his Journal more serious objections:

The College was both suspected and mistrusted for reckless irregularity and for immorality. The Duke* and Lord Petre told me that they could no longer advise any Catholic Parents to send their sons. Lord Petre's son had been culpably exposed to danger. The Bishops were informed on all sides of these evils.[61]

Capel's appointment had been made 'by the unanimous vote of the Catholic bishops', and eventually it was by their unanimous request that he had to resign. Later it was found that he had kept no books, nor had he rendered a balance sheet. After his resignation he threatened to sue the bishops for damages. At once panic seized certain members of the Hierarchy, and in particular Ullathorne of Birmingham. When Manning wrote to him, asking for suggestions for a successor to Capel, Ullathorne seized the opportunity to try and wriggle out of the responsibility for the venture. He replied:

I feel myself incompetent to give names. I do not know who would be a proper person to undertake this arduous task. . . .
A joint responsibility in all the English Bishops will not work satisfactorily. The College has hitherto been practically managed under the direction of your Eminence. Being in the Archdiocese, it is proper that it should be so, but for this reason I am still of opinion that where is the Direction there should be the responsibility and that any attempt at a joint responsibility will ultimately lead to trouble and misunderstanding. . . . [62]

Manning wrote back on 5 August 1878 to remind Ullathorne that he agreed to the joint Pastoral in 1873 and had signed the synodal letter and that it was a duty imposed from Rome on the bishops to provide some higher education.[63]

Unfortunately the reply to this letter of Manning's is missing, but apparently in it Ullathorne must have accused the Archbishop of some kind of double-dealing for Manning wrote to Ullathorne on 23 August 1878:

* Norfolk.

My dear Lord,

I have to thank you for your letter of the 19th which has just reached me* and I regret to learn from it that you are suffering. I hope your rest at Malvern will fully restore you.

I am the more obliged to you for your letter because I see with what care you wrote it at a time when you were bid to refrain from all work.

The Bishops of Clifton, Southwark and Nottingham, have twice assembled in London according to our agreement in Low Week, and every step hitherto taken has been by our common consultation.

The *Draft* Report I sent to you was intended to be *Private* and to be returned to me. Perhaps you will kindly send it back.†

In what form, or how it should be published or whether it should be published at all was what could only be decided by the advice of the Bishops.

I had intended to propose to you that we should meet at Birmingham on Aug. 16 or 17: but circumstances induced me to think that it would be better to delay our meeting till the Bishops, acting with me, had agreed to a Draft Report to be laid before our Colleagues.

On my return to London about Sept. 12 I will invite them to meet again and I will lay before them your letter in which there are many points which appear to me to be inaccurate: and some objections which I believe you will find not to be needed. There is however one point on which I may at once reply.

1. Every document from Rome relating to higher education had been laid before the Bishops.

2. No document has been asked for year after year at our meetings as well as in our Fourth Provincial Synod, which to my knowledge has any existence beyond those produced.

But I remember that in our last Council you had been misled to believe that the last document had been purposely obtained by me. But on examining the dates you withdrew the statement. I must further add that I am not aware that I have ever adduced as the authority for 'the Bishops being called on to form a College' for higher studies, any letter of the Holy See.

The Holy See has enjoined the Bishops to do two things, the one to raise our studies, 2. The other to form a body of examiners.

The founding of a College was a decision of the Bishops as a mode of carrying out these injunctions.

And I must add that though I heartily acquiesced in the decision, and have given evidence of it which in due time I will state, I was not of the opinion that it was the surer or safer way to begin.

* In Leeds, where Manning was staying.

† On uniting the Kensington University College with St. Charles' College as an advanced department. Ullathorne had broadcast the news—to Newman in particular.

My judgment on the subject is contained in the Paper I laid before the Bishops in Low Week in 1868 and it is printed with our Acta.[64]

This sharp rebuke from his Metropolitan effectually silenced the truculent Ullathorne. The reasons for the latter's sudden anger lie in the fact that Mgr. Capel during 1878–9 was trying to obtain damages from Ullathorne as a member of the body which appointed him to the Rectorship. Capel's action is interesting because it throws light upon a further—and more important—reason why the University College venture was a failure, namely the lack of episcopal co-operation. We have seen that the venture had been one undertaken by the whole Hierarchy in synod assembled. We have seen how the Hierarchy had requested Newman's co-operation. We have seen that it was the Hierarchy that appointed Capel and that later requested his resignation. Yet, when it came to a question of material support, certain of the bishops wished to regard the scheme as a diocesan undertaking by Manning—as we have seen in Ullathorne's case. As soon as the question of financial support had arisen (despite the fact that they had promised to give the Archbishop £25,000), to certain bishops it was no longer the country's Catholic university but it was Manning's university. This attitude of mind can be seen most clearly in the correspondence of Bishop Ullathorne of Birmingham in the matter of Capel's claim for damages. Capel was intending to sue the whole Hierarchy for damages, and not Manning personally. The first intimation of the matter came to Ullathorne from Capel's solicitors on 8 January 1879, and the letter read as follows:

We send your Lordship with this letter a copy of the opinion of Counsel which we have taken on behalf of our Client Monsignor Capel in respect of his claim to be repaid certain monies expended by him in forming the above University College and beg most respectfully to call your especial attention to that portion of the opinion which deals with the personal liability of the Bishops.

We beg to inform your Lordship that it is our intention to send a copy, to His Eminence Cardinal Manning, to His Eminence's Solicitors, to His Grace the Duke of Norfolk, to Lord Petre and to each of their Lordships the Catholic Bishops in England.[65]

In an undated note Ullathorne replied:

I beg to acknowledge the receipt of your letters of the 8th and 15th* in reference to a claim made by Monsignor Capel for repayment [to him

* Written because Ullathorne did not reply to that of the 8th.

of a sum of £5,521 of] money expended at the Catholic College at Kensington.

I have taken no part in the [establishment or conducting] affairs of the College, and I do not consider myself under any liability.[66]*

It is interesting to note that in the document Ullathorne crossed out the words 'establishment or conducting' and substituted the word 'affairs' for them. The bishop knew that he was as responsible as Manning for the University College, but he was unwilling to give any financial help. He had been an active supporter of Newman in the Oxford scheme and was determined to leave Manning to foot the bill for the Kensington venture. Some of the other bishops followed his lead. Ullathorne's reply was followed by a letter from Manning's solicitors which declared:

Mr. Gibson has been here several times this week to say that Monsignore Capel has returned to London and has conferred with him and that he can see no means of extricating his client under £4,000 which he would accept in full discharge of the alleged claims upon the Bishops and the Cardinal.

Further that the Cardinal has called on W. Gibson and can only probably (and that with the greatest difficulty) provide £3,000 and he begged us to inquire if the Bishops will subscribe the other £1,000.

The Bishop of Newport happening to call here at the time said he could do nothing having positively no means whatever.

The Bishop of Southwark authorises us to pay £100 and if all the other Bishops would do the same the incident and all its annoyances would be got rid of. . . .[67]

Ullathorne revealed his own attitude to the Kensington College in his reply:

In reply I beg to state, in the first instance what I have already declared to the Messrs. Gibson that I have never contracted any obligation with Mongr. Capel, or with any other person on account of the University College. I have never pledged myself to anything more than a moral support to such a College, were any Bishop to establish it in his Diocese. When I signed the joint letter, headed 'a Synodal letter' though not in fact a Synodal letter, it was with that intention, and mainly to recommend the College for subscriptions in this Diocese. . . . But by no act or deed have I ever accepted responsibility, or trust, or shared in the management of that College which, in fact, I have never seen. To avoid every appearance of any share of responsibility in that College from first to last I have declined to appear at any of its acts, however pressingly invited to do so.[68]

* In the document concerned, the words here printed in [ ] were crossed out.

Such a prevaricating letter is easy to assess. If Ullathorne did not agree with the undertaking why did he give it any support, moral or otherwise, let alone attach his name to the synodal letter? He was to a large extent annoyed that Newman's Oxford project, which he had inspired and promoted, had fallen through. Yet he had not the courage to dissociate himself from his fellow-bishops when the Kensington college was founded. His was a typical example of how little interest some of the bishops took in the University College. He confessed that he had not even seen it, and refused to give any material help or active encouragement to the establishment. In law, there is little doubt that all the bishops would have been held responsible for the College. They were fortunate in that Manning agreed to contribute £3,000 to settling Capel's claim, which he did to avoid the scandal of a public trial. The bishops, with one exception, paid £100 each towards settling the claim. The exception was Brown of Newport, who was exceedingly poor and genuinely unable to pay anything. Ullathorne paid his £100 with an ill grace; the taciturn Clifford paid his share without a murmur. The bill of discharge from Capel for Ullathorne's contribution is preserved at Archbishop's House, Birmingham. It is erroneous of Purcell to state that 'Manning acted wisely in not calling on his fellow-bishops to bear a share in the heavy losses incurred'. They all, except Brown of Newport, contributed—thereby admitting their legal and moral liability. Capel was not paid £10,000, as Purcell asserts,[69] but only £4,000.

The reasons for the failure of the university project are therefore obvious. The mistake in the appointment of Capel as Rector may largely be laid to Manning's charge. The bishops, however, did not play their part, took little interest in the scheme after the initial stages and made no financial contributions. Newman held aloof and the Jesuits disapproved. The 'Old Catholic' families were glad to see its ruin because of the hope that they might now gain permission to send their sons to Oxford and Cambridge. This latter proved to be vain. In 1882 Newman decided to appeal over Manning's head on the matter, and together with Bishop Hedley, O.S.B., of Newport, Lord Braye, and Grissell, raised the question with the new Pope, Leo XIII. They hoped that the new Pontiff would not be as influenced by Cardinal Manning as Pius IX. They were wrong. Leo XIII's name was strongly supported by Manning at the conclave on the death of Pio Nono, and Leo's pontificate was to prove

a veritable triumph of all that Manning had striven for in the realms
of labour and democracy. There was a strong affinity between the
'workers' Pope' and the 'workers' Cardinal'. The only answer Leo
made to Newman's request was to ask all the bishops to write to
Rome separately and express their views on the Oxford and Cambridge question. This was accordingly done, but in 1885 Leo announced that the Rescript of 1867 forbidding attendance at those
universities was to remain in force. Once again Manning had proved
how potent his influence was. Following this letter, Manning issued
a Pastoral on the subject, which has been described by a rather unsympathetic scholar as 'a magnificent piece of powerful and moving
writing'. The prohibition remained until the advent of Vaughan to
Westminster, when he secured its removal. Vaughan was greatly influenced by his kinsman, the Duke of Norfolk, and had been dis-
suaded from his inclination to re-open the Kensington college.
The removal of the ban was a good thing; the atmosphere at Oxford
and Cambridge had radically changed by the 1890's. 'The hostile
infidelity that had earlier characterized the Universities had died
down. Catholic works were used in the Oxford History School and
no one was *obliged* to study philosophy.'[70] Vaughan's policy was
bitterly opposed by the Bishops of Leeds, Middlesbrough,
Northampton and Salford, and Catholic youths from those dioceses
were still forbidden to frequent Oxford or Cambridge. This policy
lasted throughout the lifetimes of Bishops Gordon, Lacy, Riddell
and Bilsborrow.

The University College at Kensington had endured for four years
and in 1878, on the decision of the Hierarchy, was amalgamated
with St. Charles' College, Kensington, as an advanced department,
with Croke Robinson as Rector; the professors agreed loyally with
the change. Little more was heard of Mgr. Capel. He continued
to give trouble for a while. On 20 October 1880, Manning wrote to
Vaughan:

> The inclosed is Mgr. Capel's 2nd letter in the D. Telegraph. He is
> endeavouring to make capital out of our Middle Class movement: &
> as you see to bring in Jesuits and a St. F. Xavier's School into London . . .
> I will keep you informed for I look for trouble from Mgr. C. and S.F.[71]

Eleven days later Manning wrote: 'Mgr. Capel is beginning some
movement—and talking of an English Jury. He will ruin himself
beyond remedy.'

Capel's insubordination and moral failings led him into condemnation at Rome and he was suspended *a divinis*. He later ended his days in the U.S.A., as a distinguished but somewhat mellowed prelate.

The kind of education that had been given at Kensington during the four years of the College's existence has received high praise from Wilfrid Ward,* and from Abbot Butler, who were both students there. Butler was profuse in his gratitude, stating that he 'must gratefully acknowledge the debt he has ever since owed to the high quality of the instruction and formation received there'.[72] With a little more vision and a little less prejudice there was no reason why the College might not have flourished and persisted to the present day. It must be remembered however that after the collapse of the College, Catholics were not deprived of taking a university degree. They were urged to take the degrees of London University and this university was never subject to an ecclesiastical prohibition.

Mr. Evennett declares that 'there was a world of difference between the reality of Manning's Kensington and the ideal of Newman's Dublin'. This is indeed true, yet Newman never became fully alive to the scientific and industrial needs of the age. It is true that he did leave room for some vocational subjects to be taught in his Ideal University but as Barry declares, 'this far-reaching · movement seems to lie beyond his horizon'.[73] His opposition to London University was based on the idea that it was merely a 'bazaar or pantechnicon'. Fergal McGrath in his recent book has not succeeded in dispelling this view.

Manning, on the other hand, saw that the greatest threat to the Church lay in the scientific movement. The threat could not be circumvented by disowning the movement but only by tempering it with the doctrines of Christianity. He looked for men to fill his chairs at Kensington who had achieved a fusion in their own minds between the two ideals—men of the stamp of Mivart, Barff, Paley, Devas and Seager. These men all worked from the viewpoint that the Church had nothing to fear from the truth and that the truth could not conflict with the teachings of the Church. The future of the country, Manning held, lay in the hands of the boys of the industrial classes. These boys would find their vocation in the realms of industry and the practical application of science. If they were not to be lost to Christianity, they must be shown that the Church and

* An interesting comment on Ward senior is in the *D.N.B.* XX, p. 803. It claims that he 'proposed to dethrone classics from their place of honour'.

the scientific progress were not in conflict. If this realization were not attained, they would either leave the Church for agnosticism, or they would keep their religion in a separate compartment of their minds as something slightly unreal, as something not to be mentioned in public or applied to the everyday things of the world, as something to be preserved as a sentiment while rejected as a dogma. Manning's entire educational policy—his fight for elementary education, his provision of middle-class scientific schools, his University College at Kensington (essentially a middle-class university), his talks to working men, his lectures to Mechanics' Institutes, his membership of and lectures at the Metaphysical Society, his establishment of branches of his Academia of the Catholic Religion all over the country—are all evidences of his efforts to associate Catholicism with the 'new learning'. He was successful. Vaughan, when he succeeded to Westminster, paid a tribute to the achievement of the second Cardinal Archbishop of Westminster, declaring that Englishmen now had at least begun 'to recognize that the Catholic Church is not a petrified relic of the early or the middle ages, that she is no foreign institution alienating the affections and services of her followers from the interests of home, and moving about tentatively, furtively, on this English soil of ours, among our own flesh and blood, as though she were stranger and an alien'.[74] Manning did not make the conditions prevailing in England. He took what he found, and that meant taking the current social and intellectual trends. But instead of wistfully looking back to a former age, he transformed the new conditions and drove home the idea that truth, whether scientific or not, can never be incompatible with Christian tenets.

When we turn to consider Manning's attitude towards adult education, we find him a vigorous advocate of societies based on the principle of the Mechanics' Institutes. He frequently lectured in the Institutes themselves, and it was in the Leeds Institute that he delivered his famous lecture on 'The Rights and Dignity of Labour' on 28 January 1874. It was largely with this form of adult education in mind that he advocated the establishment of branches of the 'Academia of the Catholic Religion' in the provinces. The Academia* was a society established by Wiseman in 1861, to be a

---

* It was based on the Roman Academy. The latter was even thought of by Manning, at one time, as a possible source for providing a university training for Catholics in Rome. See Purcell, op. cit. II, p. 378.

meeting-place where Catholic men of letters could gather in London and discuss and debate learned topics and attend lectures given by distinguished Catholic Scholars. After Manning's elevation to Westminster, he broadened the basis of the Academia's purpose and turned it into a society in which *all* Catholic men could meet, if they so desired, for discussion and lectures and which would be a real educative force. This widening of the scope of the Academia, however, meant a lowering of its intellectual standards and perhaps this may have accounted in some measure for its later decline. The lectures were now to cater for all tastes, and science took a prominent place in the syllabus. The Archbishop advocated the establishment of branches of the Academia in the provinces, and Manning personally supervised the setting-up of the Manchester branch, becoming its president and delivering the inaugural lecture in 1879. The *schema* for the first two months is of interest, as showing the type of subjects dealt with. After stating that Cardinal Manning is the patron of this branch of the Academia, the programme of lectures reads:

January 10th. Inaugural Lecture by Cardinal Manning.
      ,,   18th. Canon Kershaw: 'On English Literature'.
February 1st. Fr. Perry S.J.: 'On the Transit of Venus'.
      ,,   8th. Charles O'Neill, F.C.S.: 'On The Physical and Chemical Properties of Air'.
      ,,   15th. Rev. L. Johnson: 'On the Holy Gospels'.
      ,,   22nd. A. Somers, Esq., M.D.: 'On the Unity of the Human Race'.
      ,,   28th. Fr. Harper, S.J.: 'Evidence and Certainty In Their Relation to Conceptual Truth'.[75]

As can be seen, priests, Jesuits and laymen combined in giving these lectures. The Academia, however, was established in the days of the decline of the Mechanics' Institutes. These latter had by the 1880's developed into little more than working mens' clubs, with an occasional lecture, and the Academia followed suit. Where it did not degenerate into a parish club it tended to struggle on as a highly exclusive society for the more knowledgeable parishioners. In both cases it deviated from the purposes of the Cardinal. He indeed fought to keep the basic idea alive, but to little avail. He delivered a lecture to the London branch in which he tried to reach an understanding of the 'subjects proper to the Academia'. He declared they ought to treat as the most urgent subject 'the relation of Faith and the Church to Science'.[76] 'It would be seen to be too trivial', he went on, 'to go on repeating, that between revelation and science there can be no opposition. . . . Now it will be a subject very proper to the sessions of the Academia to discuss whether science has any dependence upon Faith, or whether it can be independent in a province of its own. . . . It is not science which generates faith, but faith which generates science by the aid of reason illuminated by revelation.' Geology and biology were two subjects in particular which he wished to see discussed, for he declared:

It is much easier to trumpet about facts than fix them. Even in our own short lifetime we have seen the facts of geology to be made, unmade, remade, and made over again, I know not how many times. The nature and origin of man has been so often fixed and unfixed that I am in doubt whether I am descended, as I said, from Adam, or from an ape, or from a jelly, or from a capsule, or whether I am created at all, or am a transient manifestation of an uncreated whole, that is, whether I am man or Pan, whom I revered in boyhood, but never aspired to be.

But in spite of Manning's impassioned pleas for a widening of the subjects discussed in the branches of the Academia the local leaders did not take the advice to heart (perhaps because so many of the parochial clergy regarded science as heresy), and interest and attendance abated.

Manning's contribution to the field of historical scholarship is worthy of notice. He was responsible for obtaining permission for the Rev. Joseph Stevenson, a non-Catholic, to obtain access to the Vatican archives. Stevenson was helping in the writing of a history of England and he was the literary agent of the Master of the Rolls, Sir George Jessel. He was the first person ever to gain entry to the Vatican archives. Jessel wrote his profuse thanks to the Cardinal and quoted his agent as saying:

I am the only one who has admission to the archives. Several English have tried, French and Germans innumerable, but all have failed. My admission in the first instance, and my recent increased advantages, are all owing to the influence of Cardinal Manning.[77]

In the field of higher education, therefore, it can truly be said that Manning's chief impact was on the tone and temper of Catholic attitudes of the period. No concrete memorial stands as a direct testimony of his influence in this field. But his true memorial rests in creating a sympathetic Catholic conscience for the intellectual changes of the twentieth century.

Chapter V

THE CONDITION OF THE PEOPLE

★

A. AT HOME

TOWARDS the close of his life Cardinal Manning wrote a series of autobiographical notes, a number of which deal with the motives which he considered had inspired him in his social policy. One such note appears to express the substance of them all. In this he writes of his belief 'that if the Church is to be spread in England, it will be by its large popular sympathies identifying it, not with the governors, but with the governed'.[1] Manning in this context is especially referring to the Roman Catholic Church, but the statement was equally relevant for the other churches. For him it was impossible to divorce the social action of the Church from its divine mission and its supernatural life. Without the pursuit of social amelioration the Church would be wantonly frustrating its divine mission and drying up its supernatural life. His point of view was by no means unique. Manning lived in a period which could boast of the names of Maurice and Kingsley and be proud of the title 'Christian Socialist'. The Churches were occupied with defending themselves from the onslaughts of scientific materialism and it was but natural that what they lost in that struggle they should attempt to recover by an alliance with the democratic movement.

Fitzsimons places the date of Archbishop Manning's 'first entry into the public exercise of social charity' as 1870–1, when he was a member of the Committee of the Mansion House French Relief Fund, during the Franco-Prussian War.[2] Leslie cites the year 1872 as the one in which Manning 'took the first plunge' in social reform, when he publicly identified himself with the Agricultural Workers' Union. But his actual interest as Archbishop in this field can with greater truth be placed much earlier—to March 1868, in fact. In that month he wrote to Gladstone, who was in opposition, 'When the Poor Law Bill comes to you I will send you a memorandum.'[3] The Bill referred to was that which we noted when treating of the workhouse schools,* and which would facilitate the transfer of Roman Catholic children. Among other provisions, the Bill enforced the keeping of creed registers in the workhouses. Three months later he wrote again concerning this Poor Law Bill: 'Nothing is more sensibly felt by the Catholics in England than the treatment of our poor children in the workhouse schools. I would, therefore, ask of you, and of all you can influence to support the clauses of Mr. Villiers's Reports in 1864: and therefore your own.'[4] Manning concluded this letter by asking for an interview in order that he might specify the exact points at stake. He wrote again on the same subject on 3 July 1868.[5] That his solicitations proved to be potent is made clear by his note of 29 July 1868, when he wrote to Gladstone 'to thank you for your kindness in watching and supporting the Poor Law Bill'.[6] This incident can more truly be cited as Manning's entry into the field of social charity, for this Bill removed a very serious grievance from the shoulders of the poor, and especially the poor Irish whose children provided such a large proportion of the inmates of the workhouses.

Throughout the century the Mansion House became a pivot from which radiated the greater part of the charitable movements in the country. During the year 1870–1, the year of the Franco-Prussian War, Manning made his first appearance as a member of a Mansion House committee. In September 1870, after the surrender of Napoleon to the King of Prussia, Paris was invested by the Prussians. The siege wore on throughout the autumn, and although the French army of the Loire made desperate efforts to relieve the city it had no success. The beleaguered capital did not finally capitulate until 28 January 1871. Those four months of siege were months of desperate hardship for the people of Paris, who had run out of food and other necessities. England tried to help, and the Mansion House French Relief Fund was established and Manning was requested to join the committee. In spite of his recent exhausting labours at the Vatican Council and his arduous travels to and from Rome, he agreed to help. For his efforts in this committee and for his attempts to obtain mercy for the ill-fated Archbishop of Paris,† he was awarded a bronze medal from the City of Paris.

In 1872 Archbishop Manning was asked to preside over the

---

* See Chapter II, p. 45 supra.

† Manning had written to Bismarck to ask him to intervene and save Mgr. Darboy from the hands of the Paris Commune. He received a courteous reply—but to no avail.

International Prison Congress. The reports considered at that Congress so alarmed him that he began to solicit the help of Gladstone, who was Prime Minister at the time. The Archbishop was particularly appalled at the lack of spiritual guidance for the prisoners. He wrote urging this need in view of Sir John Trelawny's proposed private member's Bill—the Prison Ministers Bill of that year, declaring:

I will not, however, touch on any matter now but one which then [i.e. when he saw Gladstone next] would be too late, I mean the Prison Ministers Bill.

Out of 125 Prisons in England only 16 have appointed Catholic Chaplains.

I am told and taunted that whereas we are only 1/5 of the population, we have 1/5 [*sic*] of the prisoners: that our prisoners are re-convicted over and over again.

How shall they not be reconvicted if they are not reformed, and how shall they be reformed if they are deprived of the helps of their clergy and their faith?

This is hard-hearted and cruel, as well as unjust.

I do not ask for stipends. Let the clause be struck out of the Bill, but let us be allowed freely to bring the Sacraments to these poor souls.

All I ask is

1. That it be obligatory on every body of Magistrates to recognise and inscribe on the list of the officers of the Prison a Catholic chaplain.

2. That he have the same access and privileges in respect to his people that the Church of England has to his.

Now in the Name of Mercy as well as justice help Sir John Trelawny to get a time for this most just and incontestable Bill.

We are really wounded by the long delay of this hope; and by the miseries of our poor prisoners.

Do not think me too urgent: I believe you will not.[7]

Gladstone agreed to help and gave time for Trelawny's Bill, pledging Government support. The outcome was that Catholic chaplains were appointed at the prisons and they were able to do a great deal towards reforming their Irish charges.

Following the repeal of the Combination Laws in 1824 trade-unionism began to flourish in this country with an intense vigour. The Unions needed no longer to disguise their existence under the innocuous title of Friendly Societies. Robert Owen's Grand National Consolidated Trades Union was the most ambitious of these new developments. It was an impracticable gamble, a utopian scheme, which endeavoured to establish a veritable communist state in the country. It collapsed after the 1834 Tolpuddle prosecution. But it was an ideal that captured the imagination of many and stimulated new endeavours and gave rise to Chartism. By the 1850's Chartism had declined and there were arising the great new Unions. The Miners' Association was formed in 1841. In 1845 the National Association of United Trades for the Protection of Labour was formed and in 1851 the Amalgamated Society of Engineers—the last named numbering some 11,000 members. These became increasingly interested in politics and desired to return independent M.P.s—sponsored by the London Working Men's Association set up in 1866, and after 1870 by the Labour Representation League—who would join forces with Radicals and Liberals on matters of common interest. In 1871 Gladstone passed his Trade Union Act which gave added strength to the legality of the Unions and gave protection to their funds. But Gladstone's Criminal Law Amendment Act of 1871 seemed to make strike action almost illegal because of its stringent definitions of molestation, intimidation and obstruction, which it deemed criminal acts. In the early 1870's, therefore, trade-unionism was very much in the air and it is not surprising that Manning should have had to turn his attention to it and clarify his attitudes. This he did in an unmistakably clear manner by his answer to an invitation to preside at a meeting at the Exeter Hall to be held on 10 December 1872, to advance the cause of the agricultural labourers. His reply was that it might 'be detrimental to the interests of the Agricultural Union, which was then so recently established'[8] if he were to preside, but he agreed to be present and to propose the first Resolution. Mr. Samuel Morley, M.P., was asked to take the chair. Such an action called for much courage, for it was the first time that a Roman Catholic prelate had identified himself in so open a manner with the cause of Labour. Few prelates have been so intrepid as to follow his example. Manning was accompanied by distinguished personages such as Sir Charles Dilke and Sir Charles Trevelyan and he met there Mr. Mundella, Mr. T. Hughes, Mr. Potter, Mr. Odger and Mr. Arch. His action was bitterly resented by many Roman Catholics and others, and he was vigorously attacked for his 'taking part in Agrarian agitation'. His reply was defiant: 'To couple my name with that of Mr. Arch gives me no displeasure. I believe him to be an honest and good man. I believe, too, that the cause he has in hand is well founded.'[9] His experience prompted a letter to Gladstone, which Manning dated eleven days after his appearance on Arch's platform at Exeter Hall. He wrote:

As you are now somewhat less occupied I write on a subject which has now been lately forced upon me, I mean the State of our working men.

I remember your saying to me, many years ago, that the next conflict would be between the masters and the workmen. . . .

I found last week that even my Irish tradesmen are organised. They have 18 Lodges in London. As yet they have not become political, beyond Home Rule: but they might easily become republicans of the American type.

I have also lately had means of knowing what the Agricultural Unionists are, as yet they are not political. . . .

They do not coalesce with the London men; but the London men will soon make capital of them, if others do not interfere. The consequences of this would be disastrous.

My belief is that some energetic and sympathetic act on the part of the Government would avert great dangers. Could not a Royal Commission be issued, revising the last on Agricultural labour, to take the evidence of men who are now appealing to public opinion for help?[10]

Five days later he wrote again, an important letter in view of his policy and action in 1889, this time giving further concrete proposals. He asked:

Why cannot you do these things for the Labourer?*
1. Prohibit the labour of children under a certain age.
2. Compel payment of wages in money.
3. Regulate the number of dwellings according to the population of parishes, Unions, counties or what you will: and prescribe the sanitary and other conditions necessary to the moral life of men by building acts.
4. Establish tribunals of arbitration in Counties for questions between labour and land: thereby creating a public opinion which will control the arbitrary acts and wills of employers of the poor.[11]

Manning's interest in and sympathy for the agricultural labourers led him to make financial contributions to their funds in 1878 and 1879, and were perhaps influential in securing his approval in July 1881 for the Irish Land Bill then before Parliament. This intense feeling for those employed on the land was perhaps a remnant of his Anglican days when as Vicar of Lavington in Sussex he was so much in touch with the daily lives and hardships of those who were

* i.e. the agricultural labourer.

employed in eking a livelihood from labouring on the land. He himself declared at the Exeter Hall meeting: 'For seventeen years I sat day by day in the homes of the labouring men of Sussex and I knew them all and their children by name as well as I knew the scantiness of their means of subsistence.'[12] In his Charge of 1845 he referred to his agricultural labourers saying: 'They are a noble-hearted race, whose sincerity, simplicity, and patience we should buy cheap at the cost of our refinements. . . . We have a people straitened by poverty, worn down by toil; they labour from the rising to the setting of the sun; and the human spirit will faint or break at last. . . . Time must be redeemed for the poor man. The world is too hard upon him, and makes him pay too heavy a toll out of his short life. . . .'* Manning understood their hardships and needs, and the agricultural poor always found in him a stout defender.

At the Leeds Mechanics' Institute in 1874, Manning delivered a lecture which was afterwards published under the title of *The Rights and Dignity of Labour*. This lecture is worthy of detailed study because it is not only the expression of his views on the relations that should exist between Capital and Labour but also the chief written evidence of those views.

He began his lecture by referring to the great wealth of the country and he attributed this in the first place to Labour. He went on to discuss the value of mechanization in industry, and reminisced:

I can remember the time of the Swing Riots. I daresay in the North of England the fame of Swing may not be so familiar as it is to me, who have lived all my life in the South; but I remember well at that time I was living in the County of Kent, and night after night I saw the horizon red with the burning of threshing machines and of rick yards; Madness had been infused into the minds of our simple agricultural population. They believed that machinery was their ruin. We have now happily, and I think through the action of Mechanics' Institutes more than any other agency, come to a period when our whole population, agricultural and manufacturing, recognise that the advancement and multiplication of machinery is the greatest aid to them in creating labour.[13]

From this easy conversational tone Manning proceeded to his main thesis, which he expressed as being the application of the rights of Property to Labour. This was just, he contended, for

* Manning's Charge of 1845: cf. above, Chapter I, p. 13.

there is no personal property so strictly our own. The strength and skill that are in a man are as much his own as his life-blood; and that skill and strength which he has as his personal property no man can control. . . . He can buy with it, and he can sell it. He can exchange it. He can set a price upon it.

Manning asserted that Labour was 'Live Capital'—capital in its truest form—and money was simply 'Dead Capital'. This argument naturally led him to a discussion of 'freedom of association' and the trade union.

Labour has a right of liberty [he declared]. Every labourer has a right to work or not to work. . . . A labourer has a right to determine for whom he will work, and where he will work. . . . This carries with it also the right to say whether he can subsist upon certain wages. This is undeniable.

The trade unions, as he saw them, were akin to the old medieval guilds—societies for mutual protection and benefit, not political institutions.

Labour has a right, not only to its own freedom, but it has a right to protect itself. . . . I can conceive nothing more entirely in accordance with natural right and with the higher jurisprudence, than that those who have one common interest should unite together for the protection of that interest.

Following these more general remarks concerning the right of Labour to form itself into associations for its defence and advancement, he indicated the immediate ends the unions should strive for. They were practical ends but at the same time were perhaps somewhat revolutionary and far-reaching. The first of these referred to the hours of labour. He declared:

I am one of those, which is of no importance, but Mr. Brassey is also one of those, and that is of a great deal more—who are of the opinion that the hours of labour must be further regulated by law. I know the difficulty of the subject, but I say the application of unchecked political economy* to the hours of labour must be met and checked by a moral condition.

He discussed more specific outcomes of the long hours of labour, questioning:

Is it possible for a child to be educated who becomes a full-timer at ten or even twelve years of age? Is it possible for a child in the agricultural districts to be educated who may be sent out into the fields at nine? I

---

* Refers to no interference by Government in trade.

will ask, can a woman be the mother and head of a family who works sixty hours a week? You may know better than I, but bear with me if I say I do not understand how a woman can train her children in the hours after they come home from school if she works all day in a factory. The children come home at four or five in the afternoon; there is no mother in the house, I do not know how she can either clothe them, or train them, or watch over them, when her time is given to labour for sixty hours a week. I know I am treading upon a very difficult subject, but I feel confident of this, that we must face it, and that we must face it calmly, justly, and with a willingness to put labour and the profits of labour second—the moral state and the domestic life of the whole working population first. I will not venture to draw up such an Act of Parliament further than to lay down this principle.

He concluded his lecture with a passionate plea for a juster distribution of wealth in the country, stating:

The homes of the poor in London are often very miserable. The state of the houses—families living in single rooms, sometimes many families in one room, a corner apiece. These things cannot go on; these things ought not to go on. The accumulation of wealth in the land, the piling up of wealth like mountains in the possession of classes or of individuals, cannot go on if these moral conditions of our people are not healed. No commonwealth can rest on such foundations.

The lecture could not conclude without a reference to one of the foremost topics of the time—science, which he claimed 'enriches the lowest valleys and plains of labour'.

The views contained in this lecture are of vital importance in connexion with the Cardinal's intervention in the Dock Strike of 1889, for he was less of an arbitrator in that struggle than a spokesman for the cause of Labour. His sympathies throughout the struggle were with the men and he did not attempt to disguise those sympathies.

In the period between the delivery of his famous lecture at Leeds and the advent of the Dock Strike, Manning kept up his interest in the question of labour and social amelioration. He was invited to preside at a meeting of the Society of Arts in 1874 when the subject discussed was 'Thrift or the Outdoor Relief Test', and in his Lenten Pastoral of 1880 he declared:

In the midst of immeasurable wealth is a want which the poorest country of Europe scarcely knows . . .; not poverty alone, which is an honourable state, when it is *honest* and *inevitable*, but also pauperism, which is the corruption of poverty and the debasement of the poor.

In 1884 Manning renewed his acquaintance with the great Radical social reformer, Sir Charles Dilke, when he was appointed a member of the Royal Commission on the Housing of the Working Classes, of which Dilke was chairman. Their acquaintance dated from 1872 when they had appeared together on the platform of the Exeter Hall on behalf of Arch's agricultural labourers. Two years later in 1874, after the death of Dilke's wife, they began to correspond. Dilke described how on 30 July 1878 he

dined at a dinner given by a lion-hunter who managed to get together some remarkable and pleasant people—Cardinal Manning, Ruskin, Greenwood, and Borthwick. But whether it was the influence of the host or whether it was because Manning did not like his company, except me, and Ruskin did not like his company at all, the dinner was a failure. No one talked but Ruskin, and he prosed, and his prose of speech was not his prose of pen. Manning wished to see me about some education matter, and I called on him on August 2nd and from that time forward saw a good deal of the Cardinal.[14]

Between the date of this meeting and 1884 Dilke was able to be of assistance to Manning in numerous ways, and the friendship between them increased. One example of this help Dilke was able to afford Manning was concerning Nazareth House, Hammersmith. In 1883 there was a serious outbreak of typhus in the house and the medical officer had imposed conditions which Manning considered over-severe. He appealed to Dilke for help. Sir Charles visited the house in his capacity as head of the Local Government Board, and came to a like conclusion. The situation was remedied and Cardinal Manning wrote to Dilke on 27 April 1883 to thank him for his intervention, declaring that he was 'disabled and shut up, and therefore doubly grateful'.[15]

Before the appointment of the Royal Commission on the Housing of the Working Classes in 1884, Manning was already vitally interested in the problem. Writing to Dilke on 2 November 1883, he said:

Without a high-handed executive nothing will be done till another generation has been morally destroyed, but construction must keep pace with destruction. Some of my parishes are so crowded owing to the destruction without construction as to reproduce the same mischiefs in new places. You know I am no narrow politician, but I am impatient at political conflicts while these social plagues are destroying our people.[16]

From this letter it is evident that Cardinal Manning's interest in the dwellings of the poor arose primarily from a moral condition. He believed that a corrupt environment can be a potent influence in the corruption of morals, and at the same time he showed his practical appreciation of the problem by pointing out that it would not do simply to destroy slum dwellings but the people must be re-housed in new and healthier surroundings and that the two processes must keep pace with each other. It is important to observe this practical aspect of Manning's letter, in view of Dilke's later assertion that he had no *practical* appreciation of the problem.

When in 1884 the Royal Commission was set up, Manning was the first invited to serve on it and he took precedence after the Prince of Wales and before Lord Salisbury. During the meeting Dilke, as Chairman, asked Manning for his suggestions and when he got them called them 'revolutionary' and 'ill-considered' and was amazed to see 'how curiously impracticable a schemer, given to the wildest plans, this great ecclesiastic showed himself'.[17] What were these wild, revolutionary and impracticable suggestions? They numbered two, viz.:

1. Removal of Prisons and Infirmaries out of the Metropolis.
2. Re-siting of such industries as breweries, ironworks and noxious factories on the outskirts of the City.

Manning argued that these two measures would give more space for the better housing of the working classes, and improve health. His proposals would hardly raise an eyebrow today but in his day they must have caused a sensation and we can understand Dilke's remarks. He was really advocating town planning and organized development of industry. His proposals were perhaps not 'ill-considered' but were certainly in advance of his time. Manning, Dilke and J. C. Bodley* worked hard on the Commission and the final report was largely the work of Manning and Dilke, labouring together at the former's residence. Unfortunately the Commission's report was never implemented.

Manning's relations with Dilke always remained cordial and, as we shall see in the chapter on Ireland, the latter was able to give valuable asssistance in relation to the Errington Mission. The Cardinal was 'a constant correspondent'[18] of the second Lady Dilke and it was at Dilke's table that he first met von Bismarck. In

---

* Manning wished Bodley to write his life after his death.

July 1884 Dilke records that he presented a Spanish crucifix to the Archbishop and that the latter reciprocated with a picture of St. Charles, which Dilke hung in his bedroom.

In 1886 Manning interested himself in the question of colonization. In May of that year he took part in a meeting of the National Association for Promoting State-Directed Colonization. At this meeting he declared his support for the view that colonization should be systematized and organized and that settlements should be planted in the colonies in accordance with a pre-arranged plan, and that these settlements should become the nuclei of new and interesting imperial developments. This could only be achieved if it was State-directed. His speech savoured of both imperialism and socialism, but he had declared thirty-seven years previously his belief that ' the State is a sacred institution, second only in sacredness to the Church'.[19] In the same month Manning spoke at a meeting of the Shop Hours League and Trades Parliamentary Association in St. James's Hall, and during 1887-8 was a member of Lord Compton's Committee on the Distress in London.

On 1 February 1888, Manning led a deputation to Lord Salisbury advocating the institution of relief works for the distress and measures to remedy the situation for the future. But he realized, as he was to declare in the *Fortnightly Review*, that 'stone-breaking and crank-turning are well enough as a deterrent for loafers and Criminals but the workhouse is a cruel deterrent when offered to families who, by a wise assistance in time of need, may be carried through the straits of winter when in want of work'.[20] The years 1887-8 were years of exceptional crisis; European markets were being closed to British goods and European domestic industries were being improved and expanded. German and American competition was replacing imports from Great Britain, and a serious crisis in British agriculture also ensued. Manning wrote three long letters to *The Times* (2-7 February 1888) in which he urged on the Government the necessity of providing immediate relief work and guarding against such possibilities in the future. The Government had no plan or policy. But the statistician and economist at the Board of Trade, Robert Giffen, had a simple solution. He said that all those working should provide as much surplus as possible over and above the cost of production, 'for all that profit must be spent on employing somebody in some way or other'. In his letters to *The Times* Manning castigated this inanity as both 'heartless and headless', and he recommended a light hearth tax as a temporary expedient. In an article in the *Nineteenth Century* in January 1888, Manning had declared that 'every man had a right to work or bread'. But in an article in the *American Quarterly Review*, 1887, under the title of 'The Law of Nature, Divine and Supreme', he went even further and declared that a man had a natural right to life and food and therefore this right prevailed over all laws of property. A starving man committed no theft if he took sufficient food from his neighbour to sustain life. These views were anathema to *The Times*, and they branded the Archbishop as a dangerous man in the eyes of many Roman Catholics.

In the autumn of 1889, when Manning was in his eighty-second year, the dockers' strike occurred. 'The dock strike took the world by surprise, it was something quite new, upsetting all men's calculations.'[21] It was not the first manifestation of unrest at the docks, however, for there had been strikes in 1872 to increase wages from 4*d.* to 5*d.* per hour, and again in 1880. Conditions at the docks had become increasingly oppressive, and with the uncertainty and irregularity of the employment during 1888 tension and discontent had been steadily mounting.

Employment at the London docks fell into three chief categories —those engaged in unloading, those in loading, and those in the warehousing of goods. 'The labourers were employed in gangs, either directly by "quay foremen" or "warehouse foremen" in the company's employ, or by contractors to whom the work was let out.'[22] There were two classifications of workmen, those engaged permanently who received a regular wage (paid weekly), and 'casuals' who were engaged for a specific job of work and then discharged. These latter waited at the dock gates each day in the hope of obtaining a day's work. If a 'casual' proved to be a good worker and was consistent in his attendance at the dock gates, he might hope to be appointed to permanent employment. Those employed directly by the Company received 5*d.* an hour.* The other method of payment was to grant a contractor a specific sum of money for a certain amount of work and then he bargained with the men for the amount of wages. When the supply of labour was far greater than the demand the contractor was able to force wages down to 4*d.* and even 3*d.* per hour. This practice was stopped by the Joint Dock Committee at its docks before 1889 when it bound the contractors

---

* Except at Tilbury in Essex, where it was only 4*d.* an hour.

to pay 6*d*. per hour. Another form of payment which took place at the East and West India Docks was known as the 'Task' system. In this system the labourers received 5*d*. an hour from the contractor and a small share of the remaining profit after the amount paid in wages was deducted from the total amount allotted for the job. The surplus was known as 'the plus' and its allocation was a serious cause of grievance among the men. Before the end of the 1889 strike the two strong Irish Unions of Stevedores, the Thames lightermen, and watermen, sailors, firemen, porters, riggers, scrapers, ship's painters, engineers, ballast heavers, and shipwrights all joined in, and all their interests had to be dealt with in addition to those of the dock labourers.

The strike occurred as a result of a dispute that arose at the South West India Dock, regarding the allocation of 'the plus' on a particular cargo. Ben Tillett would not agree to the demand of the men that they come out on strike at once but he formulated their grievances in writing and sent them to the dock managers. The list of demands which Tillett drew up numbered three in all, viz.:

1. No man to be taken on for less than four hours at a stretch.
2. Contract and piecework to be abolished.
3. Wages to be raised to 6*d*. an hour and 8*d*. overtime.

No answer was received to the demands, and the strike commenced. Tom McCarthy, Tom Mann and John Burns were soon aiding Tillett in the organization and administration of the campaign. When the Directors did reply, they conceded the first demand; the others they refused. The Directors promised, however, that if the men would return to work they might 'think better' about the increase in wages. The men rejected the terms. The strike campaign was to last five weeks and it was evident to the leaders that all men employed at the docks or riverside must come out on strike to aid the dockers' case. The secretary of the strong Stevedores' Unions, Tom McCarthy, soon brought them into the strike. A United Strike Council was set up and the lightermen came in 'on principle'. It was not long before the strike had 'extended up and down the river, and wharves and docks were nearly deserted'.* Meanwhile rumblings were heard of a possible appeal to the other Unions and the instigation of a general strike.

* Smith and Nash, op. cit. p. 66. Belloc in *The Cruise of the 'Nona'*, op. cit. p. 235, contends that the only result of the strike was the prosperity of Southampton as a port.

The press with the solitary exception of *The Times* was on the side
of the men and was a powerful ally, for by means of the publicity
it gave to the men's cause Australia became aware of the contest
and it was not long before money was coming from there to swell
the coffers of the Strike Committee. Without the money from
Australia it would have been impossible for the strike to continue.
'The total subscriptions amounted to £30,000.' Burns kept the men
occupied by daily meetings on Tower Hill followed by a procession.
Burns and Tillett had met the Directors but the latter would not
yield on the 6*d.* per hour claim.

Cardinal Manning decided to intervene on 6 September, a day
after the dockers' leaders had issued an appeal, which was later
withdrawn, for a general strike. The dock Directors at the time
were asserting their right to buy labour in the cheapest market and
threatening to import foreign labour from Antwerp. Manning's
first act of mediation was therefore to go and try to persuade the
Directors to change their minds—but it was to no avail. He warned
them that if they persisted in their intention of bringing in foreign
labour there would be bloodshed. The original day-to-day historians
of the strike, Smith and Nash, contend that 'the Cardinal's intervention was justified, not only by his responsible public position,
but by his family connexion with dock business—his father having
been chairman of one dock company and his brother of another'.[23]
Manning himself informed S. B. Boulton how it was that he came to
intervene in the affair. He declared simply:

I found things going from bad to worse, and how much misery was the
result! At last, from positive information, I became certain that fresh
efforts which were about to be made to bring labourers from a distance . . .
would lead to violent resistance, probably to bloodshed. Finding that no
other mediation acceptable to the combatants appeared to be available,
I resolved to offer my humble services with the endeavour to bring them
to meet together.[24]

His motives were clear and unmistakable.

When Manning decided to intervene 'the fourth week of the
dispute was now drawing to its close', and Manning was 'already
thinking of an appeal to the shareholders to put pressure on the
directors'.[25]

On Friday, 6 September, a Committee of Conciliation was set
up at the Mansion House: it consisted of Cardinal Manning, the
Bishop of London, the Lord Mayor, Mr. Sydney Buxton, Lord

Brassey and Sir John Lubbock. Burns and Tillett were asked to meet the Committee. As a compromise the Committee suggested that the men should get their increase to 6*d*. per hour, but that the new rate should not become operative until 1 January 1890, that is almost four months later. Burns and Tillett promised agreement to this, provided the dock companies also agreed. Manning, together with the Bishop of London and the Lord Mayor, interviewed the Directors at Dock House, and after much wrangling—and a reminder from Manning that delay might cause bloodshed—the Directors agreed with two conditions, viz.: (*a*) that an answer of agreement be sent by the men that same night, and (*b*) that no demands for extra money for overtime be made.*

The first condition was an impossibility in view of the large number of men to be consulted, and the second was sure to be rejected. But in any case the men flatly refused to wait for their increase until 1 January. This had been the condition with which the Conciliators had bargained at Dock House. When the decision of the men was made known, the Bishop of London withdrew from the Conciliation Committee and Manning had great difficulty in persuading the Lord Mayor to remain. Tillett and Burns, however, were able to obtain the men's consent to substitute 1 October for 1 January as the date when the new increase should be available. On Sunday, 8 September, Manning 'summoned the leaders to a fresh conference in the afternoon'[26] and suggested 1 December instead of 1 October, but this was declined. He then went to see the Dock Directors on the following Monday and said 'he had had ... a longer experience of men than they . . . and he would take no answer as final until he had talked it over with [the men] all together'. On the following afternoon Manning met the strike leaders at the Kirby Street Catholic Schools, and the Cardinal argued with the men for four hours. He suggested 1 November as a compromise date. Tillett stated his objections and Manning answered them. 'He urged, with the air of gentle authority, which won the hearts of all who had dealings with him throughout the strike, that from a business point of view they would do well to accept an offer which gave them practically all they asked in six weeks time. They must consider not only themselves, but the suffering which the strike was bringing on their families, and the public issues depending on

---

* Leslie entirely ignores this second condition, and thus misses the whole significance of the consequent rejection by the men.

their action.'[27] McCarthy, Champion, Mann, and Burns supported
the Cardinal; Tillett still held out. After four hours of argument,
however, and a further passionate plea from Manning the men
gave way and accepted the November date as a compromise. It was
a veritable victory for the octogenarian Cardinal. He waited two
days, however, before communicating the offer to the Directors—
in case the men should change their minds again. On Friday he
went to Dock House, but it took him all day to persuade the
Directors to agree and it took two more days before they finally
capitulated. During this time Manning met the lightermen and
persuaded them to return to work with a promise of 6s. a day for
12 hours' work and a single job to constitute a night's work. Other
outstanding issues were left to further arbitration. The strike was
over. On his return from one of his meetings with the Directors,
the Cardinal indicated his true sympathies in the strike issue by
the remark: 'I never in my life preached to so impenitent a congregation.'

An error originating with Leslie and repeated by Taylor and
Dr. McEntee, is that Manning at the meeting in the Kirby Street
Schools threatened to break up the strike by appealing to the Irish
Catholics at the docks. No such appeal is to be found recorded in
any contemporary accounts of the meeting in the Kirby Street
Schools, nor in Manning's own account of the meeting. Neither
does it appear in Purcell, who would not have been slow to use
such evidence to buttress his view. Such a threat, in fact, would have
been just the thing to antagonize the dockers; it would have given
the impression that Manning was throwing in his hand with the
Directors. Such an action would also have jeopardized his whole
policy of attempting to identify the Church with the cause of
Labour. *The Times*, the *Daily News*, the *Pall Mall Gazette*, the
Daily Chronicle and the *Morning Post* do not record any speech by
Manning in which he threatened to appeal to the Irish with a view
to breaking up the strike, although they all give detailed accounts
of the meeting at which he was alleged to have uttered it.* These
papers all praised Manning for the part he played in the strike. The
Morning Post declared: 'The result is due in a great measure to the
individual efforts of Cardinal Manning, who has laboured assidu-
ously in spite of his eighty-one years.'[28]

* It is true, however, that Manning's known sympathy for the Irish gave him a
strong hold over the dockers, who were four-fifths Irish by birth or ancestry.

A number of permanent results ensued from Manning's action in the dock strike of 1889. It showed the power of arbitration and pointed out that the method of the conference table was better than that of the strike or the lockout. After this strike the formation of Conciliation Boards began to take place in London and elsewhere, with equal representation between masters and workmen and frequently with a neutral chairman. Cardinal Manning joined the Committee of Enquiry established in 1889 by the London Chamber of Commerce to ascertain the possibilities of setting up a Board of Conciliation for the London district. The first dispute settled by the Conciliation Board was submitted to it through the influence of the Cardinal.

We now have to deal with the effect Manning's intervention had on the Roman Catholic Church in England. He had tried to ally the Church, as represented in his own person, to Labour—but more than that, he had attempted to ally it to the cause of the worker, to the 'oppressed', to the lowest strata of society. His action gained world-wide notice. In 1891 Manning's ideas were to receive outstanding support from the Papacy itself with the issue of the Encyclical *Rerum Novarum* and later with *Quadragesimo Anno*. These Papal pronouncements, as we shall see later, were to some extent his work. Non-Catholics also appreciated the significance of the Cardinal's action and regretted that the Bishop of London had abandoned him after the serious breakdown in the negotiations. The following contribution by Canon Mason to the *Memoirs of Archbishop Temple** is illustrative of how much Manning's success as the idol of the working men was resented in certain quarters:

As soon as the main lines of the settlement were made, the Bishop returned to his holiday. It is, I dare say, true that the strikers themselves had won the main part of their cause before the ecclesiastics intervened; but the intervention at any rate brought about peace more quickly than it would other-wise have done—and especially the intervention of the Bishop of London. If the Bishop had not come, the Lord Mayor would not have come; and if the Lord Mayor had not come, I much doubt whether Manning's somewhat one-sided interposition might not even have delayed matters.[29]

But all Anglican divines were not as unappreciative as Canon Mason. Archbishop Benson recorded in his diary: 'Cardinal Manning

* Ed. E. G. Sandford (1906).

has done well in London but why has my dear Bishop of London gone back and left it to him?'[30]

In Roman Catholic circles, however, we find the two different attitudes of Canon Mason and Archbishop Benson reproduced. Much uneasiness was felt in 'Old Catholic' circles at the Cardinal's action. Social Catholicism was 'the most hateful of new doctrines to those faithful who look upon the Church as the guardian of their interests, and upon religion as the best safeguard of property'.[31] This attitude of the 'Old Catholic' families is well illustrated by the action of Cardinal Vaughan, who was himself of this class. He attributed Manning's support of Labour to senility of mind and faulty judgment. In an article in the *Nineteenth Century*, Vaughan wrote:

> While my high estimate of him* is based upon a friendship of forty years, I always appraise the last few years of his life apart, as not representing the whole man. It is said that there is one faculty which extreme old age seldom spares. It may spare the senses of the body, the intellect, the memory and the will, but rarely, indeed, does it spare the delicate balance of that sensitive faculty called the judgment. During the last short period of the Cardinal's long life the process of senile decay had set in.[32]

The man who arbitrated in the dock strike in so brilliant a manner at eighty-one years of age suffered from no faulty judgment. Vaughan was desperately searching for some way in which he could circumvent the implications of Manning's social-labour policy; he did not dare plead insanity, but he felt he could get away with the plea of senility. But Manning's spirit was destined to live on side by side with that of Vaughan and it steadily gained ground.

Manning referred to the dock strike of 1889 in a commentary which he wrote for the *Dublin Review* in 1891 on the recent Papal Encyclical *Rerum Novarum*. His reference is worth quoting for its contemporary colour:

> For a month the streets of London were choked day by day with processions of tens of thousands. Disorder and horseplay, which at any moment may turn to collisions; these were sharpened by disappointment, and irritated by refusal of an additional penny an hour. At any moment a drunkard, or a madman, or a fool might have set fire to the docks and warehouses. The commercial wealth of London and the merchandise of the world, the banks and wharves of the Thames might have been

---

* i.e. Manning.

pillaged and the conflagration might have spread for hours before order, at unimaginable loss, could be restored. And all this because a strike is 'a matter between us and our men'. They were reminded that there were two other parties interested besides masters and men, the multitude of suffering women and children, and the whole peaceful population of London. At a certain stage of such a conflict, either or both of these parties have a social, civil, and natural right to intervene to protect the public safety. Leo XIII . . . affirms that the State may intervene.

In the same article he describes unmistakably his attitudes towards strikes in general:

A strike is like war. If for just cause a strike is a right inevitable, it is a healthy constraint imposed upon the despotism of capital. It is the only power in the hands of the working men.[33]

'What we may hope will come from this strike is a registration of labourers and an organization of labour', declared Manning in 1889, and it is undoubtedly true that from this time dates the great and powerful organization of labour of the twentieth century. Writing to Lord Buxton on 27 December 1889, Manning was able to state categorically: 'I have been turning over the strike matters, and the more I think, the more I am on the side of Labour.' In reply to those Catholics who asserted that it was the Church's duty to teach the working men not to be always seeking for material advantage but to be contented with their lot and resigned to the condition of life in which God had placed them, the Archbishop rejoined: 'Where there is no proportion, or no known proportion, between enormous and increasing profits and scanty and stationary wages, to be contented is to be superhuman.'[34]

In a letter to Gladstone dated 27 August 1890 Manning gave an account of his experiences the previous year, and declared:

This time last year forced [the question of the relations between capital and labour] upon me, and since then I have been in full communication with the heads and leaders of the Strike of last year. I find them very reasonable, many of them Total Abstainers from all drink, and many of them sincerely religious. Further they have broken with the Socialist Theories and are simply industrial and economic. They want to reform not to destroy. They both come to me and write to me, and twice last winter they listened and undid an imprudence which they had done.

They are now more I fear near the rocks. The Dock Labourers Union has shown an intention of closing their books, on the ground they have enrolled enough men for all the Dock Labour. This looks like a Monopoly and a Corner. On the other hand the 'Refuse' at the docks, constantly recruited from the country, will certainly pull wages down to a minimum on which no *home* can live.

'The Times' of to-day has an article which to me is brutal. It claims for Capital the absolute dictatorship of labour.

My belief is that in justice, natural and supernatural, there is a proportion between profit and wages.[35]

Obviously, Manning was following very closely the day-to-day relations of Capital and Labour. He was in close contact with the leaders of Labour in London and John Burns, especially, was a frequent visitor at Archbishop's House. Burns has been described as being unable to 'resist the fascination of Cardinal Manning while in his presence'.[36] Although Burns's diary for the year of the Strike of 1889 is unhappily missing, his diary for 1891 contains an entry which is illustrative of how he admired the Cardinal. The entry reads:

18*th March Wednesday.*—Went to Battersea Vestry about Local Improvements etc. . . . Thence to Cardinal Manning's where I found the old chap in wonderful health and spirits for 82 years of age. He expressed the opinion that England would go through her Labour troubles with perhaps a few broken windows but was doubtful of the Continental movement. We chatted for over an hour and after getting his signature to two Burns' books I left, cheered up by the opinion of the old fellow.[37]

The dockers revered Manning. After the strike they presented him with a gift of £160 which he gave to the London Hospital to endow a bed, and when he died they staged a huge demonstration at the funeral. The delegates of the London Trades Council passed a resolution

to the effect that the Cardinal, by his tender sympathy for the poor, and his fearless advocacy of justice, especially for the poor, and by his persistent denunciation of the oppression of the workers, has endeared his memory to the heart of every true friend of Labour.[38]

B. ABROAD

Manning's reputation as a friend of Labour and as a social reformer spread abroad, and not only to the English-speaking world. The Bishop of Liège, Mgr. Doutreloux, invited him in 1890 to attend the famous Social Congress at Liège and give an address. Owing to his advanced age Manning was unable to attend, but he sent a letter in which he advocated Sunday rest, freedom of association and arbitration, the limiting of children's and women's labour and an eight-hour day. He wrote that he favoured 'a just and suitable standard regulating profits and salary' as a guide for 'free contracts between capital and labour'.[39] He was amused when he was told later that his letter had caused a flutter among the foreign bishops who attended the Congress.*

Manning was a correspondent of such firm continental reformers as Von Ketteler (1811–77), who had begun his career as a lawyer and later became a priest. Von Ketteler had been a member of the Frankfurt Parliament of 1848, and Bishop of Mainz since 1850. He was the inspiration of the Centre Party led by Windthorst and was himself a member of the Reichstag in 1871. Von Ketteler greatly admired Manning's efforts in his attempt to affiliate the labour movements to the Church and he himself advocated in Mainz the formation of trade unions and co-operative societies.

Another correspondent of Manning was Cardinal Mermillod (1824–92), Bishop of Geneva. He was similarly interested in social problems; and the Swiss, Descurtins, corresponded on social matters with the English Cardinal. Miss Crawford records that Manning 'was held in the highest esteem by Cardinals Capecelatro and Mermillod, by Vogelsang, de Mun and Descurtins, with all of whom he was in correspondence, and his name was revered in workmen's clubs in France and Germany and Belgium no less than by the Irish dockers in the East End'.[40] Cardinal Capecelatro, the Archbishop of Capua, wrote in his book *Christ, the Church and Man*:

I know none among Catholic Socialists (let the name be permitted me) braver than my late beloved friend, Cardinal Manning, a social student fearless in speculation, effectual in enterprise. . . . Manning, living as he did in the midst of the independent and tenacious English people, did not hesitate to put himself at the head of Christian 'Socialism' . . . Temperance, arbitration, peace-making, public charity, had in him an eloquent, a persistent, a fearless advocate.[41]

Such praise was praise indeed, coming as it did from perhaps one of the greatest social reformers the Italian Church has produced.

Manning enjoyed his greatest influence, however, in the United States of America. Here he was able to exert his influence in regard to Henry George and the Knights of Labour, and his Irish

* Cardinal Achille Liénart, the present Bishop of Lille, is a firm disciple of Manning.

sympathies always gained him a hearing among American Catholics. Manning's first contact with American problems, and one which tended to remove some of his original prejudice against the country, was through Henry George. The latter regarded land nationalization as a cure for all social ills and gained wide influence over Archbishop Walsh of Dublin and Croke of Cashel and the Irish Land Leaguers. George visited Manning for the first time in 1866 and the Cardinal gave him an encouraging welcome. As Manning was later to point out to Walsh, and Walsh agreed with him, there was nothing wrong about land nationalization provided a just compensation was paid to the owners before it was effected. George, however, was against the principle of compensation—but this did not appear until later. In his interview with Manning, the Cardinal informed him that he had read *Social Problems* and found nothing to censure in it. George went away elated and gave his news to the press. In later editions of the work George was to refer to Manning in the following address to Leo XIII:

Your Holiness will remember the great London dock strike of two years ago, which, with that of other influential men, received the moral support of that Prince of the Church whom we of English Speech hold higher and dearer than any prelate has been held by us since the blood of Thomas a' Becket stained the Canterbury altar.[42]

As a motto at the beginning of this volume we find that George appended the following quotation from Manning, taken from the latter's well-known pamphlet to Lord Grey on Ireland:

The land question means hunger, thirst, nakedness, notice to quit, labour spent in vain, the toil of years seized upon, the breaking up of homes, the miseries, sicknesses, deaths of parents, children, wives; the despair and wildness which spring up in the hearts of the poor, when legal force like a sharp harrow goes over the most sensitive and vital right of mankind. All this is contained in the land question.[43]

From these references it is evident that George was intending to use Manning's name as a passport for his somewhat impracticable ideas. The reformer had established a close friendship with Michael Davitt, and largely through this association was able to secure a strong following among the Irish in America.

His platform was based upon the single land tax, which was to be the first instalment of the remedy for all the political and agrarian

discontent of the day. George soon came into conflict with certain
Roman Catholic ecclesiastical authorities in the United States—
and especially in regard to the 'McGlynn Case'. Edward McGlynn
was the parish priest of St. Stephen's Roman Catholic Church in
New York City and, because of George's support of Davitt, he had
soon identified himself with George's policy. McGlynn was a
staunch supporter of the Knights of Labour, and the George
movement had by 1882 become ancillary to the Knights of Labour.
In 1882 Michael Davitt visited the United States to gain financial
and moral support for the Land League, and appeared on a number
of public platforms with Henry George. McGlynn was prevailed
upon to attend these meetings and in this way the countenance of
the Church was given to the proceedings. Dr. McGlynn's views
on land nationalization were reported to Rome, and after examination there were condemned by Cardinal Simeoni, who reported
Father McGlynn to his bishop, Cardinal McClosky, for disciplinary action. McClosky was sympathetic towards the labour
movements in the States and was unwilling to antagonize them by
any condemnation of McGlynn. He saw the latter privately and told
him of the views of Rome but took no further action, and McGlynn
carried on in much the same fashion as before. But McClosky was
succeeded by Archbishop Corrigan, and he was to prove to be largely
antagonistic to the cause of Labour. From the outset Corrigan
hounded McGlynn, and he found his excuse for stricter measures
in the election of 1886 for the New York Mayoralty. Henry George
stood as a candidate for election and McGlynn promised to support
him on the public platform. Corrigan intervened and, when
McGlynn did not obey the order to refrain from supporting George,
suspended him. McGlynn was defiant, and although summoned to
Rome to state his case he refused to go. Corrigan deposed him from
his benefice. Up to this point the McGlynn case had been a purely
domestic quarrel and as such would be of little concern to us, but
the great excitement whipped up by the press over the supposed
antagonism of the Church to the cause of Labour gave the quarrel
a much wider significance.

Archbishop Walsh of Dublin wrote to Manning in reply to a
letter from him dated 17 August 1886, saying that there was nothing
morally amiss in the teachings of Henry George provided compensation for the owners of the land was admitted and that in that sense
he supported George's ideas. Walsh declared that he deprecated

most strongly the action of Archbishop Corrigan who, he declared, was hounding one poor priest and undoing all the good work that prelates such as Manning were trying to do for the cause of the Church and Labour. Manning in his reply expressed agreement and likewise deprecated Corrigan's action.[44]

Manning's earnest disciple in the United States was Cardinal Gibbons of Baltimore. Gibbons was to pass his life doing, in the United States, the same kind of work that Manning was doing in England. He wished to wean the Church from the privileged and well-born to the worker and the poor immigrant. Indeed his public pronouncements show a great similarity to those sentiments of Cardinal Manning on this matter. Further proof of this is hardly needed than Gibbons's statement at Wilmington, North Carolina, which ran: 'I would rather grasp the soiled hand of the honest artisan, than the soft, kid-gloved hand of the dandy.'[45] Gibbons was a keen supporter of the trade unions and later a staunch defender of the Knights of Labour. It was inevitable that he should regret the action of Archbishop Corrigan in the McGlynn case, for it struck at the very roots of his policy and prejudiced its outcome. Gibbons urged McGlynn to take his case to Rome 'to unfold a principle'.[46]

While Cardinal Gibbons was in Rome concerned with the case of the Knights of Labour he learnt that not only was McGlynn to be excommunicated, but that the whole movement with which he had identified himself was to be branded by Henry George's *Progress and Poverty* being placed on the Index. In a panic Gibbons wrote to Manning begging him to help. The threat to place the book on the Index had originated, Cardinal Gibbons declared, with 'a certain quarter in this country'; and 'he concluded by saying that since Manning had given so much help to him the previous year in the Knights of Labour case he was prompted to call on him again'. Now Manning was himself the senior Cardinal who was a member of the Congregation of the Index and he immediately informed Gibbons that he would help and assured him that George's work would never be placed upon the Index. It never was. This was only one of the ways in which Manning was able to forward the cause of Labour in the United States. The English prelate was to live to see his good work repaid when the Papal Ablegate to the United States in 1891, Archbishop Satolli, examined Dr. McGlynn, found nothing to condemn in his beliefs, attitude, or writings,

lifted the excommunication and restored him to his positions. By
so doing, Satolli acted on authority from Rome and set the seal of
approval upon the Henry George movement. This was of especial
significance to Cardinal Manning, for he and Walsh had constantly
been quoted as sympathetic to George's cause and it was known
that the English Cardinal had been responsible for thwarting the
attempts of Corrigan to get George's movement condemned.

Bound up closely with the McGlynn case was the question of
the Knights of Labour. The Knights of Labour had been founded
in 1869 by Uriah S. Stephens, and the belief behind the foundation
can be described in the words of Edmund Burke—'When bad men
combine, the good must associate, else they will fall, one by one, an
unpitied sacrifice in a contemptible struggle'—and the aims were
largely 'the eight-hour day, the "establishment of co-operative
institutions productive and distributive", the use of arbitration as a
substitute for strikes, and such legal innovations as were calculated
to improve the status of labour'.[47] It was hoped that the Knights of
Labour would develop into one large trade union, embracing all
kinds of occupations and to which anyone could belong, whatever
his colour, his race or his religion. Until 1878 the Knights did not
attract any great influx of membership but after that date, and until
about 1888 when a decline ensued, the Knights grew in popularity
and attracted a large membership. This increase in power and numbers coincided with the rise to leadership in the movement of a
Roman Catholic, Terence V. Powderly.

Prior to the rise of Powderly, the Knights of Labour had adopted
many of the externals of the European Continental Secret Societies,
such as a grip, a password, an oath, an initiation ceremony and stringent secrecy. These were the marks of Continental Masonry, and
the latter had fallen under the ban of the Roman Catholic Church.
It was estimated that at least two-thirds of the membership of the
Knights was Roman Catholic, and naturally because of this the
attention of the bishops of that Church in America was turned
towards the movement. All they saw were the excessive secrecy,
the ritual and the various symbols of the Order and they concluded
that because of these it was under the ban of the Church—together
with Masonry, Oddfellows, and Knights of Pythias. The initial
opposition to the movement among the Hierarchy came from Archbishop Seghers of Oregon City and Bishop Chatard of Vincennes.
They soon received support from other members of the American

Hierarchy. With the rise of Powderly to the leadership of the Order, the problem took on a more urgent aspect: here was a Roman Catholic head of a Labour Society, two-thirds of its members being Catholics, which was suspect in the eyes of ecclesiastical authority. Powderly was especially desirous of gaining Church approbation for the Knights, as he was himself a devout and sincere Catholic. 'Part of Powderly's task in reconciling the Church to the Knights of Labour was to show that [the] secrecy was harmless to ecclesiastical and civil society.'[48] He began by abolishing much of the ritual, proclaiming the name and aims of the Society at large and removing much of the secrecy.

The greatest antagonists of the Knights in the United States were the Jesuits and the Redemptorists. Proof is given of the fact that wherever these two Orders had Houses or flourished, the Knights consequently declined. 'In the city of Philadelphia where the bishop had blessed the Order, the missionaries were refusing members absolution', and it is recorded that a parish priest wrote to Powderly for a copy of the constitution and by-laws of the Order 'as I have a Jesuit mission now in progress'.[49] But as the policy of Powderly resulted in the Order foregoing much of its secrecy the attacks were less common, and later it was a Jesuit, Aloysius Sabetti, who advised Cardinal Gibbons to persist in his policy of favouring the Knights.

Meanwhile danger was approaching from another quarter and it was because of this that Cardinal Manning was drawn into the contest. For years Manning had been fighting for the appointment of a Cardinal to give representation in the Sacred College to the dominions of the British Empire. His representations were rewarded in 1886 when the Hat was awarded to Elzéar-Alexandre Taschereau, Archbishop of Quebec. Prior to his nomination Taschereau had viewed with great disapproval the growth of the Knights of Labour in Canada; and had petitioned the Holy Office to support him in condemning the movement. This had been done but did not prove satisfactory to Taschereau. The latter declared that no Catholic might join the Knights of Labour, but his statement was contradicted by Archbishop Lynch of Toronto who forbade the promulgation of the Holy Office decree in his diocese. His lead was immediately followed by Edouard Fabre, Archbishop of Montreal. Other bishops followed suit and Taschereau realized that he was being made to look the fool. The whole question must be cleared up and the recalcitrant prelates ordered to promulgate the decree. A bishop who was especially anxious about the situation was the Bishop of Portland, Maine, Mgr. Healy. His diocese was bordering on the area where the Knights were condemned, and yet in the United States Cardinal Gibbons was giving active and positive encouragement to the Order. Gibbons declared that 'any and every movement consistent with justice and fair dealing toward their employers and having for its end the amelioration of the conditions of the labouring class deserved encouragement'.[50] He also somewhat over-optimistically asserted that 'the Catholic prelates will to a man declare in favor of the organisation of labor'.

Taschereau learnt of Gibbons's sympathy and petitioned Rome for a condemnation, not just for Canada but for the Knights of Labour as a society wherever it might exist, asking that its decision be communicated 'to all prelates of Canada and of the United States, with the *obligation* of promulgating it and *demanding* its execution'.[51] At once Gibbons was up in arms, for it was estimated that at least half a million Roman Catholics in the United States were members of the Order, and after consulting the Rev. Aloysius Sabetti, S.J., and Cardinal Manning he immediately wrote to Rome protesting against Taschereau's request. Taschereau and Gibbons both left for Rome, where the McGlynn case and the theories of Henry George were to confuse issues and where they were both to receive the Cardinal's Hat. Before sailing Taschereau informed reporters who questioned him concerning the Knights: 'I shall do what I can to have it denounced.'

It was at this juncture that Cardinal Manning intervened decisively. He knew Taschereau personally and had recommended the Hat for him, but he knew him to be stubborn and tenacious of purpose. Gibbons, on the other hand, he had met in Rome in 1880, and he had been his guest at the American College. He feared he was too meek to fight Taschereau successfully and that the latter would be more likely to prevail at Rome. Manning, therefore, declared his sympathies at the outset. He wrote to his friend Bishop Keane of Richmond, U.S.A.—who was in Rome at the time—a letter in which he publicly identified himself with the cause of Gibbons, declaring that he would support him 'in preventing a hasty decision'.[52] Manning was always listened to with awe at Rome because of his great record in the shaping of Church policy and because of his particular interests in the field of Labour–Church relations. Long before the ship carrying Gibbons and Taschereau arrived in Rome, the Curia were already informed of the true state of affairs from Manning. Keane had written to Manning begging this action and declaring that he hoped the English prelate would request the Pope 'not to order or permit any overt decision of the American social questions at present, both because they had not ripened yet and taken shape, and because the action of the Holy See would hardly fail to be odious to the whole American public and to split up Catholic unity'.[53]

When Gibbons arrived in Rome he presented his side of the case to the Curia in a written Memorial on the Knights of Labour and in this he took care to quote Cardinal Manning 'to the effect that the Church had no longer to deal with parliaments and princes but rather with the masses, and from this he educed a warning against the danger to the Church of alienating the working classes'.[54]

On 28 February 1887, Keane wrote again to Manning to tell him 'the good service that the latter's utterances . . . had done for the Cardinal of Baltimore'.[55] Manning replied with advice on which member of the Curia to approach and whom to consult and whose opinion was worth winning over, and similar valuable information. Keane meanwhile (in agreement with Manning) published, both in Rome and in America, Manning's correspondence with him on the Knights of Labour. All this was aimed at securing a favourable verdict for Gibbons. Meantime Gibbons himself had begun a correspondence with Manning. On 14 March he wrote: 'We are indebted more than you are aware to the influence of your name in discussing these social questions and in influencing the public mind.'[56] And earlier in the same letter he said: 'I cannot sufficiently express to you how much I felt strengthened in my position by being able to refer in the document to your utterances on the claims of the working-men to our sympathy and how I am cheered beyond measure in receiving from your pen an endorsement of my sentiments and those of my American colleagues now in Rome.'

Keane made public another letter of Manning, dated 11 March, which stated: 'The Church is the mother, friend, and protector of the people. As the Lord walked among them, so His Church lives among them. The Cardinal's argument is irresistible.' A month later Manning wrote: 'We must deal with facts, not with memories, and lamentations. And to deal with facts we must go down into the midst of them. The Incarnation is our law, and wisdom.'[57]

Replying to Manning, Bishop Keane gave an interesting comment on the condition of the Curia. He declared: 'The Vatican seems open to living ideas,—but the Propaganda and Holy Office keep doors and windows closed to the new light.'[58] Seven days after this letter Manning silenced English Roman Catholic criticism of the Knights of Labour by an outspoken letter written in the *Tablet*, which was acclaimed in many countries. In this letter Cardinal Manning openly praised the Knights, and declared: 'The Knights of Labour and the English trade unions represent the right of labour and the rights of association for its defence.'[59] Dr. Browne relates how the latter was copied and published with comment in *Unita Catholica*, the *Germanic*, the *Reichzeitung*, the *Vaterland*. The last-named Viennese paper declared that it was an indication that ' the old principles of Christian morals are to serve social justice'.

The conclusion of the struggle is well described in two letters from Keane to Manning. The first declared:

The clear, strong, wise words of your Eminence's Letters will be a bulwark to the truth and a rebuke to mischief-makers. The impression produced here seems to be excellent. Nay, our victory is already won. Cardinal Taschereau has gone home with directions from the Holy Office to grant absolution to all the thousands of poor fellows, who have been cut off from the Sacraments by the condemnation in Canada, and there does not seem to be any danger now of a condemnation for America. Deo Gratias.[60]

The second letter was written a month later:

I explained to Cardinal Simeoni how an advocacy of popular rights was no friendliness to Socialism, and that our aim was—recognising the inevitable tendency to Democracy—not to leave it to be ruled by the devil, but to hold it in the ways of God. . . . We can expect from him only the toleration of our ideas. . . . The times are certainly critical, but we know we are advancing truth and justice.*[61]

Gibbons was so grateful for Manning's decisive intervention that he journeyed direct to London to thank the Cardinal personally

* In a personal letter to the writer, Professor John Tracy-Ellis declared that in his opinion 'Gibbons, Ireland, and Keane deliberately brought [Manning] into the discussion while they were at Rome in the winter of 1887 because they knew of his powerful position in the Roman Curia, and especially as a member of the Congregation de Propaganda Fide. Moreover, they may have been aware of Henry George's previous contacts with Manning and, therefore, turned to the latter for that reason when the Henry George case was up at Rome. The two memorials of Gibbons to Propaganda were signed the same week, as you may recall, on February 20, 1887 (Knights) and on February 25 (George).' (Letter dated 26 February 1957).

and to be his guest at Westminster for a short while. When Gibbons was in London, Manning won him over to the policy of opposing a permanent Apostolic Delegate or Nuncio for the United States. This was consistent with his policy in England, for he considered that the bishops, and they only, were the proper channels through which Rome should act.

Cardinal Gibbons never forgot Manning's kindness and in 1889 he wrote to congratulate him on his silver jubilee, saying:

Your private virtues and apostolic life, your public discourses delivered in season and out of season, your prolific writings in defence of religion and sound morals, your untiring zeal in the cause of temperance, your readiness, at the sacrifice of health, to co-operate in every measure affecting the interests of humanity, are a source of constant edification to one and all, and an incentive to emulate so bright an example.

A gift of $540 from the United States Hierarchy was enclosed.

In the *Dublin Review* in April 1917, Cardinal Gibbons wrote:

I can never forget the anxiety and distress of mind of those days. If the Knights of Labour were not condemned by the Church, then the Church ran the risk of combining against herself every element of wealth and power. . . . But if the Church did not protect the working men she would have been false to her whole history.

He attributed the final result to 'the indomitable courage and perseverance of Cardinal Manning'.

When Gibbons died the panegyric was preached by Archbishop Glennon of St. Louis—and it is significant that he classed Manning as one of the three greatest Roman Catholic Churchmen who had radically altered the existing attitudes of ecclesiastics of their time. To ally the Church to the cause of the working man was a challenge, and to make it, Glennon said, 'Divine Providence had raised up three men who had boldly proclaimed the Supernatural and divine truths for their generation and these three were Leo XIII, Manning of Westminster, and Gibbons of Baltimore'.[62] Of these three, Leo and Gibbons were disciples of Manning.

Before his death Manning was able to see his beliefs receive papal approbation in the great encyclicals of Leo XIII. Proof can be advanced to illustrate the impact Manning had made on Leo. Bishop Vaughan wrote to Manning from Rome in reference to Leo's campaign against slavery in 1880:

Bilio said only the other day: 'The Pope was telling me that this last Encyclical is Manning's. It was he who put the idea into my head to do something for the slaves. He is a man *di vaste vedute*, and his conversation is full of suggestion. I have written this Encyclical in consequence of my conversation with him.'[63]

The encyclical *Immortale Dei* of 1 November 1885, dealing with the relations between Church and State, illustrates how deeply Leo had become imbued with 'Manning-ism'.

But when we review Leo's great encyclicals on the Labour question we encounter more direct evidence. In January 1891 Leo wrote directly to Manning, saying:

It is not unknown to you, dear son, how anxious we are made by the fortunes of Ireland. No less is the care which touches you as to the condition of the working-men. We are engaged in the consideration of each matter, and as soon as we are able we will take pains that neither our duty nor charity are lacking to either cause.[64]

This private letter was followed by one from Archbishop Walsh of Dublin, who declared from Rome:

The Holy Father is in wonderful spirits. He spoke at great length to me about the coming Encyclical. . . . After a good deal of talk he said that the English translation was to be taken in hand by your Eminence and me. . . . I think I trace your Eminence's Influence in this as in many other things that I have noted here during this visit.[65]

Leo XIII sent a copy of the encyclical to Manning (11 May 1891) and declared in the letter that he was 'grateful for the important communications' Manning had made to him. The letter charged him with the duty of translating the encyclical together with Archbishop Walsh, and added: 'the English edition is to serve for circulation in America also, and it will be therefore necessary to send some thousands of copies to Cardinal Gibbons.'[66] Sir Shane Leslie in his book has made a close parallel between the wording of Leo's *Rerum Novarum* encyclical and Manning's letter to the Congress of Liège of the previous year, and although too much ought not to be made of the point when we consider that Manning was the English translator of the Encyclical, it is obvious that Leo had read the Liège letter and had been influenced by it.

Rerum Novarum was the seal of approval set upon the labours of Manning. Everything he had striven for was concerned with the forging of an alliance between Christianity and the 'New

Democracy'. That alliance had now been achieved in its most important field—the field of Labour. Manning himself expressed this view in the commentary on the Encyclical which he wrote for the *Dublin Review*:

For a century the civil Powers in almost all the Christian World have been separating themselves from the Church, claiming, and glorying in their separation. . . . And now of a sudden they find that the millions of the world sympathize with the Church, which has compassion on the multitude rather than with the State or the plutocracy which has weighed so heavily upon them.[67]

When Manning died in 1892 the funeral eulogy was preached by a prelate who in the past had had little in common with the Cardinal, Bishop John Cuthbert Hedley, O.S.B., of Newport. Manning died less than eight months after the promulgation of the encyclical *On the Condition of Labour* and Hedley referred to it, saying that it

owes something, beyond all doubt, to the counsels of Cardinal Manning. And there is one sentence in that letter which, if it was not his in form, most certainly expresses his conviction: 'There is a dictate of nature more imperious and more ancient than any bargain between man and man, that the remuneration of the wage-earner must be enough to support him in reasonable and frugal comfort.'

Chapter VI

IRELAND AND GLADSTONE

★

IN June 1866 Lord Derby became Prime Minister at the head of a Conservative Ministry in succession to Russell's Whig-Liberal Government, which had held on to office precariously for eight months (October 1865 to June 1866). It was at this time, at the outset of his episcopal career, that Manning first turned his attention to Ireland; a time when the Fenian agitation was at its height.

To explain and understand much of his policy and the opposition to it, it is necessary to bear in mind the situation of Anglo-Irish relations within the Roman Catholic community during the reign of Manning's predecessor.

The growing conflict of view and attitude between the 'Old Catholics' and the converts, together with the steady influx of Irish immigrants since the 1830's, had made it imperative for Wiseman to attempt to reconcile these discordant elements. He had not the elements of greatness or genius to enable him to rise to such a difficult task. Although he was an impulsive and warm-hearted man and in sympathy with the converts, he realized that the easiest way to pacify and reconcile the militant 'Old Catholic' faction was to allow it to retain positions of authority and control within the Church. His policy was well described by a reply of Manning to a letter of Gladstone in 1890:

You are right about Cardinal Wiseman. He was a Tory without Irish sympathies, though himself an Irishman. But he knew nothing of politics. He came into the ring of the 'Old Catholic' families and never went beyond them. They as you know and see are nine times English.[1]

But in addition to being insular and contemptuous of things foreign, the 'Old Catholics' were very conscious of their class, their breeding and their proud history. They were particularly determined that the Roman Catholic Church in England should in no way be identified with the mass of ignorant and pauperized Irish Catholics that were teeming in the new towns and bringing in their wake a new class of Irish clerics, many of whom were of mediocre intellectual quality and tainted with anti-English sympathies. This attitude is well illustrated in the case of Mrs. Charlton, a wealthy English Catholic of aristocratic stock. In 1860 she was a guest at the house of the Marquis of Westminster and the latter, in order to protect her from any stray insults, informed his guests in Mrs. Charlton's presence that she was a Roman Catholic. The refined lady immediately added: 'Yes, but an English Catholic, not an Irish one, which is all the difference in the world.'[2] This same lady relates how she had 'to suffer from the tyranny of the [Irish] priest, who never seemed to bear in mind that but for my husband, who paid so liberally towards the expenses of St. Oswald's Mission out of his own pocket, he might never have been there at all'. She stigmatized the Irish Catholics as 'all dirty and helpless . . . and unworthy objects', and declared that she 'never knew to what degree of perfection Irish filth could be raised until I visited the Hibernian colony in Bristol, and duplicity went hand in hand with dirt'. Mrs. Charlton was related by marriage to the old recusant family of that name at Hesley-side and was herself of 'Old Catholic' stock, being a member of the Anne family. Her attitude was unfortunately typical of many of her class.

There was then a distinct refusal on the part of the 'Old Catholics' to recognize Irish Catholicism as an integral part of their Church. It was foreign, unsavoury, dirty, embarrassing, and something to be tolerated in a patronizing way but by no means encouraged or accorded formal recognition. Wiseman had never the courage to assault this citadel of privilege within the Church, but trusted to the passage of time and the gradual increase in the Irish population in England to remedy the situation.

Manning, in 1865, inherited an unenviable position. He was known to be sympathetic to the converts and to the Irish and to be antipathetic to the 'Old Catholic' groups.

It was evident to him that in order to placate these various groups within his Province he would have to tread warily, and in no matter was this more the case than in his Irish policy. Throughout Wiseman's episcopate a feeling of antipathy, if not of downright hostility, existed between the Irish Roman Catholic Hierarchy and the English bishops. It was to the removal of this feeling that Manning first had to direct his energies. This end could not be achieved in a day, neither could it be achieved by words alone. He set out to

divine some way in which he could publicly identify himself with
the aspirations of the Irish episcopacy. That opportunity was not
long in forthcoming.

The Archbishop of Dublin (since 1852) was Cardinal Cullen, a
man who, according to Professor Denis Gwynn, directed 'all his
great influence to discourage the restless tendencies of Irish nationalism'.[3] Cullen was by no means as much of a 'Castle-Bishop' as
has been represented. He was fully acquainted with the misery
and unhappiness of his people, and the following picture he gave
in a letter to Manning (dated 8 April 1867) is indicative of his
feelings as well as being a very graphic pen-picture. Cullen wrote:

The last twenty years have pressed very heavily on Ireland, and afford
little ground for expecting future prosperity. We have lost about three
millions of our population, about a million of acres of land has been
withdrawn from cultivation, our principal towns have been decaying,
hundreds of villages have altogether disappeared, more than three hundred
thousand cottages of the poor have been levelled to the ground, the
working classes have become poorer than ever, trade has been reduced
to a very low state, and whatever manufactories were in the country
have ceased to give any remuneration if you except distilleries, breweries,
and establishments for spinning and weaving linen. I know that Lord
Carlisle and many other statesmen have been accustomed to boast of the
prosperity of Ireland, but it appears to me that the picture I have drawn
of the country is quite correct, and I could find statistical reports to
confirm the accuracy of my statements. . . . Unfortunately our rulers
either do not believe what is palpably true, or they do not wish to act,
or do not know what measures to adopt in order to check the progress of
ruin. It is this state of things that in my opinion creates so much discontent, and I think that until something effectual shall be done for the
country, it will be impossible to put down Fenians or to establish order
in the country.[4]

Manning realized how completely Cullen understood Irish
Catholic life and how completely he dominated the Irish episcopacy,
and that he himself could not hope to do anything for Ireland if he
did not first win the confidence of Cullen and the Irish bishops.
In 1866 Cullen and his bench of bishops issued Pastorals condemning Fenianism and its consequent violence. This action provided
a good opportunity for Manning to identify himself with the policy
of the Irish bishops and at the same time to convince the 'Old
Catholics', who were loud in their clamourings against the Fenians,
that he was not a revolutionary. He therefore issued a condemnation

of the Fenian outrages—being careful to condemn only these and not the movement itself, which he neither praised nor attacked.* In spite of its inadequacy, the statement won him the respect of the Roman Catholic bishops of Ireland.

If we look for the reasons for Cullen's antagonism to the Fenian movement we find that they revolved around the questions of education and disestablishment of the Protestant Church in Ireland. Writing to Manning on this latter point in 1867, he declared:

the Irish bishops are persuaded that peace and love for authority can never be established in Ireland as long as the Catholics shall be obliged to support a Protestant establishment and to submit to a Protestant ascendancy. . . . The total disendowment of the Protestant church would put an end to a grievance and insult, and to the continual invective of our Protestant Ministers against Catholics which keep up ill-will, and distrust between landlord and tenant; a good system of education would also do away with a great deal of bad feeling—but all this will not be enough unless something be done to encourage and protect agriculture and industry. I beg your Grace will excuse me for mentioning all these matters. I have ventured to do so because I know you are most anxious for our welfare and desirous to aid us.[5]

Cullen's two chief immediate aims, therefore, were (a) the removal of the ascendancy of the Established Church, and (b) the provision of Roman Catholic education at all levels for Ireland. Fenianism, he felt, would only harden the Government's attitude—therefore it must be condemned.

Regarding the statement attributed to Manning, which he is said to have made in Birmingham in 1867: 'Show me an Irish Catholic who has lost the Faith, and I will show you a Fenian', we can no longer accept Purcell's interpretation that this meant that all Fenians were condemned by the Church as bad Catholics. This is evident from a letter which Manning wrote to Ullathorne, Bishop of Birmingham, when the latter had reversed the statement and declared: 'Show me a Fenian and I will show you a bad Catholic.'[6] Manning said: 'I do not believe the converse of my words to be true. I feel sure that multitudes of good Catholics are misled by various causes into Fenianism.' The violence of the Fenians may have deserved condemnation but not the Fenians themselves who, according to Manning's views, had been goaded into pursuing a violent course by genuine provocation. This attitude is further

* Pastoral for 1866 (Bayswater collection).

made clear by the speech which Manning delivered at a public meeting in May 1866, on the Fenianism but recently condemned:

No greater self-deception could we practice upon ourselves than to imagine that Fenianism is the folly of a few apprentices and shop-boys. Fenianism could not have survived for a year if it were not sustained by the traditional and just discontent. . . . This feeling is to be found . . . amongst those who are in immediate contact with the land question, that is, in the occupiers and tenants, and in the labourers, whose lot is better or worse as the occupiers prosper or are impoverished. These are neither apprentices nor shop-boys, neither are they a handful, but a population in close kindred and living sympathy with millions who have tasted the civil and religious equality, and are thriving under the laws of the United States.[7]

He concluded:

Four millions and a half of the Irish in Ireland turn instinctively to five millions of Irish in America.*

At the time when Manning was uttering such a speech (1866), Gladstone was advocating a policy of coercion for Ireland and had not yet grasped the essential nature and remedy of the troubles. He wrote:

We must, without hesitation, though not without grief, use every method, adopt every measure that may be necessary to maintain the authority of the law, and to preserve the peace of the country.

The age-old policy of force was his proposed remedy.

In order to understand the Land Question, it is essential to make a few general observations on the nature of Irish land tenure. Property in land in England rested on a somewhat different basis from that in Ireland. The Irish system had developed from the tribal, the English from the feudal. Under the feudal system a landowner held his land from the Crown and in that capacity was exclusive owner of it. The tenant simply had to pay rent or render services to the landowner in return for the use of the land and a certain protection of his interests. But he did not possess any ownership in the land which he was using—that was exclusive to the landlord. In Ireland, on the other hand, the tribe possessed the land originally and although the tenant had to pay a specific amount of tribute to the head of the tribe, he was nevertheless regarded

---

* Writing to Ullathorne at this time, Manning equated Fenianism with Mazzinianism (see Leslie, op. cit. p. 195).

as a co-owner of the land—that is, he possessed inalienable rights of property in the land he worked. The Irish, therefore, regarded the land in a different light from the English tenant. With the advent of the English landlord to Ireland, the position was radically altered. It can truly be said that it was an application of English ideas of land tenure to Ireland that formed the basic cause of Irish unrest. By 1881 'there were approximately 600,000 agricultural holdings in the country, and, due allowance being made for a dual ownership and occupancy, between three and a half and four millions of the people were directly and indirectly dependant on the land. This single fact stamped the land question as a central and vital issue in the Irish politics of the period.'*

The landlords in Ireland did not normally grant long-term leases and often issued them only for one year at a time. It is obvious what kind of evils would ensue from such a system—refusal of renewals, refusal of compensation for improvements, and evictions. Manning became more and more convinced that the solution of the Irish problem lay in the solution of the land problem.

Gladstone was soon (in 1868) to succeed Russell as leader of the Liberals, and Disraeli was similarly to succeed Derby as leader of the Conservatives. On 5 April 1867 Manning wrote to Gladstone: 'I send you the inclosed as it treats of Fenianism which will give you and me much trouble, unless we adopt a just and wider legislation for Ireland.'⁸ The letter included a copy of Manning's Pastoral of that year on the Fenian outrages.

This was one of the first of those highly intimate communications on the Irish problem that were to pass between the two men. A few months after this letter was dispatched, we find Manning writing to Gladstone again—this time because he was worried about the general political situation of the world. He laments 'Garibaldi's relation to the Reform League', 'the Fenian affair at Manchester', and 'the Peace Congress'.⁹ He was afraid that the trade unions in England were following the Continental pattern, becoming excessively political, anti-clerical, secret† and criminal. Then he refers to what was uppermost in his mind: 'I look with

---

* Patrick J. Walsh, *William J. Walsh, Archbishop of Dublin* (Longmans, London 1928), p. 98. See also the letter of Ullathorne dated 4 Feb. 1881 in this connexion (in *Letters of Archbishop Ullathorne* by Mother Francis Raphael, O.S.D., London 1892, p. 406).

† It was the excessive secrecy surrounding Fenianism and the Knights of Labour that antagonized men like Cullen and Corrigan.

great anxiety to this next year. If Parliament deals uprightly and justly with Ireland we may become an united people. If not, I am afraid to look on.' He pointed out the influence of the Irish population in the United States, declaring: 'The American Irish are practically without religion, except a burning hate of England for the religious persecutions in Ireland.'

In February 1868 the tottering ministry of Lord Derby finally collapsed, owing to lack of adequate support in the Commons; and a new, re-invigorated, reinforced Conservative Ministry under the new leader Disraeli took office. Almost immediately Manning became more prolific in his letters to Gladstone and in giving what he considered to be good advice. On 15 January he had written in anger 'to express my indignation and shame at the conduct of *The Times*, in publishing ten days ago a letter recommending Martial Law for Ireland, and still more, today the letter recommending "Plantation", and extermination of the Irish race'.[10] He concluded: 'This diabolical spirit will provoke civil war.' In a cooler moment he was able to give more constructive and specific remedies:

The distribution of Patronage down to the most trivial places to Protestants and Orangemen has produced a despair of obtaining anything from Parliament, and a willingness to listen to bad counsels. Ireland is becoming Republican: not red but American republicanism, a calm, and reasonable preference for the civil and religious equality of America rather than the irritating and impoverished inequalities of the United Kingdom's spreading. This is invading the clergy: and if it establish itself in the Pastors you will have lost the people. I see no hope for Martial Law, and another '98 is not hope—but in gaining the confidence of the Irish. You can do it. They are looking to you. . . . One word more: I am afraid of the educational question. Unless the denominational system is maintained in all its integrity, and extended to Ireland, there will be a split with those whose support is now with you.[11]

From this letter it is obvious that he had recognized that the demand for Home Rule—or as he termed it 'American republicanism'—was destined to play a large part in Anglo-Irish relations in the future. It is also obvious that Manning when writing the above to Gladstone, at a time when the latter was in Opposition and had only recently succeeded to the leadership of his party, had little confidence either in the stability of the Conservative Ministry or in the capacity of Disraeli to deal justly with Ireland. His political sympathies were with Gladstone, and he knew his man. These views did not, however, prevent him from treating with the Conservatives. He had already openly identified himself with the aspirations of the Irish bishops and he now set himself to achieve something more concrete for them, in order to establish firmly the alliance.

As already stated, Cullen was especially interested in two schemes, the disestablishment of the Irish Protestant Church and a reform of the education system in Ireland. Manning attempted to forward these two schemes. 'The Irish University Question and Protestant Disestablishment became the two subjects of active and offensive alliance between the Irish and English Primates.'[12] The Conservatives would never consider disestablishment, so Manning concentrated his attention on the education scheme. He had already referred to the matter in the letter quoted which he had written to Gladstone on 11 February 1868, and a month later he wrote to him again, giving as his opinion that ' a true, full, unimpeded, Catholic education is the only hope I know, of keeping Ireland from American anarchy'.[13] The chief factor in the education problem was the provision of adequate university education for the Roman Catholics who were forbidden by the Hierarchy to attend Trinity College, Dublin and the Queen's Colleges. A Roman Catholic College in Dublin known as University College, Dublin (which had been established after Newman's dismal failure) did provide higher education for the Catholics but it was not recognized by the State, was not empowered to award degrees, and received no endowments. Manning determined to open negotiations with Disraeli on the subject (March 1868), and was soon acting as intermediary between the Government and the Irish bishops. Disraeli proved amenable and was willing to grant a charter to a Roman Catholic University in Ireland: he was not willing, however, to give any endowment. Manning communicated with Cullen and advised him to accept the offer. The Archbishop of Dublin gave a guarded acceptance, declaring:

Though the charter is not what we would wish, yet I think it ought to be accepted with some modifications. The chancellor's election ought not to be left to convocation—as for the election of the six laymen. I suppose it might be left to the graduates though it would be safer in the hands of the Senate.[14]

It may be noticed that Cullen made no objections to the lack of endowment, nor gave any indication that he would not accept the offer, provided the modification he mentioned was made. Manning passed on the gist of Cullen's letter to Disraeli. But Cardinal Cullen had promised hastily! When the Irish bishops held their next gathering he found himself completely at variance with the wishes of the Irish Episcopate. And, after all, there was little he could do: the Archbishop of Armagh was the Roman Catholic Primate of All Ireland, not Cullen. Disraeli had introduced his Bill when three Irish bishops saw him in London and, unknown to Manning, expressed the view that the University charter would be unacceptable if it was unaccompanied by endowment. Up to this point, of course, the Prime Minister had been working on the assumption that it would be accepted. It is not surprising that when the Government was defeated over the matter Disraeli should have accused Archbishop Manning of having 'stabbed him in the back'. Some little time elapsed before Manning was able to clear himself of the charge to Disraeli.* He was unable to do so at the time because it would have presented an unpleasant alternative to him—either to declare in public that he disagreed with the Irish bishops' decision (and thus sacrifice the recently-won friendship and alliance), or to complain of how shabbily he had been treated by Cullen (and thus set a number of Irish bishops against their Archbishop, for they probably were unaware of his letter of 15 March to Manning). He decided to remain silent, and thus much odium attached to him as the one responsible for bringing about the defeat of the new Government. Disraeli said later that he would have resigned if superior political considerations had not prevented him.[15] Manning attempted to clear himself of the charge in a letter which he sent Gladstone on 24 March 1868: 'I have done all I can to separate the Charter and the endowment questions. But I have not the ability to do more in a case out of England than give an opinion.'[16]

Gladstone became Prime Minister for the first time in December 1868. Manning now directed all his energies to the second plank in Cullen's platform—disestablishment of the Protestant Church in Ireland. The first intimation of this activity, after the accession of Gladstone to power, was the famous pamphlet *Ireland: A Letter to Earl Grey* (12 March 1868). In this pamphlet dedicated to the elder statesman, Manning boldly and fearlessly recommended a series of radical reforms, which he said would help to pacify Ireland. He held that Fenianism was but a continuation of the

---

* Time enough for Disraeli to retaliate by making Manning a character in his *Lothair* —the suave Cardinal Grandison.

insurrectionary movements of 1798, 1828 and 1848, and that the
root causes were the same then as now. He instanced the need for
five major reforms:

(1) An Act of Parliament summed up in one clause which would recite
and repeal all penal enactments against the Catholic Church and religion
still lingering in the Statutes of these realms.

(2) The Church of the people [in Ireland] must be placed upon the
perfect equality which it enjoys in Canada and Australia.

(3) Such a modification of the National Education Board as shall
make the existing schools 'bona fide' denominational schools of the
Catholic and of the Protestant populations respectively.

(4) Disestablishment of the Protestant Church in Ireland.

(5) [The land question] is the chief and paramount condition on
which the peace of Ireland depends.[17]

Together with these suggestions Manning appended a series of
examples of evictions and other grievances, and raised the ire of *The
Times* and the 'Old Catholics' by his statement that

A starving man commits no theft if he saves his life by eating of his
neighbour's bread so much as is necessary for the support of his existence.
The civil law yields before the higher jurisdiction of the divine, as the
positive divine law yields before the natural law of God.

These sentences were held by his opponents to be a veritable encouragement of Fenianism and reprisals and a relaxation of the moral
law. In fact some Catholics were adverse even to the disestablishment of the Irish Church and especially a Catholic Peer, Lord
Gormanston, and, strangely, James Hope.

One day before the actual release of this pamphlet, Manning sent
a personal copy to all the leading statesmen, including Gladstone.
In the letter accompanying it to Gladstone, Manning wrote:

It gives expression to feelings and convictions which powerfully govern
the great mass of our people, who desire to see Great Britain and Ireland
strong and peaceful. Believe me, the only hope of restoring Ireland to
social order and peace is to give free course to the only powers of Christianity which control it.

Now Gladstone had for long been convinced of the uselessness
of upholding the Irish Establishment, but he had not yet been
convinced that the time was ripe for Disestablishment. Writing on
13 February 1865 to Robert Phillimore, Gladstone had declared:

I would treat the Irish Church, as a religious body, with the same respect and consideration as the Church of England, and would apply to it the same liberal policy as regards its freedom of action. But I am not loyal to it as an establishment.[18]

It is true that both Manning and Bishop Wilberforce had argued about the use of maintaining the Irish Establishment long before the former became a Roman Catholic, and Professor Chapeau has shown very convincingly that in these early days Manning had influenced the forming of Gladstone's views on this matter.

But in the letter to Phillimore quoted above, Gladstone concluded: 'I will never be a party, knowingly, to what I may call frivolous acts of disturbance, nor to the premature production of schemes of change.' Morley states that in regard to disestablishment Gladstone 'was careful to explain in public correspondence that the question was out of all bearing on the practical politics of the day'. That was in 1865, and the fact remains that both in 1865 and 1866 Gladstone voted against the disestablishment of the Irish Church. But in 1865 Manning had urged Disestablishment! Morley declares, referring to Manning: 'One acute observer who knew him [Gladstone] well, evidently took a different view of the practical politics of the day, or at any rate of the morrow',[19] and he quotes a letter of Manning of 1865 in which he states: 'I read your speech on the Irish Church, which set me musing and forecasting. It was a real grapple with the question.' It is not unlikely that Manning's pamphlet to Earl Grey finally convinced Gladstone that the time was now ripe for Disestablishment. Gladstone received Manning's pamphlet on 12 March 1868; four days later, on 16 March, he rose in the House of Commons and declared: 'The time has now come when the Church of Ireland as a Church in alliance with the State must cease to exist.'[20] There is little doubt that Gladstone was interested in capturing votes from the new electorate,* but at the same time it is an equally tenable view that the change in his attitude may have been due in some extent to Manning's influence and pamphlet.

The effect of the pamphlet was equally startling on certain members of the English Roman Catholic Hierarchy. It won for Manning the unquestioned support of Dr. Ullathorne, a support he was to

* Derby's Reform Bill of 1867 granted household suffrage. He described his own Bill as 'a leap in the dark'.

retain in Irish matters throughout Ullathorne's life.† The latter wrote to Manning:

I wish to tell you how pleased we all are here with your letter to Lord Grey on Ireland. The exposition of the sentiments which animate the Irish bishops and clergy and the rebuke to the cold and stolid tone of English depreciation of the Irish mind, are particularly happy. I am sure the letter will be very acceptable in Ireland, and will do good in more ways than one amongst the Irish Catholics in England.[21]

Writing about his *Letter to Earl Grey* to his nephew John Anderdon, who had sent his congratulations, Manning declared: 'I am glad you liked my letter. I never wrote anything with a firmer conviction of its truth and justice.'[22] Referring to the effect it had had on Gladstone and the 'Old Catholics' he declared: 'It seems as if a light had fallen suddenly upon men's minds. I never thought to live to see what is passing now. My belief is that if Ireland were like Canada or Australia these Kingdoms might yet be united. The main cause of all division, conflict, and animosity is the Irish Establishment.'

In the meantime, Manning continued to supply Gladstone with his views. From 12 March, the date of the publication of the former's pamphlet, until December 1868, when Gladstone took office, Manning wrote two or three letters to him on Irish disestablishment. On 28 March he wrote:

The Irish Establishment is a great wrong. It is the cause of division in Ireland, of alienation between Ireland and England. It embitters every other question. Even the land question is exasperated by it. All relations of life are tainted by it. The fatal ascendancy of religion over religion. If this wrong were righted everything else would be easier. I do not think it a leap in the dark, but a step onward into the light.[23]

Again on 8 April he wrote, this time quoting Cullen of Dublin:

I am convinced that if the Irish Church were disestablished, even though it retain all its endowments, the vastest step to mitigating and extinguishing the religious animosities of Ireland would be made.[24]

When Gladstone formed his first Ministry there was some hope that much of what Manning desired at this time for Ireland might be obtained. For the Radical wing of Gladstone's party was also

---

† There is no justification for Dr. Mathew's statement that Ullathorne regarded Manning 'with the suspicion of a bull mastiff'—see *English Catholics, 1850–1950*, p. 525.

pushing for the achievement of this programme. Dilke's views on the Irish question may be taken as typical of a large section of the party and they are of interest to us in view of the very close friendship that sprung up between this extreme Radical and Manning. Dilke's views are stated clearly:

After the Church should have been disestablished, the land system reformed, and a wide measure of Parliamentary reform given to Ireland; after they shall have passed Fawcett's Bill 'for throwing open Trinity College, Dublin, and destroying the last trace of that sectarian spirit which has hitherto been allowed to rule in Ireland'—they might hope not perhaps for instant quiet in the country, but at least for the gradual growth of a feeling that we have done our duty, and that we may well call upon the Irish to do theirs.[25]

How closely akin were the views of Dilke and Manning!

In 1869 Gladstone disestablished the Irish Church. Manning had to restrain the zeal of the Irish Members from demanding a share in the spoils of the endowments; the Irish Hierarchy was totally opposed to any share, for the bishops considered that such an action would alienate the people. Manning wrote to Gladstone on 14 July 1869 about this matter:

The old endowments cannot be applied to *religious* purposes without breaking peace, wounding ability and *hindering religion*. . . . Let all that can, be applied to charitable uses sensible to the whole of Ireland. Finally if any part can be so applied as to relieve the land question, it is given to the poor.[26]

The outcome was that the funds of the old Establishment were equally divided between Protestant Ministers in Ireland and a fund established for the relief of the Irish poor. Professor Denis Gwynn regards the disestablishment of the Irish Protestant Church as unquestionably 'the most important concession for Ireland since the Emancipation Act of forty years earlier'. But even so, it did not materially affect the real basis of Irish discontent. Gladstone became disappointed at the very small response the measure had evoked. This is evident from the fact that in November 1869 Manning was writing from Nice to him:

Do not be discouraged about Ireland. We have to deal now not with Ireland but with America in Ireland. The Nemesis is upon us. The Famine year and the emigration in despair have made Ireland more American than Irish.

Following the disestablishment of the Irish Church, Gladstone's attention was turned to the Land Question. The Archbishop had always contended that this was the root of the Irish problem. As we have seen, he held that Fenianism would directly lose its appeal if it were divorced from the cause of agrarian discontent. He had an intense suspicion of anybody talking of the freedom of Ireland in the abstract, and of any society governed by excessive secrecy and mystic signs. He grew tolerant of Fenianism only when it allied itself to the advocacy of social reform, and ceased to talk of 'freedom' in a vague way. This change in the aim and direction of Fenianism was effected by Michael Davitt, himself a frequent visitor at Archbishop's House, Westminster, and a man who had the greatest respect for its occupant. The effect this change wrought in the movement has been described by Davitt's biographer as follows:

The leaders of Fenianism . . . had made the error of thinking the common man, taken in the mass, would or could be ready to risk his all for the freedom of Ireland in the abstract. . . . Fenianism did nothing to remedy his immediate grievance. . . . Davitt determined to remedy this by making the land question the motive power of the open agitation.[27]

In order, therefore, to remedy some of the more flagrant abuses in the Irish land system, Gladstone introduced in 1870 his Land Bill. He wrote to Manning to explain that the Bill was intended to prevent the landlord from using the terrible weapon of undue and unjust eviction, by so framing the handle that it shall cut his hands with the sharp edge of pecuniary damages. The man evicted without any fault, and suffering the usual loss by it will receive whatever the custom of the country gives, and where there is no custom, according to a scale, besides whatever he can claim for permanent buildings or reclamation of land. Wanton eviction will, as I hope, be extinguished by provisions like these.[28]

These hopes were to prove over-sanguine. Yet Manning shared these hopes. He wrote to congratulate Gladstone, and declared:

Yesterday I had a long conversation with two very advanced Irish politicians. They assured me that three years ago the desire for separation from England was greatly in the ascendant. That now the desire is equally strong for the integrity of the Empire. They ascribed this to a revived confidence in Parliament, and that to your two chief Irish measures. You have fairly earned this, which no English statesman has yet deserved.[29]

This letter illustrates clearly how limited were Manning's own Irish aspirations at this time and how over-optimistic were his views for the future.

During 1870 Manning was engaged in the business of the Vatican Council, and what little spare time he had to write to Gladstone was used to express his views on the impending Education Act. He did, however, convey to the Prime Minister the suggestion that the establishment of land-courts would provide a more perfect guarantee for Ireland. The Land Bill of 1870, however, was a first step in the right direction and became a basis for all future legislation on the matter.*

The Prime Minister next turned his attention to the vexed question of Irish education, which it will be remembered had been the third item in Manning's pamphlet. The main difficulty here was university education. We have seen that Disraeli had already failed to settle the question, and that Manning's attitude had more in common with that of Disraeli that with that of the Irish bishops. When Manning learned, therefore, of Gladstone's purpose he wrote to warn him of the danger of the question:

Nothing would so wound all that is sound in Ireland as anything adverse to the popular instincts of the country in matters of education. . . . If their religion were touched in matters of education, I should have great fear.[30]

Gladstone decided, however, to go ahead and try to solve the impasse. His offer was that Dublin University should be a federal body consisting of Trinity College, University College, the Queen's Colleges at Belfast and Cork, and any other colleges capable of justifying their existence as colleges of advanced education. All these were to be constituent members and equal in rank. But there were to be provisos: (1) no religious tests to be allowed; (2) all teaching of theology, modern history, moral and mental philosophy were to be excluded from the University (though not from the constituent colleges). Again Manning urged acceptance, but Cullen (chiefly because it would exclude his beloved Maynooth— the chief theological seminary in Ireland—from the constituent membership of the University) rejected the offer and dubbed it 'godless'. The Bill was defeated at the second reading (by three votes), and Gladstone resigned. Although Gladstone resumed office, it had been proved that the Irish education question was able, once more, to bring about the defeat of a British government.

* Lawyers soon devised ways to evade its main provisions; the Bill was somewhat ambiguous in expression.

The remaining part of Manning's recommended programme for Ireland was that there should be an Act of Parliament repealing any traces of penal enactments still left in the laws of the country, and this Gladstone accomplished in 1871 with the removal of the Tests and the freeing of most positions at Oxford and Cambridge to all shades of religious opinion.

If we ask ourselves how it was that Manning was able to support so wholeheartedly Gladstone's Irish policy in his first ministry we must remember that the Archbishop was thoroughly acquainted with the texture of Gladstone's opinions and with the nature of his Liberalism, and that he knew how to seize on the weak points in his political theory. This latter is well illustrated in the correspondence between them over the Temporal Power,* and how Manning was able to utilize the opportunity to benefit Ireland. Gladstone was unable to see the justice of the Pope's invoking French aid to protect his possessions from the Italian nationalists, and he expressed these views in a letter to Manning. The latter replied:

I am also altogether unable to maintain the justice of our holding Ireland if the Pope had not a just sovereignty over Rome. My belief is that the action of Italy upon Rome is like the action of America upon Ireland. I have never heard of this argument met by reason, but only by Sir Robert Inglis's 25,000 men: or by a raid of Lowland Scots from Belfast to Cork. But this is the policy of Russia in Poland.

If you wish to know the will of Ireland ask the Irish in our Colonies and in the United States. You will never get it in Ireland with 30,000 English and Scotch bayonets. The political representation of Ireland by 30 Catholic members out of a hundred with a population four fifths Catholic is like the Roman Plebiscite. . . .

All this will sound to you very wild, but it is the judgment of all the world outside our four seas. . . . Do not believe me, if you like. But do not disregard me. Steer your course as if the rocks I have laid down in the Chart were as certain, as you may perhaps think them to be moonshine.[31]

The underlying insinuation of this letter was that while Gladstone could recognize and was willing to sponsor any kind of liberal insurrectionary movement on the Continent, he was at the same time blinded to the fact that the Irish movement was a liberal rising of an oppressed people. The charge was painfully obvious to Gladstone, as can be seen from the weakness of his reply, viz.:

* There is a great deal of material extant on the relations between Gladstone and Manning on the Temporal Power—but the subject falls outside the scope of this present work.

I cannot accept your belief as to the people of Ireland. I know of no proof that they desire separation from this country. . . . The bayonets in Ireland are Irish as well as English, and Scotch, but I know of no influence which they do or can exercise on the free expression of opinion.[32]

This correspondence illustrates how easily Manning was able to drive home a truth. It also points out that he was attempting to convince Gladstone that there was an ever-increasing demand for Home Rule in Ireland. If it be asked when Manning first *advocated* Home Rule for Ireland the question is more difficult to answer, for to Manning 'Home Rule' meant different things at different times. In the letter to Gladstone of 11 February 1868, already quoted, Manning recognized that Ireland was moving towards some form of Home Rule, which he described as 'Republican: not red but American republicanism, a calm, and reasonable preference for the civil and religious equality of America'.[33] But American republicanism meant total separation from the mother country. This surely was a recognition of Home Rule in its most extreme form. Again in November 1869 he wrote: 'We have to deal now not with Ireland but with America in Ireland.'[34] This was also a recognition that there was a fervent desire for total separation in Ireland. In the letter to Anderdon, however, of 2 April 1868, Manning had declared that if 'Ireland were like Canada or Australia' all would be well. This statement would simply seem to imply some form of 'dominion' self-government but not total separation. Manning always claimed that it was a reading of Butt's *Land Tenure in Ireland* which converted him to Home Rule. Proof that Manning was thinking seriously about his attitude towards the various forms of Home Rule occurs in 1871, when he wrote to Cullen to ascertain the true situation in this regard in Ireland, and the attitude of the Irish bishops towards it. He always wished to co-operate with the Irish bishops whenever possible and not to prejudice their actions. Cullen replied as follows:

I beg to state that I have determined to have nothing to do with the home rule movement for the present. The principal leaders in the movement here are professors of Trinity College who have never heretofore manifested any good feeling towards the people of Ireland, and Orange men who are still worse. Their object appears to be to get out the present ministry and get Disraeli into power when they will all give up the present agitation, and declare against home rule. The other leaders are editors of half Fenian or anti-religious newspapers and some few wrong headed or disappointed Catholics who are ready to engage in any new project whatever it may be. Very few, perhaps ten or twelve, priests have taken a part in this agitation, but I think all the bishops and the great mass of the clergy seem determined to keep aloof.

In the Saunders [?] newspaper of this morning I find the enclosed notice which seems to indicate a union of the advocates of home rule with the International. If this statement have any foundation, it cannot but excite alarm in reference to home rule.

The great mass of the people in Ireland are always ready to join in any movement which is presented to them as something patriotic, but I think that the home rule is still looked on with suspicion by them on account of its leaders. . . . The line of action I am determined to follow is to look on until we shall know more about the tendencies of the system and its leaders. . . . I have not thought it necessary to do any more at present than to observe passing events.[35]

In view of this letter and the declared policy of the Irish Hierarchy, Manning could not openly express his mind on the Home Rule idea. But Leslie claims that Manning was 'perhaps the first Prelate in the world to welcome' Home Rule, and quotes letters to Ullathorne of 1873 in which the former declares himself 'very tolerant about it' because it 'reclaimed many Fenians'.[36] But we must remember that this was the Home Rule of Isaac Butt and not of Parnell. We are right in surmising, however, that Manning would not agree with Cullen's policy of simply 'observing passing events'. He felt that the Church ought always to identify itself with the legitimate aspirations of the laity. The Church should place itself at the head of the popular movement. Otherwise it was in danger of becoming identified with the oppressors in the mind of the laity. We must never lose sight of the fact that most of Manning's public attitudes rested on such a basic ecclesiastical policy.

Gladstone fell from office early in 1874, and at the ensuing election (during which a secret ballot was used for the first time) Disraeli was returned to power at the head of a Conservative ministry strong enough to endure six years of office. The result of this change, as was to be expected, was that Manning's political influence immediately declined. As pointed out elsewhere, Manning was not particularly sorry to find that Gladstone was to spend a period in opposition. He had feared the growing influence of Forster and the advocates of secular education, and the growing reliance of the Liberals upon the Nonconformists.

Disraeli attempted to settle the Irish university question for the second time, and this time his Bill reached the Statute Book in 1879. This established the Royal University of Ireland. In the meantime Cullen had died and had been succeeded by his Auxiliary as Archbishop of Dublin, Dr. McCabe. The latter shared to the full Cullen's prejudices and animosities and even succeeded in having the militant Archbishop of Cashel, Dr. Croke, summoned to Rome *ad audiendum verbum* for his violent support of the Irish movement. Croke was described by Davitt as the 'stoutest defender and strongest supporter among the Irish Hierarchy' of the nationalist movement.[37] He was able to clear himself at Rome, and returned to his see bearing no little resentment against the Archbishop of Dublin. The latter was one of those unfortunately weak leaders who are unable to follow a firm policy, but to the consternation of everybody are addicted to the habit of rapidly reversing their decisions. This became evident in the matter of Disraeli's Act. The Royal University was to be merely an examining body; the old Queen's University was dissolved. The Queen's Colleges were to retain their endowments; Trinity College was to remain outside the scheme altogether. The Royal University was to examine and grant degrees to anybody, no matter where they had studied. McCabe waxed enthusiastic over the scheme, even consenting to be a member of the Senate. But when a certain reactionary core among the Maynooth professors objected to his membership, he resigned. Later he rejoined the Senate, and still later resigned a second time. The quarrel was over the endowment (the Catholic colleges received only £6,000 out of a total of £30,000) and over the unsatisfactory way in which examination papers were set and assessed.

At the time that Croke was considered to be a violent partisan of the Land League, McCabe went out of his way to condemn it. He condemned, in addition, the Ladies' Land League, in such a way as to cast suspicion on the purity and morals of its members; this action resulted in a public rebuke from Croke. McCabe was widely regarded as a 'Castle-bishop' and was very sympathetic to Disraeli's Government. Manning, while keeping on friendly terms with McCabe, held his peace during these years and did not directly interfere in Irish problems. He was distrusted by Disraeli and ignored by McCabe. It is hardly true to describe Cardinal Manning, as O'Brien in his *Parnell* does, as seeing in Archbishop Croke 'the hope of moderating a movement which he disliked'.[28] As we have seen,

Manning did not *dislike* the Irish movement and Croke was a militant and advanced advocate of the Land League.

Gladstone returned to power in April 1880, to head his second great ministry. He indicated at the outset that he wished to introduce a new Land Act that would go further than the Act of 1870. Consequently the Bessborough Commission was set up in 1880, and reported that 'the Land Act of 1870 had completely failed to protect tenants' property in their improvements'. The result was Gladstone's Land Bill of 1881. Writing to Dr. Walsh, the President of Maynooth, to ask him to write a simple layman's account of this Bill, Bishop Butler of Limerick amusingly referred to it as the most abstruse document since the Apocalypse was written, going on: 'the meaning when there is any, is so veiled and hidden away that ordinary men cannot even take a decent guess at it.'[39] The result must have been creditable, for the *Tablet* asserted that ' the famous "Exposition" of Gladstone's complex and controverted Land Act made that measure clear, amongst others, to the author of it'.[40] The Act recognized fixity of tenure and established fair rent courts. Manning acted throughout this year 'as a constant intermediary between the Government and the Irish bishops'.[41]

Gladstone in 1881, finding Manning* to be wholly sympathetic to the Land League and a staunch defender of Croke, was unable to ask him to use his influence with the Irish bishops against the retaliatory measures undertaken by the Land League, which the latter had intensified after Gladstone's Coercion Act of that year. Manning's pro-League sympathies made Gladstone decide to try his hand with one of the chief champions of the 'Old Catholics' and someone whose influence he felt sure would bear weight at Rome—Newman. He knew the latter was antipathetic to Manning and disliked the Irish temperament after his failure at Dublin, and he decided to ask him to get Rome to condemn the Land League and quieten Croke and his friends. The correspondence was of course carried on unknown to Manning. Gladstone wrote to Newman:

Some members of the Roman Catholic priesthood in Ireland deliver certain sermons and otherwise express themselves in the way which my enclosures exhibit. I doubt whether if they were laymen we should not have settled their cases by putting them in jail. I need not describe the sentiments uttered. Your Eminence will feel them and judge them as

---

* Manning was made a Cardinal in 1875 by Pio Nono.

strongly as I do. But now as to the supreme pontiff: you will hardly be surprised when I say that I regard him, if apprised of the facts, as responsible for the conduct of these priests. For I know perfectly well that he has the means of silencing them, and that if any one were in public to dispute the decrees of the council of 1870, as plainly as he has denounced law and order, he would be silenced.[42]

The Prime Minister concluded his letter by asking Newman's good offices with the Pope. The letter is interesting because it is the first intimation of that policy on the part of the British Government, to assume threatening magnitude later, of trying to conquer Irish discontent by soliciting papal condemnations. Newman, never well acquainted with political strategy and decidedly anti-Irish in his feelings, somewhat naïvely agreed to help, saying that he would gladly find himself 'able to be of service, however slight it might be, in a political crisis which must be felt as of a grave anxiety by all who understand the blessing of national unity'.

Manning would have opposed any English intrigue at Rome, because he rightly realized that once it was suspected by the Irish laity the clergy would lose their hold on the National Movement and it might then assume the same proportions as the Continental movements and become violently anti-clerical.

Little seems to have resulted from Newman's intervention; Manning was the head of the Roman Catholic Church in England, and ultimately his counsels must prevail at Rome. Newman, whose orthodoxy was suspect, was certainly not the kind of man Rome would heed in matters of political magnitude.

Meanwhile, during the year 1884-5, Manning became involved in the Irish 'Central Board' scheme, supported by Dilke and Chamberlain. And this became further complicated by the 'Errington Mission' and Manning's action in the general election of 1885.

In February 1885 the unexpected death of Cardinal McCabe occurred. It was extremely important from the point of view of the British Government that his successor should share his views and those of his predecessor, Cardinal Cullen. Both Salisbury and Gladstone were anxious for an amenable prelate in Dublin. The three chief names forwarded to Rome from the vacant see were Dr. Walsh, President of Maynooth College; Dr. Donnelly, Auxiliary Bishop of Dublin and Titular Bishop of Canea; and Dr. Tynan, private secretary to the late Cardinal. Walsh, who was the favourite, was a friend of Croke of Cashel and a keen supporter of the Land

League. Tynan was a dark horse, whom neither side could be sure about. Bishop Donnelly was a colourless ecclesiastic, suitable as a conscientious parish priest but weak and, if anything, mildly antagonistic to the Land League. Lord Granville, who was the Foreign Secretary in Gladstone's Ministry, employed 'Mr. George Errington . . . an active, officious, though not an official agent'[43] in order to work at Rome for the interests of the Crown. Errington was an 'Old Catholic'. Granville was in favour of Donnelly's candidature, while Errington was pressing at Rome for the appointment of either Donnelly or Dr. Moran, Archbishop of Sydney and a nephew of Cardinal Cullen. At the same time Granville was engaged in 'trying through Cardinal Newman, to induce the Pope to bully the Irish bishops'.[44]

Manning became aware of these intrigues, largely through information supplied to him by Sir Charles Dilke. Dilke was a great admirer of the Cardinal and a close friend, and in his capacity as Under-Secretary for Foreign Affairs in Gladstone's Ministry was able to pass on valuable information to Manning. Dilke strongly disapproved of the episode, but nevertheless encouraged Errington to write to him in order that he might offset his influence more successfully. As early as 28 October 1881, Dilke records that he 'saw Errington, who was in Paris on his way to Rome with letters from Lord Granville, based on the request of Spencer and Forster that he, Errington, should represent the Irish Government at Rome during its great struggle with Parnell'.[45] The Errington affair nearly led to the fall of the Government. Dilke declared: 'The Errington Mission led to strained relations between Lord Granville and myself. . . . There never was a more discreditable piece of business than the whole of this Errington matter. . . . It is the Government and not Errington that must be blamed.' Chamberlain wrote to Dilke on 25 April 1885, 'Do not let Mr. Errington meddle with the Archbishopric of Dublin.'

In his articles in *Irish Historical Studies* for September 1953 and in the *English Historical Review* for January 1947 and October 1950, Mr. C. H. D. Howard seems to be unaware of how really serious the Errington Mission was. He declares that Manning 'was suspicious of the activities in Rome of George Errington, who he had reason to believe was attempting, on instructions from Granville, to influence the appointment to the See of Dublin.' It was far more than suspicion. The Ministry was split. Dilke records,

'On Tuesday, 28 April, the Cardinal again spoke to me as to the Archbishopric of Dublin, expressing his great vexation as to Spencer's action through Errington.'[46] The groups in the Cabinet now begin to stand out clearly: Granville, Spencer, Harcourt, Carlingford, Hartington for the Mission; Dilke and Chamberlain decidedly against; Gladstone 'sitting on the fence'.

Into this complicated diplomatic skein a new factor was about to enter. Errington was an 'Old Catholic' and he enlisted in his support such stalwarts of the faith as the Bishop of Clifton (Dr. Clifford) and the Duke of Norfolk. This faction began by supporting the candidature of Donnelly but soon transferred their support to a more reliable ally, Dr. Moran of Sydney. 'The British Government [now] desired the appointment of Dr. Moran, whom they expected to be another mild politician.'[47]

The whole situation became tense when a letter written by Errington to Granville, in which he talked about the 'strong pressure I can still command' being used 'at the right moment', was published in *United Ireland*.[48] Ireland was thrown into a furore at the revelation, and this was not quieted by a series of defamatory articles against Dr. Walsh which began to make their appearance in *The Times* about this time. There was no time to be lost in nullifying British intrigue. Garvin asserts that 'backstairs interference of this kind with their politico-spiritual affairs was peculiarly hated by Nationalist Catholics'. Davitt sped to Rome to canvass Walsh's nomination and Manning, through the agency of Dilke, watched closely and passed news to Croke and Walsh. Dilke himself wrote to Gladstone to protest formally 'against the secret arrangement', adding 'the last straw has been the resistance to Walsh'.[49]

On 1 May 1885 we find Manning writing to Croke of Cashel: 'Let me hear of our affairs at Rome. . . . And let me know whether I can be of any use.' Croke replied: 'The setting aside of Dr. Walsh *for anyone* would raise such a storm in Ireland and in the United States that his Holiness should be solemnly warned against doing so. Your Eminence alone can give such a warning and I earnestly ask you to do it.'*

Manning at once complied and he also wrote to Dilke: 'My first and chief anxiety is that the Government shall in no way either

---

* There was a suggestion later (attributed to Croke) that Manning be translated to Dublin. But he was of far more value to Ireland where he was.

officially or officiously, through Mr. Errington or any other attempt to influence the election.'[50]

To show the impact of these events and the value of Manning's aid to Ireland, the following letter from Archbishop Croke is enlightening. He was writing to Manning:

Things look very threatening here. The people cannot be persuaded that the Pope has not entered into some sort of agreement with the Government. . . . Dangerous indeed it is, if it should turn out that English influence proved to be so potent in the Vatican as to cause His Holiness to discredit one of the foremost ecclesiastics of the day, simply because he happened not to be a 'Persona grata' to the Government. . . . I write to your Eminence as to the highest and most influential ecclesiastic within the realm, with the hope that you may have it conveyed to the proper quarter.[51]

To reassure Croke, Manning replied that he had already written fully to the Pope in the sense suggested, and assuring him that he might confide on his [Manning's] leaving nothing undone that he could do.*

The Cardinal's next move in the question was to arrange for Dilke to meet Dr. Walsh at dinner, in order to form a personal estimate of the man. Dilke was favourably impressed and no doubt informed Walsh of Manning's great efforts to secure his appointment—for we find a correspondence beginning between Walsh and Manning after this time.

On 27 June Gladstone had irritated Manning again—by the conferring of a baronetcy on Errington. Dilke was equally perturbed and wrote to Gladstone to express his dismay at the honour 'at a moment when it will be felt by the great majority of people who do not see round corners that he is rewarded for the fight made by him on behalf of the (defeated) policy of resistance to the selection as Roman Catholic Archbishop of the accomplished gentleman on whom the whole Irish Roman Catholic Clergy and people had set their hearts'.[52] He threatened to leave the Liberal Front Bench because of it. Chamberlain wrote to Dilke: 'I would cordially join in a protest against this, although, as I have already told you, I do not think the last proceeding—in the matter of Errington—will justify a formal secession.'

* 'Dr. Croke looked upon Manning as the most honest Englishman he had ever known—a man absolutely fair and friendly towards Ireland' (Walsh, p. 160).

Quite suddenly Gladstone's Ministry was, in June 1885, forced out of office by the Irish vote. As soon as Salisbury became Prime Minister, Manning saw the new Viceroy for Ireland (Lord Carnarvon) and 'impressed upon him the dangers of interference'[53] in the Dublin appointment. But within a few days the Pope made a personal decision and appointed Dr. Walsh Archbishop of Dublin. Letters of congratulation to Manning were profuse. That this appointment owed much to his intervention there can be little doubt. Writing to Vaughan of Salford after the trouble was over, Manning declared:

> I thought my last letter to Leo XIII would have vexed him. We have been on the brink of an enormous scandal. Rightly or wrongly, the feeling in Ireland was full of danger.[54]

Throughout the period of the contest for the Dublin appointment Manning also became involved in Chamberlain's 'Central Board' scheme for Ireland. Garvin maintains very convincingly that Manning's interest in Chamberlain's 'Central Board' scheme was largely in order to defeat the Errington intrigue. By supporting the limited self-government plan sponsored by Chamberlain and Dilke, Manning hoped to win their support in the Cabinet against the Errington Mission. He also maintains that Manning's 'political views exactly coincided with Chamberlain's',[55] thus implying that Manning's conception of Home Rule at this time was simply one of local self-government as envisaged in the 'Central Board' plan and that he did not desire a policy of *total* separation for Ireland. 'As regards the Imperial connection ', he contends, 'he was emphatically a Unionist at this time, but in favour of ample devolution for Irish internal affairs.' On the other hand, O'Brien states that 'it may well have been Manning who briefed Chamberlain on the whole local self-government idea. As early as 1883 he had written to Leo XIII : "Amministrazione domestica, ma Parlamento no : sarebbe preludio di confitto e di separazione." '[56] But O'Brien sees in Manning's intervention an even deeper motive than the Errington affair:

> The readiness of the bishops to do business, politically speaking, with Chamberlain at this time was probably directly related to the abhorrence with which they regarded his ideas. 'Local self-government' would make Irish education safely—and quickly—out of reach of such irreligious innovators as Joseph Chamberlain.[57]

Perhaps the true reason for Manning's interest lies in an amalgam-ation of both these. Chamberlain knew that a general election must be held not later than 1886 and that owing to the new franchise the Irish electors would hold the balance, and he also knew that Gladstone's Coercion Act of 1882 would come up for renewal before the dissolution and that the Irish members would try to prevent its renewal. A constructive policy for Ireland was urgently needed. Chamberlain's 'Central Board' scheme involved 'the creation of an essentially legislative body with powers over land, education and communications, which would serve to relieve the congestion of the overworked House of Commons'. On reading Chamberlain's Cabinet memorandum on 'Local Government in Ireland' (Shane Leslie informs us) Manning had an interview with Parnell. When Mr. C. H. D. Howard contends that all Manning had to do was 'to steer a course between English Catholics, many of whom were hostile to Irish political aspirations, and Irish National-ists'[58] he is missing the entire significance of Manning's actions in 1885. He was obviously trying to gain any kind of amelioration in Ireland's condition, combined with an ecclesiastical *coup* of the first magnitude. This becomes self-evident when, on 22 April 1885, Manning informed Dilke that five Irish bishops and Archbishop Croke had been staying with him recently and that they viewed Chamberlain's scheme with approval.[59] On 30 April Manning saw Parnell and told him that the bishops would support Chamberlain's scheme, and both Chamberlain and Dilke interviewed the Cardinal on this matter. 'Needless to say', Chamberlain's biographer declares, 'as the Cardinal desired [Dilke and Chamberlain] were filled with zeal for the appointment of Walsh to the see of Dublin, and, with desire as Ministers to frustrate "backstairs diplomacy" at Rome.'[60] Manning's part in the negotiations seems to have been that of intermediary between Chamberlain and the Irish episcopate on the one hand, and between Chamberlain and Parnell on the other. But the 'local government' scheme was bound to fail, and it is surprising that Manning did not realize that a separate Irish Parliament was by this time an essential ingredient of Irish nationalism, and what is more this had commanded 'at least the tacit approval of the Irish bishops'.[61] It would have been a very unwise move for the bishops to denounce this in favour of any form of local government which meant abandoning an Irish Parliament.

But on Friday 15 May a split on the question of a new Coercion Bill occurred in the Cabinet, and Childers, Dilke, Chamberlain and Lefevre felt bound to resign. After this meeting Chamberlain's scheme was a dead letter. Much has been made of the fact that on 24 June of this year, 1885, Manning refused to give Chamberlain letters of introduction to the Irish bishops in order to conduct a campaign in Ireland in favour of his scheme. But the reasons for his action are clear. Parnell was no longer interested in Chamberlain's policy and was negotiating with the Tories, and Manning would no doubt have perceived the change in his attitude. In addition Chamberlain was vigorously advocating 'secularism' in education; and Manning himself was beginning to think that perhaps, all in all, a better provision might be obtained from the Tories and the well-meaning Carnarvon. What with secularism, coercion and the Errington Mission, he was little pleased with recent Liberal policy.

In November 1885 there was a general election. Before the election Parnell had approached the leaders of the two parties to see if he could extract promises of what they would do for Ireland if in office. Gladstone refused to promise anything until the wishes of the newly-enfranchised Irish electors had been made clear at the polls. Parnell therefore, in his famous Manifesto, pledged his supporters to vote against all Liberals and Radicals (excepting those he would specifically exempt).

C. H. D. Howard contends that Manning's action in the help he gave to the return of Salisbury is to be interpreted wholly in the light of the educational problems of the Catholic Church.[62] It is true that Manning directed questions to be put to prospective candidates referring to the Voluntary Schools. But the schools question was by no means the only reason why Manning wished to see the defeat of Gladstone. He felt that it would be beneficial to Ireland to reject him for a while. Gladstone was held by Manning to be the person responsible for the Errington Mission, and Dilke's correspondence with the Cardinal illustrates the fact that Gladstone had done nothing to prevent Granville from pursuing the intrigue. He could have prevented the Mission if he would. He had been (despite his professions to the contrary) in favour of the Mission, as Dilke feared. Gladstone's letter to Newman (previously quoted) soliciting the latter's aid illustrates his policy of trying to conquer Ireland through Rome. The policy had very nearly succeeded—Dr.

Moran had at one stage been summoned from Sydney,* and it almost seemed as though Errington's Mission would have been successful. Add to these facts Gladstone's growing impotence at the hands of the Nonconformists and the Birmingham Radicals and the fact of the failure in Cabinet of Chamberlain's 'Central Board' scheme, and it will be seen that Manning's opposition cannot be ascribed to any single cause. That Manning considered Parnell's policy in its anti-Liberal front was the correct policy for Ireland at this time becomes evident when we consider the correspondence between Walsh and Manning. Walsh wrote on 27 December 1885 to complain of the tendency of English Catholics to subordinate Irish affairs to the English Education Question.[63] Manning replied: 'I will say at once that I know of no one who desires to subordinate the Irish movement to English education', and again in the same letter: '*You may rely on me* for refusing to subordinate the Irish movement to any English question.'[64] Is it likely that such promises would be given by a man who one month earlier had subjected the Irish Question to the English Education Question? His letter also disproves Howard's contention that Manning was searching for a *via media* between English Catholic opinion and Irish nationalism.[65] He was not willing to subject the cause of Ireland to *any* English matter.

Mr. Howard gives the impression that Manning was largely uninterested in the Parnell issue and was supporting the Conservatives with his questions because of the education issue. The view that Manning was against Home Rule, limited as his conception may have been at this time, as Howard implies,[66] is at variance with his action in 1885 over the 'Central Board' scheme. His conclusion, therefore, that it is impossible to say which of the two appeals, Manning's or Parnell's, was more completely obeyed by the Irish electors, is irrelevant; they were both pursuing a common object and they obtained it. In those constituencies where the advice conflicted, Manning was quite prepared that Parnell's candidate should be elected. The Irish Question was paramount over the Schools Question—Manning explicitly said so to Walsh. Neither is Mr. Howard's statement that the Roman Catholic clergy 'were primarily

---

* It later turned out to be to receive the Hat. Moran, himself, thought he was going to Dublin and had prematurely packed his belongings. Rome had changed its mind. There is little doubt that when he was originally summoned it was to be appointed to Dublin. Cardinal Howard, a relative of the Duke of Norfolk, had worked for Moran's appointment to Dublin.

concerned not with the demand for home rule, but the threat . . . to the Church's schools' very convincing. When we consider that two-thirds of the clergy were Irish by birth or sympathetic to Ireland, and when we consider the furore in the Irish and English Press but recently over the Dublin appointment, such an attitude is certainly unlikely. Throughout this time the *Catholic Times* always subordinated the Schools Question to Home Rule. In this very year, Manning had been willing to help the chief advocate of secular schools, Chamberlain, in his 'Central Board' scheme for Ireland.

Basically, Manning always believed that Gladstone would only be liberal towards Ireland while he was dependent on the support of the Irish Members. When early in 1874 Gladstone, after his parliamentary defeat, had retired temporarily from public life and consequently no longer needed the Irish support, he published his attacks on Papal Infallibility and what he termed 'Vaticanism'. It would not do Gladstone any harm in 1885 to let him see that the Irish vote could make or mar him.

Manning had for some time been increasingly aware that the only real solution to Irish discontent was some form of Home Rule. At first, as we have seen, this did not mean for him separation (for he feared the effect of the loss of the Irish members at Westminster), but a large share of self-government, leaving to the Imperial Government the control of defence and foreign policy. He wrote to Gladstone, only three months before the latter introduced his first Home Rule Bill, that he had 'always thought that if Ireland could do for Irish affairs what Manchester could do for itself with extended powers for Education and public works it would be on a level with England and Scotland: and this equality seems to me to be absolutely vital. . . . From the knowledge I have of the Bishops and Clergy of Ireland and also of the Irish members, my belief is that such a valuation justly and not evasively given, would be willingly accepted.'[67] But Gladstone's proposal for a separate Parliament at Dublin split his party and led to his fall, after six months of office. The next six years saw a Conservative Ministry under Salisbury, and Manning's influence and impact on policy was immediately to wane; he was not to live to see Gladstone Prime Minister for the fourth and last time. But during these last six years of Manning's life he became increasingly convinced that a more radical conception of Home Rule than what he had previously held was necessary to solve the Irish difficulties. It seems as though finally at the end of his life he was prepared to accept the idea of a separate Parliament. This view becomes tenable when we read his unpublished letter to Sir Charles Gavan-Duffy of 19 August 1887, which is given here in full. Sir Charles had produced his basic plan to solve the Irish problem, and Manning wrote to him:

Aug. 19. 1887.

Dear Sir Charles,

I have read your article with much assent—but in a matter so complex and many sided, I am, without knowledge, mistrustful of my own judgment.

Nevertheless *I will say this, it is the most adequate, and safely guarded outline that I have seen.* You write with the great advantage of experience in Government, and of Colonial Legislation. And the tone is just, sincere, and practical.

I am inclined to agree with the Archbishop of Dublin on the presence of Ecclesiastics. They would not prevail by numbers; and we can prevail by reason without being entangled in a political state *which is more safely dealt with by absolute independence.*

The financial argument is very strong. It ought to be worked out in a separate article: *and its effect in behalf of separation would be irresistible,* if the facts cannot be denied. This argument is unknown to Englishmen, and it is thoroughly English—I believe it would cause a strong re-action. I shall much like to hear what Lord Hartington would say.
Believe me,

        Yours faithfully,

                HENRY E. Card. Archbp.*[68]

This letter proves beyond doubt that in 1887 Manning had moved towards a position where his idea of Home Rule had embraced the idea of a separate Parliament for Dublin. It is but a short step from this to total separation.

As a consequence of Manning's acceptance of 'Home Rule' in its more advanced sense, he became more and more distrusted by the 'Old Catholics'. Referring to the latter in a letter to Gladstone, he divined their opposition accurately: 'They think me past praying for, because I would not denounce Parnell and I would defend Archbishop Walsh.'[69] Writing to an American friend at the same time he asserted:

The time is come when Ireland shall be handed over to itself. Its people have attained their majority. . . . We are beginning in the nineteenth

* Italics mine—V.A.M.

century to undo the miseries of the seventeenth and eighteenth. But let us not excuse ourselves by alleging the faults of national character. If our Irish brethren have faults they are for the most part what England has made them.[70]

Manning's final considered views on Ireland are to be found in a letter written to Gladstone on 5 December 1890:

I hope,
  1. that you will refuse all discussion,
  2. that you will refuse all pledges, except one,
  3. that your one pledge shall be
'I will endeavour to frame a scheme of Home Rule which shall be *acceptable to the people of Ireland. If they* shall *refuse to accept it* I will relinquish the work to other hands and leave public life.'[71]

Manning's active work for Ireland did not cease, however, during Lord Salisbury's ministry (1866–92). These were the years which were to bring the Persico Mission, and were troublesome for his Church.

Soon after the appointment of Walsh to Dublin the new Archbishop gave a series of interviews (with Davitt's enthusiastic support) to the Press, in which he manifested his open support for the Land League, land purchase, Home Rule and even land nationalization. Manning, although he had met and liked the great advocate of the single land tax, Henry George,* and supported his advocacy of land reform,† was a little surprised at Walsh's talk of land nationalization and asked for a clarification of his views, writing:

I know what Henry George means by 'nationalization' of the land, but I am not sure of your meaning, unless it be that the Irish people shall re-enter into the possession of their own soil. The garrison must give way to the nation.[72]

Walsh's reply was that he supported George's plan for land nationalization entirely—with the proviso that compensation be given to owners.‡ Manning was satisfied. There is no ground for Purcell's statement that Manning found in George's work 'grave

---

* George dedicated his *Progress and Poverty* to Manning.
† 'Manning held drastic notions as to ownership of land, but it cannot be said that he accepted Mr. George's social panacea'—Leslie, op. cit. p. 354.
‡ Meantime both Walsh and Manning were condemning certain members of the American Hierarchy (notably Corrigan) for opposition to George and persecution of Dr. McGlynn.

cause for condemnation'—all evidence indeed points to the contrary.*

Views of the nature held by Walsh were bitterly resented by Roman Catholic opinion in England, especially among the aristocracy, and this opposition found public expression in the pages of the *Tablet*, which had even opposed Irish disestablishment. The proprietor of this weekly paper was the Roman Catholic bishop of Salford, Dr. Herbert Vaughan, an intimate of the Duke of Norfolk† and bitterly opposed to the Irish movement. The leader of the lay opposition was Norfolk.

The editor of the *Tablet* after 1884 (till 1920) was a kinsman of Vaughan and later his somewhat uncritical biographer, J. G. Snead-Cox. Snead-Cox, 'by origin an English country gentleman, was naturally and by conviction a Conservative'.[73] Under his editorship the *Tablet* turned into a decidedly anti-Irish weekly and gave great offence by its personal attacks on Archbishop Walsh and his views. These attacks invited retaliation, and on 4 April 1887 the Archbishop of Dublin publicly attacked its policy. 'I regard *The Tablet*' he declared, 'as responsible for practically all the soreness of feeling that now exists to so large an extent between the Catholics of the two countries'[74]; and later in the *Tablet* itself he referred to it as 'a Tory anti-Home Rule organ, sailing under the figure head of an extract from a Papal letter, and persistently assailing Home Rule so as to imply that it may be at variance with Catholic interests'.[75]

Manning was naturally perturbed at this rupture, and wrote to Walsh saying: 'Let me ask you always to let me know what you find amiss in it (the *Tablet*). I will always do, as I have always done, my best to correct it.'[76] Many times during 1885 and 1886 Walsh found it necessary to protest to Manning over the *Tablet*.

Manning himself was not immune from open attack, and not only in the *Tablet*. For instance a Roman Catholic wrote to *The Times* in 1881:

The public regard a man of profound piety and zeal like the Archbishop of Westminster as our public spokesman, but we, absolutely one in faith, are not bound to approve his politics. Perhaps the less English Catholics as such have to do with politics, but especially Irish politics, the better.[77]

---

* Manning declared that he saw nothing in George 'to censure as unsound'—Leslie, op. cit. p. 353.

† Norfolk and Vaughan 'shared the same political approach and there was an easy intimacy between Vaughan and Howard families'—Dr. Mathew, in *The English Catholics, 1850–1950*, op. cit. p. 239.

The sentiments expressed were typical of the anti-Irish Catholic.

By 1886 the policy of the 'Old Catholics', headed by the Duke of Norfolk and the Earl of Denbigh, had assumed a more militant programme. They realized that in all matters concerning England the Pope sought and acted on the advice of Manning. But this would not be the case if the British Government were to establish diplomatic relations with the Vatican. The chief plank, therefore, in the 'Old Catholic' platform was to achieve this end. In that way Manning's influence would be negatived—there would be little trouble in getting an amenable prelate (such as Cardinal Howard had been) appointed. Manning was aware of the move, and had early set out to win Gladstone to his opinions. The Cardinal had become seriously alarmed at the time of the Errington Mission, and also at the time when a papal envoy was sent to Victoria's Jubilee, that an attempt would be made to establish diplomatic relations with the Vatican; but Gladstone told Dilke that 'he was bitterly opposed to the notion of re-opening relations' and that 'he assented most unwillingly to the views of Spencer, Forster and Harcourt in favour of the Errington Mission'.[78] Again he wrote to Dilke when the latter protested against Errington's being made a baronet: 'As to "diplomatic relations" with the Pope, I am entirely opposed to them.'[79] It is, therefore, obvious that Manning's viewpoint had prevailed at home. Manning held that the bishops of England had their fingers on the pulse of the nation and that they and they only were competent to advise Rome.* Manning knew that the kind of situation that had arisen over the Dublin appointment would be made more frequent if diplomatic relations were established.

The Duke of Norfolk publicly attacked Walsh when addressing the Primrose Dames in 1886, and he demanded that Rome issue a rebuke to the Irish bishops. Walsh immediately wrote to Manning in consternation:

Has your Eminence seen the extraordinary speech of the Duke of Norfolk on the Catholics of Ireland? To me it seems one of the most unprovoked attacks upon the people of this country that I have met for a very long time.[80]

In his reply Manning showed that he was in full control of the situation. After referring to Norfolk's inexperience, he said:

---

* Manning opposed the appointing of a Papal Nuncio to the U.S.A. for the same reasons.

14

In the time of my predecessor there was a great breach between English and Irish Catholics. For twenty years I have laboured to heal it. It is unhappily again open. But the English Catholics are few. The mass of our people are Irish and united with Ireland.[81]

It is significant that when Walsh was asked by the *Pall Mall Gazette* in 1887 concerning his views on the establishment of diplomatic relations with the Vatican, he replied:

I am able to state with the very highest authority . . . that such a step will not be taken . . . during the pontificate of Leo XIII without provision of the most effective kind being made to safeguard the interests of Ireland from any English interference at the Holy See.[82]

That Manning had won his point is evident from his letter to Walsh of June 1887, when he said: 'The Duke (of Norfolk) wrote to me . . . and said: "The Pope sees that your views and mine about Ireland do not agree, and I am sorry to say that he trusts yours rather than mine." '[83]

Rome had, however, to pay some attention to the charges of the 'Old Catholics' that the Irish Hierarchy was encouraging violence and agrarian crime. A Commission was sent to Ireland to investigate the charges. It consisted of an Italian friar, Mgr. Persico, and he was assisted by Don Enrico Gualdi. At once Manning wrote to Walsh:

You may like to know that Monsignor Persico and Don Enrico Gualdi are intimately known to me. The latter was for fifteen years a priest in this diocese. . . . Monsignor Persico I have known for thirty-six years. . . . He translated a book of mine.[84]

On Manning's advice Persico called on the Lord Lieutenant as well as visiting all the Irish bishops. The envoy was a fair-minded man and set out on his job impartially and conscientiously. He was a Capuchin with wide and varied experience—he had been a missionary in India, a bishop in the U.S.A., and had ruled three Italian dioceses and was now a distinguished member of the Papal Court and shortly to be made a Cardinal. Never had the Capuchins such a famous son since the days of Father Joseph. In December of 1887 he reported to Manning:

My intercourse with the bishops has been straightforward and loyal, and nothing underhand has passed between me and them. I have strictly confined myself to the object of my mission—to observe, to study, to know—and in due time to make my Report. . . . But I may even now tell Y.E. that I have said that whatever is deemed necessary or useful for Ireland must be done *with and through the bishops*.

Persico was going to recommend with Manning that diplomatic relations should not be established. That this decision was largely influenced by the Archbishop of Westminster is obvious from a letter to him from Persico, three weeks later:

I agree fully with your Eminence that 'the true *nunciatura* for England and Ireland is the episcopate'. If the bishops do not know the state of the country they are not fit to be bishops. If they do, what more can *una persona ufficiosa o ufficiale* do for the Holy See?

And, more explicitly:

I have given my *negative* opinion in my reports, and that is against the appointment of a permanent Apostolic Delegate.

Persico had been entirely converted to the side of Manning and Walsh, and was angry with the 'Old Catholics' and Vaughan. Croke of Cashel wrote to Walsh about Persico: 'He denounces the English Catholics most vehemently for their hostility to Ireland ... "Nominatim" he is death on Salford.'[85]

The Persico mission finally settled the question of diplomatic relations in favour of Manning's view.

In 1888 Archbishop Walsh went to Rome for Leo XIII's sacerdotal jubilee, and while there was asked to prepare a memorandum on the Land Question. But before this was ready Leo XIII issued a condemnation of the Plan of Campaign and the practice of boycotting. The condemnation surprised Ireland, Walsh, Persico and Manning; its effect was electric. Manning, unable to divine what had happened, wrote at once to Walsh:

Pray without delay let me know the history of the Decree. Had you any knowledge of it? Had Mgr. Persico?
1. While it stands all must submit.
2. But the reasons may be analysed and laid before the Holy Office.

Persico meanwhile wrote to Manning: 'I did not expect at all the said Decree, and I was never so much surprised in my life.'

Walsh was astounded. He immediately left Rome and went direct to London to see Cardinal Manning before returning to Ireland. Only one Irish bishop* promulgated the decree. While Walsh was in London Manning advised him to give three interviews to the Press, explaining the decree and explaining that it in

* Limerick.

no way condemned the Irish nationalist movement or the Land
League. Walsh also gave a decisive rebuke to the *Tablet*, which had
claimed the decree as a victory for the 'Old Catholics'. Coincident
with Walsh's return to Dublin another letter arrived from Rome,
excusing much of the decree and saying that it had been mis-
interpreted and misunderstood. This letter was given to the Press
(it was undoubtedly a result of Manning's representations), and it
did much to undo the ill effects of the decree.

Michael Davitt attributed the condemnation (unjustifiably) to
Mgr. Persico,* and asserted that 'Cardinal Manning, staunch and
true friend of Ireland as he was, intrigued with the worst of our
English Catholic opponents'[86] in 1886. In other words, he blamed
Manning for the Persico mission and Persico for the condemnation
of the Plan of Campaign and boycotting. These opinions no doubt
gained currency among nationalist circles, and a cloud of suspicion
and mistrust descended upon all the ecclesiastics.

The last two years of Manning's life, beginning in 1890, have been
appraised by some (notably by Dr. McEntee[87]) as a period of re-
trenchment in his Irish policy. This is because he supported the
demand for the removal of Parnell from the leadership of the Irish
parliamentary group, at the time of the divorce scandal. In other
words, it is said that he placed personal prejudice and religious
bigotry before the Irish cause. But Manning had supported Parnell
at the time of the Pigott forgeries, and the reasons for his actions
in 1890 are plain. He wrote to Walsh:

> I have found that the judgment here of the most *vital* friends of Ireland
> is that if the leadership of the Irish members is to remain unchanged,
> the bishops, priests, and people of Ireland, will be seriously affected in
> the judgment of all English friends, or the chief of them. Already this
> has been shown by the Nonconformists and it is certain of a great part of
> Mr. Gladstone's supporters. Moreover, I am sure of the judgment and
> feeling of Rome.[88]

Gladstone thought likewise. So did Croke. The English Nonconformist leaders 'sought Parnell's retirement', and there were 'increasing signs of uneasiness among liberal supporters'.[89] Walsh
was vehement in his views, declaring to Manning:

> To my mind, the one straight course for the members was, and is, to
> say, 'this protracted proceeding is simply playing into the hands of the

---

* His final report had not been sent to Rome at that time.

enemy: from all we now see Mr. Parnell is a man absolutely unworthy of trust in public or in private affairs: the Westminster Palace Hotel speech of June 30, six months after the Hawarden interview, now put side by side with his recent "manifesto" takes away his last vestige of standing ground: we have nothing to do with what Mr. Gladstone, or any one else, may or may not have to say about the police force in Ireland: the one question is whether Mr. Parnell is fit to be our leader: we now see clearly, beyond all question, that he is not: the "Irish people" may have him if they like: *we* will not have him: we hereby declare the Chairmanship vacant: we shall answer to our constituents at the general election which now, as the result of his treason to Ireland, will in all probability end in disaster.'

But they will not do this. They will be led on from point to point, their position gradually becoming weaker and weaker, and their majority dwindling away, at each successive demonstration of their miserable inability to hold their own.

I have written strongly to Mr. Murphy, one of our City M.P.'s, and I have authorised him to show my letter to Healy, Sexton, and to 'one or two others' if he thinks it advisable.[90]

O'Brien contends that in moving against Parnell, Manning was holding out to Walsh 'the tempting baits of restored Ecclesiastical supremacy in Irish politics and restored Irish influence in Rome'.[91] This is undoubtedly true but it does not tell the whole story. He knew there would be little hope for Irish aspirations if the English Liberals were irrevocably alienated.

Neither Manning nor the Irish Hierarchy made any public declarations—until Parnell turned and attacked Gladstone; then Croke and Walsh spoke. Manning wrote a letter to Walsh on 4 December 1890, intended to be given to the Press, which stated: 'Ireland by its fidelity has outlived all that politics can do against it: and by the same Christian and Catholic fidelity of its Pastors and people it will win all the rights it has so long striven by suffering to attain.'[92] Archbishop Walsh did not think fit to publish this letter, for as he wrote to Manning: 'Some of the Tory papers here started the cry last week that your Eminence acting through Arthur O'Connor, was the real author of the revolt of the Party against Parnell.'[93]

The Nonconformists, however, were loud in their clamourings against Parnell. Manning urged the Irish Hierarchy to speak out against him, otherwise they would be accused of political expediency in the eyes of Gladstone, Rome and the Nonconformists.

He was in almost daily communication with them. In the meantime he did not neglect Gladstone. He wrote: 'Gratitude, blind loyalty, and just anger at English violence will make the Irish people refuse to forsake Parnell. I feel for them, and, in a sense, with them. But I hope their Bishops and Priests will bid them be silent.'*

On 14 January 1892 Cardinal Manning died, and if he had but lived six months longer he would have been able to prevent another great injustice to Ireland. By that time Herbert Vaughan had become Archbishop of Westminster and exerted all his influence in order to prevent Archbishop Walsh of Dublin from being made a Cardinal. Vaughan had always disliked Walsh's attitude to his beloved periodical the *Tablet*, and also his friendship with Manning. Archbishop Walsh's biographer relates that 'Dr. Vaughan himself more than once told a venerable Prelate who is still living that it was his opportune intervention which had decided Leo not to create Dr. Walsh Cardinal'. Thus the first instalment of the revenge of the 'Old Catholics' was accomplished less than six months after the death of the prelate of whom Archbishop Walsh had written, in a private letter to a friend in 1887: 'We can never make him a suitable return for what he has done, and is doing, to help on the Irish cause.'94

* G.P., Manning to Gladstone 22 Nov. 1890. Gladstone was on familiar terms with Manning until the latter's death. It is pleasant to find Manning writing to him on 27 Nov. 1890: 'Take care of this sudden cold and do not walk about without your hat.' (G.P. in B.M., Manning to Gladstone 27.11.90.)

Chapter VII

PHILANTHROPY

★

RUSKIN, great artist as he was, was led into the field of social reform largely because he felt that it was useless to attempt to inculcate a love of beauty in his fellow-men when all the latter saw was the misery and ugliness of their own lives and those of their friends. For Ruskin, Art and Life were interconnected. Herbert Spencer brilliantly summed up this feeling when he declared: 'You cannot get golden conduct out of leaden instincts.' Manning was influenced by a comparable thought. The environment of the working man and the conditions of his existence, it seemed to him, were militating against his endeavour to lead a more perfect, a Christian life. Hence it was the duty of the Church and of the true follower of Christ to attempt to ameliorate those conditions. 'Christ had compassion on the multitude', and Manning added: 'Compassion is fellow-feeling, and a share in the sufferings of others.'[1] But 'sympathy' unallied to 'action' was for him hypocrisy. The evil once perceived must be attacked until it no longer existed! He had written:

The bloated and brutal man, if he had been nurtured by a loving mother in a pure home fit for man to live in; if he had grown up in the consciousness of Divine law and presence; if he had lived in honest labour, found as a rule in the labour market, or as an exception, in times of distress, provided by the compassion of a wise charity, or of a law wisely and charitably administered, he would not have become the wreck in body, mind, and speech, which we may see in our streets every day.

This passage clearly indicates the connexion Manning believed to exist between the physical conditions of life and Christian morality. For him it was impossible to advance the latter without also attempting to ameliorate the former, and it was this basic belief that led Manning to identify himself, as we have seen, with practically all major philanthropic schemes and social reforms of the second half of the nineteenth century.

But there are some movements that owed much to Manning's support and which we have not yet discussed. The chief of these is the temperance movement.

In 1853 the United Kingdom Alliance was formed. The Alliance was not particularly interested in the legislative control of the drink trade, but in what might be termed a widening sympathy for temperance—or, as Carter expresses it: 'If, by *general consent*, the gin-shop and beer-shop came under a swift and common doom, then the individual, the family and the State would achieve great moral gain.'[2]

Dr. Handley declares that 'excessive drinking had been common among all classes throughout the eighteenth century, both in rural areas and in towns and villages',[3] but he adds that 'it was in the cities of the nineteenth century that its brutal effects spread deepest and widest'. It was estimated that in 1838 in Glasgow there were ten thousand men 'who got drunk on Saturday night, were drunk all Sunday, were in a state of intoxication or half-intoxication all Monday, and began their week's work on Tuesday'. In fact, as Professor Denis Gwynn asserts, 'drunkenness was the most demoralizing and debasing feature in the whole social life of the poor of all sorts during the later years of the century'.[4]

Vigorous campaigns in favour of both total abstinence and temperance had been carried on in the nineteenth century before the advent of Joseph Livesay and the United Kingdom Alliance. The great Irish Capuchin apostle of temperance, Father Mathew, who had been converted to the cause by a Quaker, visited Great Britain. In August 1842 he went to Glasgow, where he preached at the opening of St. Mary's Church, and he visited Edinburgh, Liverpool, Manchester, Salford, Huddersfield, Wakefield, Leeds and London. 'By the time he left London he had administered the pledge to 600,000 people, and by so much reduced the mass of misery and crime.'[5]

But unfortunately Father Mathew's campaign was to develop into an anti-Fenian organization. He undid much of his previous good work when he declared at a temperance meeting in Tipperary:

I have seen with the deepest regret that it has been imputed to the district of Newport that secret societies exist there. This I am afflicted to hear, that any district where the temperance cause has been established could harbour such societies. I have earnestly, perseveringly, emphatically cautioned the people against these societies; because they are filled with danger, with vice, with iniquity; because they cut at the roots of social order; because they are the blight and bane of social happiness.[6]

And again:

Oh! in the name of God, hold fast to the temperance pledge, and shun as you would the plague the company of those who seek to entrap you into secret and illegal associations, the authors of every wretchedness.[7]

As soon as Mathew's temperance campaign became identified with an Irish repressive policy it began to lose its hold upon the Irish population in England and Scotland, as well as upon Ireland itself.

Manning became interested in the temperance movement, not, as one might have expected, through Father Mathew but through the agency of the United Kingdom Alliance. In a speech entitled 'The Temperance Reformation, the United Kingdom Alliance, and Local Option' which Manning delivered at Newcastle-on-Tyne on 4 September 1882 and which was later published in behalf of the United Kingdom Alliance, the Archbishop declared:

I have to thank the United Kingdom Alliance for having aroused my attention to this subject, about fifteen years ago* when, after a long life already spent, believing myself to know the condition of the people . . . I for the first time came to a knowledge of the real demoralizing power of this drink traffic. I came to this knowledge through a deputation of good men— members of the United Kingdom Alliance—who wrote to me and requested an interview. They came to my house, and the arguments they lay before me aroused my attention.[8]

But in 1865 Manning had set on foot a committee to enquire into the drink evil, following the report of a Committee of the House of Commons which had sat during 1853–4 on the subject. The Provincial Committee recommended the formation of a temperance society, and after Manning became interested in the United Kingdom Alliance in 1867 it was obvious the line his policy would take. He called alcohol 'that most destructive of all poisons which destroys the reason of man'. He soon moved away from the original intentions of the United Kingdom Alliance, however, by his adoption of a political programme. Both the Alliance and Father Mathew's campaign had been interested primarily in a reformation of the habits of the people; their agitation was based on a reformation of morals. Manning realized that this would have little practical effect without action also being taken at parliamentary level. It was with the intention of creating a powerful and unanimous body of public opinion that would have an effect upon Government, that he founded the

* i.e. in 1867.

'League of the Cross'. Its origins are interesting, for they show how entirely Manning understood the strongest feelings of the Irish heart.

For many years the feast of St. Patrick (17 March) had been held by the Irish in London to be an excuse for excessive drinking and for brawling. The police courts for the days after the feast were always filled with offenders. Manning decided to prevent these degrading scenes from occurring in 1867. A few days before the feast, he issued an appeal for what he termed a 'Truce of St. Patrick'. The idea behind the Truce was that all the Irish should pledge themselves to abstain from intoxicating drink for three days—the eve of the feast, the feast itself and the day following—and in return for the faithful observance of this the Pope had agreed to grant an indulgence, under the usual conditions.* The result was a great success. Purcell records:

Order and sobriety took the place of the customary orgies which had so long disgraced the Festival, and had brought into public disrepute the Catholic faith and the Irish name. The public-houses during the Truce of St. Patrick were religiously shunned. The police-courts were empty.[9]

The reasons for this success are not difficult to divine. Manning had truly discovered the two strongest sentiments in the Irish heart —religion and nationalism. By combining the two in his 'Truce' he had ensured its success. He tried to follow it up by extending the pledge to include avoiding public houses on all Saturdays and Sundays throughout the year, but although it had some success it lacked the personal appeal of the 'Truce of St. Patrick'. Something more colourful and personally appealing was needed. The Archbishop looked around him for guidance, and his eye fell upon the phenomenal success of the Salvation Army. In 1872, Manning took the Pledge and announced the formation of the 'League of the Cross', organized on the same external basis as the Salvation Army. He himself was the head of the League and monthly meetings were held at Archbishop's House, Westminster. The League was divided up into Officers, Captains and Body-Guards, and a distinctive dress consisting of a bright scarlet sash was given to them. This dramatic and personal appeal to the display-instinct of the Irish met with outstanding success. Every Whit Monday there was a

* These conditions were (1) Confession (2) a reception of Holy Communion and (3) a faithful observance of the 'Truce'.

great procession in London. 'The march past the Cardinal at the Crystal Palace, and the beating of drums, and the marshalling of the soldiers of the League of the Cross by the Cardinal's "Guards", excited enthusiasm and attracted public attention.'[10] The League gained recruits by the thousand. Purcell quotes the *Standard* of 1874, which declared:

The League has been formed mainly by the untiring exertions of that great apostle of Temperance, Archbishop Manning, who has never ceased to strive for the cause, not only of temperance but of total abstinence. That he has been to a great extent successful may be judged by the fact that the League now numbers many scores of thousands throughout the United Kingdom, and that in London alone their 28,000 members shows that the Association has done good work amongst the humbler classes of the Catholic population of the metropolis. Very many of these have now taken the pledge, and have kept it most firmly. Thus habits of temperance become, as it were, inoculated and habitual. Of the value of such a League no man can doubt. . . . Certainly the cause of Abstinence has never found a more able advocate, and we wish his Grace every success.

In company with Bishop Hedley, O.S.B., of Newport and Menevia, Manning travelled all over the country addressing public meetings in behalf of temperance. Commenting on the importance of the League, Professor Denis Gwynn declares: 'Among the Catholic reformers Manning's League of the Cross represented the most powerful influence for counteracting the tendencies which kept the poor in their abject condition.'[11]

Meanwhile, Manning's connexion with the United Kingdom Alliance was strengthened. In 1867 he spoke at the annual meeting of the society at Manchester, as well as at Newcastle. In 1871 Manning was a Vice-President of the Alliance and addressed a meeting in St. James's Hall, London, in support of Sir Wilfrid Lawson's Permissive Bill. Commenting on Manning's and Lawson's support of this Bill and their entry upon a political agitation, Carter declares: 'It should be remarked that individual supporters of the United Kingdom Alliance did not at all times regard themselves as bound by its past or contemporary judgments. A case in point was the endeavour of Cardinal Manning. . . .'[12] He thus indicates that the political agitation that Manning was about to embark upon did not meet with the entire approval of the Alliance and can, therefore, not be regarded as the policy of the Alliance.

As early as October 1868, in regard to the proposed Permissive

Bill, Manning had written to Gladstone, who was shortly to become
Prime Minister:

Let me know your mind about what you call 'local option' in respect to
the traffic in drink. . . . I am for the Permissive Bill, but with such riders,
or adjuncts as shall make its execution reasonable and not extreme. In
fact, I think the evil so widespread, complex, tenacious, and deadly that
I am for every measure which is practicable from the restriction on
Licences, under the Permissive Bill.[13]

But by 1882 Manning had publicly accepted Local Option. He
declared at Newcastle in that year: 'There is at this moment a
licensing power which can place in the midst of any population a
public-house whether that population wills it or no, and what we
ask is this: that there shall be given to the people of these localities
the power, when the licensing authority is prepared to put down
a public-house, of simply saying, "No".'[14] He claimed that in the
last election the Government was returned 'by the influence of the
great drink traffic', and added: 'Thirty-three millions of revenue
have been raised annually by a tax upon intoxicating drink. I can
well understand why no Government is ready to put a check upon
this great trade in intoxicating drink.' He defined Local Option as
being 'a popular veto' on the drink trade, and declared: 'I am one
of those who do not believe that drunkenness is characteristic of
the working man. . . . It is in every class. It is the shame, the burning
shame, of every class and I am indignant when talk of temperance
and the putting down of drunkenness as a remedy for the evils
among the working men and their families.' This last statement is
very characteristic. Manning was widening his attack on intemperance and had now begun to address himself 'not to the poor, and
the rude, and the turbulent, whose riot is in the streets, but to the
rich and the refined and the educated . . . sheltered by the high
civilization of our social life from all grossness, and who would choose
rather to die than to be marked by an act of excess, or even suspected
of it.'[15] At once the Jesuit organ, *The Month*, which peculiarly
represented the 'Old Catholic' families and the Catholic nobility,
took up the opposition to Manning and gave expression to their
views. It declared in February 1879: 'The alcohol drinking nations
taken comprehensively, are superior in mind and body to the
abstaining nations, and as this result has been achieved in spite of
all the acknowledged damage done by the intemperance of successive
generations it might be fairly argued that the superiority would

be even more marked than it is, if the alcohol drinking races had practised more self-control in their potations.'[16] Referring more specifically to Manning's campaign, it declared:

Each man must be his own physician in this matter. If he cannot trust his discretion to keep within bounds, then for his own sake, he must refrain from alcohol altogether. . . . If he has some higher motive of the service of God and the love of his neighbour,* and commits himself to tea and coffee and lemonade because the abnormal misery of the poor around him requires in his opinion the strong temporary check of total abstinence which he cannot spread effectively if his example does not bear out his words, then he deserves the admiration even of those who do not share his convictions.

The Month knew how to 'damn with faint praise'!

In 1884 a series of attacks on Manning and his policy, in the form of letters from correspondents, were published in the *Tablet*.[17] They 'were marked by unusual violence on the part of those opposed to the Cardinal's advocacy of total abstinence, one of the writers in particular rejoicing that expression had at last been given to the reflections and conversations of thousands of Catholics against the un-Catholic speeches and sentiments of fanatical teetotallers'. One of these letters, however, advocated a new brand of temperance reform. Why not make the pledge only against beer and spirits and not against wine? As Miss Taylor has felicitously expressed it: 'In other words and plainer language, why should not the poor be induced to abandon their luxuries, whilst the rich would remain in undisturbed possession of their own?'[18] Even the Bishop of Nottingham, Mgr. Bagshawe, attacked Manning under the pseudonym 'Senex'. The 'Old Catholics' reported Manning's doings on behalf of temperance to Rome, and declared that he was making heretical statements. Rome asked him for an explanation, and in reply he gave a horrifying report of the dangers of drunkenness among the poor of London. No condemnation issued from the Vatican, but a request urging him to continue the good work.

In 1871 Manning supported Sir Robert Anstruther, M.P., and Dr. Temple, Bishop of Exeter, in behalf of Bruce's Licensing Bill, then before Parliament. Among other things this Bill proposed a new classification of licences, a rate-payers' veto, and that the number of publicans' licences was not to exceed a scale based on a ratio of

---

* Referring more closely to the fact that Manning had taken the pledge as a total abstainer.

these licences to population. Now Manning, at this time, was a Vice-President of the United Kingdom Alliance and the latter disliked this association with a political measure. But Manning declared: 'The Bill introduced by the Government must, if possible, be carried. I look upon the Bill as the first honest and earnest grappling with this question.'[19] Carter adds that although Manning was for the Bill, 'as regards the greater part of the organized Temperance Movement, the Alliance then held the key to legislative policy, and its attitude was negative'.[20] Although Manning was unable to persuade the Alliance to adopt the Bill, and although Bruce's Bill failed, Manning continued to press for Government regulation.

'In 1890', as Carter records, 'G. J. Goschen, Chancellor of the Exchequer under Lord Salisbury, proposed in his Budget speech to set aside a sum from the proceeds of taxes on spirits and beer for the purchase and extinction of publican's licences.'[21] Hutton contends that 'the withdrawal of the Government's scheme for compensating publicans (1890) was reckoned as due in great measure to the imposing forces that Cardinal Manning was able to marshal in opposition to it'.[22]

Manning himself always considered that his work on behalf of temperance was one of the major charitable works of his life. His considered judgement is contained in a Note which he wrote towards the end of his life. He declared:

I have deliberately made myself 'a fool for Christ's sake' in this matter and set my face as a flint. When I thought in Paris that I might never come back in 1877,* one of my happiest thoughts was that 'we had saved many poor drunkards'. I hope whosoever comes after me will have the courage to face the criticism and the ridicule of not the fools only, but the half-hearted wise. Our poor men are an example and a rebuke to us. They founded and have maintained the League of the Cross: we have only led it.[23]

Purcell and Leslie both contend that Bishop Vaughan of Salford did not see eye to eye with the Cardinal on the temperance problem —but in December 1875† Vaughan in a pastoral letter announced that special sermons would be preached on the subject in the diocese and that an active crusade would be conducted in the diocese of

---

* He had a serious illness on his way to Rome.

† Vaughan's pastoral letter to the diocese of Salford, 13 December 1875 in Wardley Hall archives, Salford, Lancs.

Salford in behalf of temperance. He may not have been as passionate in the cause as Manning, but Vaughan was certainly not opposed to it.

We have seen how Manning copied the external organization of the Salvation Army when he formed his League of the Cross, and it is true that the Cardinal conceived a great admiration for the practical Christianity which was pursued by the Army. Bramwell Booth records how Manning once wrote to the founder:

You have gone down into the depths. Every living soul cost the Most Precious Blood, and we ought to save it, even the worthless and the worst. After the Trafalgar Square miseries I wrote a 'Pleading for the Worthless', which probably you never saw. It would show you how completely my heart is in your book.* No doubt you remember that the Poor Laws of Queen Elizabeth compelled parishes to provide work for the able-bodied unemployed, and to lay in stores of raw material for work.[24]

Bramwell Booth says that he had contact with Cardinal Manning on many occasions and that he frequently visited Westminster, where 'more than once we spoke of the most intimate spiritual experiences'. He adds:

The Salvation Army was not within his Church, but it was at least within the protection of his Church's prayers. He joined heartily in several attempts to raise funds for us. He saw the worth of those whom Society esteemed as worthless, and he liked the Army because it saw the same thing, and said so, and went to work to help them.

Manning's friendship with the Salvation Army led him to turn his attention to the Social Purity Crusade. This aspect of his social policy has been severely criticized. Purcell declares that the connexion was a 'grave . . . error of judgment on the part of Cardinal Manning [which] can only be accounted for by the isolation in which he lived at the time, by the absence of contact with the outer world, with men of sound sense and sober judgment and knowledge of the reality of things'.[25] There is little foundation for Purcell's harsh charge. The originators of the Social Purity Crusade were both 'men of sound sense and sober judgment and knowledge of the reality of things'—W. T. Stead and Bramwell Booth. The beginning of the Movement has been well described by Booth himself:

From our earliest years as the Christian Mission, there came, occasionally to our penitent-form in Whitechapel, unfortunate girls who looked to us for some means of enabling them to throw off the fetters of their

* In Darkest England and the Way Out.

deadly calling. . . . This work into which The Army, without any set
purpose of its own, was gradually led, was placed under the personal
supervision of Mrs. Bramwell Booth. . . . Before she had been at her task
for six months, it was brought home to her that a frightful state of things
existed in London. She was prepared for the evidence of widespread
prostitution, terrible as that is, but it came upon her as an appalling
revelation to find that young girls—children, really, of thirteen and
fourteen—were being entrapped by a vicious network of carefully devised
agencies and in their innocence condemned to a life of shame.[26]

Booth was urged to take up this work by Mrs. Josephine Butler
and Benjamin Scott, and actual cases of young girls being sold into
this kind of slavery were soon discovered.

In 1885 the age at which the girl's consent could free her seducer
from any kind of responsibility was only thirteen, and Booth decided
that the most necessary reform was to have this age raised. Parliament would not take action without the pressure of public opinion,
and it was with the intention of arousing the latter that Manning
and W. T. Stead were approached. Manning could lend his powerful
influence to the cause, and pledge the support of his Church;
Stead, as editor of the *Pall Mall Gazette*, could exert the influence
of the Press in favour of the reform. The *Pall Mall Gazette* 'Extra'
of 6 July 1885, in which Stead described 'The Maiden Tribute
of Modern Babylon', took the public by storm and undoubtedly
had some effect on Parliament.

'On the day of the publication of the first of the articles,' Booth
noted, 'Lord Salisbury's new Ministry had met. A day or two later,
evidently prompted by the state of feeling outside, the Home
Secretary, Sir Richard Cross'[27] proposed to debate the question.
The outcome was that the age when the girls' consent would free
their seducers of responsibility was raised from thirteen to sixteen.

Later Stead and Booth were both charged with the abduction of
a young girl. But it was obvious that the alleged abduction was only
in the nature of an experiment, on the part of Booth and Stead, to
prove how easy it was for a child to be ensnared into a vicious and
immoral life. Booth was acquitted but Stead was imprisoned for
three months. Purcell records that Manning kept up correspondence
with Stead while the latter was in prison, and regarded him as a
martyr to the cause of purity.

Purcell was particularly anxious to condemn W. T. Stead, whom
he regarded as unworthy to 'defile even this unhappy page in the

life of an austere and holy prelate', and whom he accused of wanton sensationalism and 'gross imaginings'.[28] But Bramwell Booth testified that Stead 'always subordinated his journalism to what he believed to be right', and added: 'Religion with him was service. He set out, heart and soul, to serve his generation. The world was cleaner and sweeter for his eloquent voice. He aroused the nation on the social question.'[29] Manning certainly thought highly of him. Whatever the true merits of Purcell's argument may be, the fact remains that Manning by his support of Booth and Stead in the Social Purity Crusade had a share in forming that public opinion which in its turn resulted in an Act of Parliament, more humane and a greater safeguard to the morals of the young than had hitherto existed.

Manning's broad sympathy for the oppressed and the persecuted led towards the end of his life to a like sympathy for animals and as a result he developed into a vigorous anti-vivisectionist. He was a Vice-President of the Victoria Street Society from its foundation in 1876 till his death in 1892, and he frequently attended meetings. On 20 March 1876 he joined a deputation to the Home Office, consisting of the Earl of Shaftesbury, Earl of Minto, Sir Evelyn Wood, Mr. Froude, Sir F. Elliot, Mr. Mundella, Lord Mount-Temple and Mr. Leslie Stephen, 'to urge the introduction by Government of a Bill to restrict Vivisection'.[30] Dr. McEntee states that 'such a bill was introduced and, with many changes, became the Act 39 & 40 Vict. C.77'.[31] He worked with many famous personages for the cause. He spoke at the first General Meeting of the Victoria Street Society at the Westminster Palace Hotel on 10 June 1876, where Shaftesbury was chairman and where fellow-speakers were the Marquis of Bute and the Earl of Glasgow. He spoke at the meeting of 22 April 1877 along with the Anglican Bishops of Winchester, Gloucester and Bristol, and Prince Lucien Bonaparte and Lord Mount-Temple. At the 1881 annual meeting he described the practice of vivisection as 'a detestable practice without scientific result, and immoral in itself'.

The theological reasons given by Manning for his opposition to vivisection are interesting while rather erratic. He declared in 1882 at a meeting in Lord Shaftesbury's house, Grosvenor Square:

It appears to me that as we have the uncertainty of the result, and the certainty of atrocious and unimaginable suffering we have a case so strong that I cannot understand any civilised man countenancing the continuance of such a practice. . . . I am somewhat concerned to say it, but I know that an impression has been made that those whom I represent look, if not with approbation, at least with great indulgence on the practice of vivisection. . . . There is not a religious instinct in nature, nor a religion of nature nor is there a word in revelation, either in the Old Testament or the New Testament, nor is there to be found in the great theology which I do represent, no, nor in any Act of the Church of which I am a member; no, nor in the lives and utterances of any one of those great servants of that Church who stand as examples, nor is there an authoritative utterance anywhere to be found in favour of vivisection. There may be the chatter, the prating, and the talk of those who know nothing about it.

He then went on to state that he had written very urgently to the Pope and that when the facts had been made known to the papal Curia 'they experienced a revulsion of feeling' and inclined to his view.[32]

The interesting thing is that Manning should have become an anti-vivisectionist, when his work in so many other fields had been to advance the claims of science in the eyes of Catholics. But when his desires for a *via media* between Catholicism and science conflicted with his intensely personal feeling for the suffering, it was obvious what his policy would be. He declared himself on this very point:

I believe that Science consists in the knowledge of truth obtained by the processes which are in conformity with the nature of God, who, the Holy Scripture says, is the Lord of all sciences. . . . I believe in science most profoundly with its own limits; but it has its own limits, and, when the word Science is applied to matter which is beyond those limits, I don't believe in it.

One of the last public acts Manning performed, which to us seems narrow and short-sighted, was to write his name to the Memorial which the Victoria Street Society presented in October 1891 to the Home Office, petitioning that a licence for vivisection be refused to the Institute of Preventive Medicine.

Manning persuaded Cardinal Gibbons to join the Society, as he had already won him over to the cause of temperance and to an admiration of the Salvation Army. The only other Catholic members of note in the Society were the Marquis of Bute and Lord and Lady Clifford of Chudleigh. Their common interest in anti-vivisection brought Shaftesbury and Manning together. Shaftesbury declared: 'the Victoria Street Society would not have been founded in vain had it only served to bring together to work at one Committee-table' himself and the Cardinal. When Manning was told of this remark 'a tear sprang in his eyes and he said with deep emotion: "Did Lord Shaftesbury say that? I loved Lord Shaftesbury!" '.[33]

'Cardinal Manning', declared the journal *The Zoophilist*, 'was the first great divine of the Church of Rome to define the existence of any moral obligation of humanity towards the brutes', and was 'a Captain in whom any host in the moral battle of humanity might justly glory'.[34]

We began this discussion of the major philanthropic schemes with which Manning was associated by a reference to John Ruskin, and it is fitting to conclude it with an account of the Cardinal's relations with this great social thinker. They probably became acquainted with each other, in the first place, at the meetings of the Metaphysical Society, of which they were both members, and 'Ruskin used to call on Manning at Archbishop's House'.[35] We know also that Manning worked with Ruskin on the Committee for the Unemployed and on the Committee for the Relief of Paris.

On the publication of Ruskin's *Fors Clavigera* Manning wrote an interesting letter to him, which explains a great deal of his social doctrine and policy. In *Fors Clavigera* (Letter 76) Ruskin declares that 'the teaching of Art as I understand it, is the teaching of all things', and in this book he defines the relation between art and ethics. For him as for Manning, the separation of material from spiritual progress is an impossibility. The awakening of the spiritual within the material was the aim of both men, and this affinity in belief is clearly shown in Manning's letter. The latter is dated 21 October 1873, and reads:

My dear Mr. Ruskin,

. . . I cannot say with what interest I have read 'Fors Clavigera'. It is like the beating of one's heart in a nightmare. You are crying out of the depths of this material world; and no man will listen. You can now understand what we feel. We cry and cry, but the nineteenth century looks upon us as deaf and impassive as the young Memnon. There are no breaks in the woods on the horizon to let us into infinity. We are hedged in by the 3 per cents, iron-clads, secularism, and deified Civil Powers. The God of this World has got his day for a time. Irving said forty years ago: 'The physical sciences have taken the whole breadth of heaven to themselves, and the spiritual sciences have gone down into the earth and are to be no more found.' It is very true. Could the Ape theory ever have come up in any mind if they had not just lost spiritual

instincts, and intuitions of the intelligent and moral nature of man?
With a theist I have sympathy, with an atheist or an agnostic I can find
no human hand or heart to lay hold of. What room for the καλόν or
'pulchrum' physical, moral, spiritual, ideal in men who feel that they may
be the sons of an ape?

Your 'Fors' is a vigorous and human protest against this degradation
of man and of Society, which next after the Church is God's greatest
work. I hope you are well.

> Believe me, always, my dear Mr. Ruskin,
>   Yours faithfully,
>   HENRY E. Archbp. of Westmr.[36]

Ruskin became very attached to Manning and described him in
letters to his friends as 'my dear Cardinal'. He dined with him
frequently and took him to see Burne-Jones's studio. He wrote to
Manning on 25 January 1878:

My dear Lord Cardinal,

It was a great joy to receive your letter, in all but that it told
me you had been ill. There are few people now left for me in the
world whose illness troubles me;—yours does, both for my own heart's
sake, and in its anxiety for the good of the Christian Church (when does
one get over that wicked foolishness of anxiety?)—which can ill spare
you, it seems to me.[37]

A letter to Elizabeth Barrett Browning of 13 May 1861, by contrast,
indicates how out of sympathy with Newman Ruskin was.[38]

Manning was also able to be of much use to Ruskin in his literary
and academic work. We find Ruskin writing to Mrs. Arthur Severn
from Talloires on 17 November 1882:

I wonder if Arthur would mind calling at the Archbishop's House to
ask how he is, and if he's well, asking for an interview to give him a
message from me; and then explaining to him a little of what I've been
about these three months, which it would really take too much of my
scrawling to tell him, and then—this is the message, with my love, that
I want to have the early authentic forms of the Rule of St. Benedict, and
the Rule of Citeaux, and that I don't know if I can lay my hand on them
at Geneva, and that if the Cardinal's secretary would be so very good as
to write out the essential heads of them for me—and send them me to the
Hotel des Bergues—I should be so grateful; and so comfortable in quoting
at my lecture.[39]

Obviously Ruskin and Manning were on a footing of complete
intimacy and friendship. It was to endure although Ruskin never
became a Roman Catholic as Manning may have hoped he would.

Chapter VIII

EPILOGUE

★

IT only remains for us now to attempt to assess the nature of the impact that Henry Edward Manning had upon English life in general and upon the Roman Catholic Church in particular; how far he was a typical product of the nineteenth century and to what extent he achieved his aims.

It is undoubtedly true that history is the story of the gradual development of man from the savage to modern civilization, and in that story certain personalities dominate in each successive century. One of the dominating characters of the later nineteenth century was that of Henry Edward Manning, and yet few characters have been as little understood or appreciated as his. He has been described as 'ascetic', 'austere' and 'frugal',[1] and the total picture that emerges from the pages of Purcell and Lytton Strachey is that of a cold, ruthless schemer, unattractive in personality, guided by an intense personal ambition and always searching for ways and means to advance the claims of his flock. Such a picture is somewhat distorted and unhistorical.

On the personal level, Manning has been described as living in a very frugal way: a slice of mutton with mustard 'formed the hygienic staple of his mid-day meal'. But this kind of austerity is not what we perceive described in a letter of John Ruskin to Miss Susan Beever, dated September 1880, and telling of a visit to the Cardinal.

Ruskin declared:

Now you're just wrong about my darling Cardinal. See what it is to be jealous! He gave me lovely soup, roast beef, hare and currant jelly, puff pastry . . . raisins and almonds, and those lovely preserved cherries like kisses kept in amber. And told me delicious stories all through lunch. *There*![2]

And again,

I lunched with Cardinal Manning, and he gave me *such* a plum pie. I never tasted a Protestant pie to touch it.[3]

The truth is that Manning was a brilliant social host and knew
how to mix in all kinds of company. It was this latter quality that
enabled him to preserve lasting friendships with men so completely
different from each other as J. E. C. Bodley, General Booth and
Bramwell Booth, John Burns, Gladstone, Archbishop Croke,
Ruskin, and W. G. Ward. He possessed in a marked degree that
rare quality of being all things to all men. It was this broad and liberal
acquaintance with men of all shades of opinion and belief that
allowed Manning to develop such a shrewd analysis of the condition of society in his day, and this knowledge allied to a broad
sympathy with the poor and oppressed helped him to systematize
his ideas on social reform. Bramwell Booth thought Manning a
saint and yet when in the Cardinal's presence he always seemed to
suffer from an inferiority complex. He was over-awed by the man
and declared: 'There was an undercurrent of subtlety about him
which made one never quite sure of one's grip.'[4] He seemed to be
wise as a serpent and yet as gentle as a dove. Booth's testimony is
of importance because he described vividly how Manning really
felt when confronted with social evil. He states:

I have seen him in various moods. I have seen him intensely critical,
arguing with the most subtle skill with those who sought to cross swords
with him. I have seen him angry, with flashing eyes and emphatic gestures
denouncing iniquity. And I have seen him tender, with the tears running
down his ascetic cheeks, moved by some tale of sorrow, especially where
little children were concerned. . . .[5]

Manning was a man of intense feeling, and in this respect he was
perhaps a child of his age, a typical product of the nineteenth
century. For the latter was an intense age and one characterized by
its production of men who felt intensely about social evil, men of
the calibre of Charles Dickens, Charles Kingsley, Charles Reade,
Walter Besant, James Rice and Richard Whiteing in the literary
field, and F. D. Maurice and the Positivists in the more practical
field. And yet, in a quite different way, Manning's path towards
social reform was a highly individual one. The Christian Socialists
had a morbid tendency to regard life as a constant diorama of
crises. Following upon the removal of one evil another was sure to
arise. Thus life was to be one struggle after another against social
evil. There was no hope of a redemption. This pessimistic note
found no welcome in Manning's heart. His whole life was interfused
with his religion; it permeated and transformed every action and

policy that he pursued. He worked for the education of the poor children, because he considered it to be his duty as 'a father in God'. He worked for the cause of the working men and for Ireland from a like motive. Bramwell Booth once gave expression to this basic characteristic of Manning when he declared:

I do not think that outside the Salvation Army I ever met a man who more uncompromisingly brought his religion into everything he touched, into everything he wrote, into everything he planned. He did it with the most exquisite tact, and without the slightest suggestion of putting himself forward, but he did it.[6]

Manning's religion was the driving force of his humanitarianism, hence he did not owe any fundamental debt to the Christian Socialists or to the Positivists. The material end was the same, perhaps, but Manning's policy was invigorated by a highly personal sense of religion, of practical Christianity. This sense removed his natural tendency towards insularity and enabled him to work for the cause of the oppressed in the United States of America, France and Europe. His correspondence with the great Continental Christian social reformers reveals, as we have seen, a world-wide interest in social problems. He had a great belief in the sanctity of the family, and he believed that the majority of the political troubles of the nineteenth century sprang from a destruction of domestic life. He declared:

A large proportion of the people in London are herded in places not fit for human habitation. . . . What moral influence or formation of life and character of children is possible in overcrowded dens where all is misery and confusion?[7]

The rich, he felt, were doing little to help, and in some cases were aggravating the evils. He declared

The ostentation of luxury is a sharp temptation to men in despair. It is not only the hunger that pulls down a man's own strength, but the cry of those who look to him for bread that sounds daily in his ears, and haunts him wherever he goes. They must know little of life who do not know what ruin of men and of women comes from the straits of poverty.

Yet he felt that the Roman Catholics in England had little appreciation of the problem. The influential 'Old Catholics' were living a narrow isolated life, withdrawn from and uninterested in their humbler Irish brethren. Manning's lifelong problem was how to make these 'Old Catholics' socially conscious and to bring them 'out of the sacristy' to take their full share in the work of amelioration. He was only partially successful. The 'Old Catholics' were determined to resist, and looking for a rallying point for their cause they found it in John Henry Newman. In sympathy, tastes, feelings and insularity, Newman closely resembled the 'Old Catholics' and his name was used unscrupulously to thwart Manning's policies. Any opportunity for causing pain to the Archbishop was eagerly sought for and used. This was especially true of *The Month*. On the elevation of Newman to the Cardinalate, this magazine used every literary method to exalt the nature of the honour conferred on him and by implication minimize the fact that Manning held the same honour. *The Month* referred to Newman as 'the most distinguished and the greatest Englishman who will ever have worn the Roman Purple'[8] and it made the comparison more odious by continuing:

It is not policy, or the favour of high personages, or the accident of important services in some negotiation or cleverness in smoothing over some embarrassing difficulty, or the long pursuit of the ecclesiastical 'carriera' or high birth and connections, or great position in the Hierarchy, or any other similar cause, which has brought the name of the new Cardinal before the notice of the Holy Father.... Had Dr. Newman been the Head of the new hierarchy, or some distinguished member of the Catholic Episcopate in this country, there would have been an official character about his nomination which would have excited a comparatively languid interest amongst Englishmen outside the narrow pale of our own community.... Catholics know how Dr. Newman set the public mind right after the Church had been assailed by the blundering sophistries of the 'Eirenicon' and the fanatical virulence of Mr. Gladstone, and how they have always instinctively looked to him as the champion to whom Englishmen would listen with confidence in any hour of need or danger.

The bare fact remains, however, that Newman's honour was far from a spontaneous grant of the Holy See but was made precisely by 'the favour of high personages', the Duke of Norfolk and Lord Ripon. They desired the honour not so much for Newman, as Newman, but for Newman the champion of 'Old Catholic' interests. Manning, from the outset of his episcopal career, attempted to reconcile the 'Old Catholics' to his policy. He remained on cordial terms with many of them and attempted to meet them half-way in many matters—for instance, in his appointing Mgr. Capel to the Rectorship of the Kensington University College and in his frequent compliments to their tenacity in adhering to the faith in Penal times. His recommendation of Dr. Errington to restore the Scottish Hierarchy was an indication of his willingness to heal the breach.* When Manning received the Cardinal's Hat in 1875 he spoke of those in particular who 'have preserved unbroken the tradition of the faith'† in England. But despite his overtures the 'Old Catholics' refused to co-operate. To achieve the success of his policy of weaning the Church from the cloister to the public life, from the aristocratic to the democratic, Manning had to employ other forces. During the pontificate of Pius IX all appointments to English sees as they became vacant were Manning's appointments. Before Pius died in 1878, Manning had succeeded in establishing in five sees bishops of like mind to himself: bishops who would work with and not against his policy. Under Pius IX he was completely successful in this, but his influence with Leo XIII who succeeded to the triple tiara in 1878 proved to be no less great.

By his skilful exclusion of the 'Old Catholic' families from episcopal office Manning went a long way in democratizing the Roman Catholic Church in England. After his death his ideas were sure to live on, and they came to life again in the policies of Archbishops Keating and Downey and Cardinal Hinsley. The latter openly declared Manning to be his model.

The Papal Encyclical *Rerum Novarum* indicated that Manning's policy had been accepted by the Church as a whole; it was a policy that he had forged and one which Leo XIII, as we have seen, himself declared was of Manning's making. No longer could the Church be regarded solely as an ally of Capital.

Manning's public life and social influence can be said to have been a success in so far as he had reconciled the new learning and the Church in his own attitude, and hence shown the way to the reconciliation of dogma and science. On hearing of Manning's death Leo XIII declared 'A great light of the Church has gone out'.[9] But although he was dead his light was to shine on, re-invigorating men's minds with a clearer perception of the meaning and truth of the phrase 'practical Christianity'.

* See my article, 'Documents Relating to the Appointments of a Delegate Apostolic for Scotland, 1868', in the *Innes Review* (Scottish Catholic Historical Society), Autumn 1957.
† Second draft speech of Cardinal Manning at English College, Rome, on receiving letter of nomination to the Cardinalate, 15 March 1875. In National Library of Ireland, Dublin.

A NOTE ON THE SOURCES

(A) Manuscript Sources

The chief manuscript source for any study of Cardinal Manning is the collection of his papers and diaries preserved at the Church of St. Mary of the Angels, Moorhouse Road, Bayswater, London, W.2. The collection is a private one and not open to general inspection as such. For a number of years, Professor Chapeau has been engaged in arranging the papers in preparation for the definitive biography. Partly owing to the action of Purcell and partly owing to war damage, the extant papers represent only a portion of the original collection. However, there is still at Bayswater much material not used by Purcell and whose existence was unknown to him. The indexing and cataloguing of the papers is not yet complete and it is impossible to give references to file-boxes. In the notes this collection is referred to as M.P. (Manning Papers). (See Appendix I.)

The Gladstone Papers, housed at the British Museum, are of the greatest importance, for they contain two folios (Add. MSS. 44249 and 44250), which consist entirely of letters to and from Manning. (See Appendix II. Here and in the Notes, Manning's name appears as M. and Gladstone's as G.) In addition to the Gladstone Papers, the British Museum has the John Burns Papers but, unfortunately, only his diaries covering the years 1888–1902 were available for public inspection at the time of writing (Add. MSS. 46310–46320). The most important diary for the Strike Year, 1889, is missing, but those for the other years contain references to Cardinal Manning and are of especial value for the light they throw on the relationship between the Cardinal and Burns.

For internal Church History, the writer has made use of the following manuscript sources:

1. Letters and speeches in the archives of the Rev. R. A. Coffin, C.SS.R., who left the Oratorians to join the Redemptorists and who later—in 1885—became third bishop of Southwark. The archives are in a private collection at the Church of Our Immaculate Lady of Victories, Clapham, S.W.4.

2. Letters from Manning to Newman (and vice versa) in the archives of the Oratory, Birmingham. These letters are the ones which Purcell claims were destroyed by Newman 'subsequent to his correspondence with Archbishop Manning in 1866' (p. 309, I, n. 17). The letters preserved at the Oratory escaped both Purcell and, strangely, Leslie. (See Appendix III.)

3. Letters in the archives of Archbishop's House, Norfolk Road, Birmingham, 15. Here are five unpublished letters on the Kensington University project, which throw light on the reasons for its failure and on the character of its Rector, Mgr. Capel.

4. The Clifford and Errington Papers preserved at St. Ambrose, Leigh Woods, Bristol, 8. (See Appendix IV.)

5. A number of individual letters have come to light from various sources and these have been acknowledged in the notes.

In referring to manuscript sources in the notes, I have used N.P. for the Newman Papers, U.P. for the Ullathorne Papers, G.P. for the Gladstone Papers, &c., and this system has been followed uniformly throughout.

(B) Primary Printed Sources

Of primary importance among the printed sources within this category is E. S. Purcell's *Life of Cardinal Manning, Archbishop of Westminster*, in two volumes, published by Macmillan in 1896. It is a source that has to be handled with great care. The effect of the work is to show that Cardinal Manning and Ambition are almost synonymous terms. Purcell paid no attention to the Cardinal's printed writings and he saw only a small fraction of Manning's papers. He saw none of Manning's letters to Gladstone, or to Archbishop Ullathorne, Vaughan and Walsh and he failed to gain access to Manning's letters to Newman and to Cardinal Cullen. To hide these omissions Purcell stated that Manning destroyed the relevant correspondence (I, pp. x, 65, 309, n. 17). In actual fact these letters remain and Purcell's work therefore fails to give a full and accurate picture. In a similar way, when handling the sources, Purcell easily becomes confused. This is seen most clearly in I, pp. 286–8 when he is relating the story of Manning's holidays of 1844. He jumbles into one a visit to Normandy of 1844, a visit to Paris of 1845 and a visit to Wales and Scotland of 1849. All these become a holiday in Wales in 1844 to Purcell, and it is very difficult to see how he could have made the mistake because the dates of each year are clearly embossed on the cover of each diary and in more than one case a date has been altered: 'September 29th, 1844, Rouen' in the diary is changed in Purcell to become 'August 6th 1849, in Wales' (pp. 285–6). Similar errors can be shown throughout the work and especially in the extracts he made from Manning's Journal of 1847.

The whole of the second volume of Purcell is badly written and out of proportion to the first. Far too much space is given to the differences between Newman and Manning and hardly anything is said about Manning's social and political achievement. Approximately 249 pages are allocated to the Cardinal's public work and policy out of a total of 818 in the second volume. The Manning-Talbot correspondence is printed without any kind of historical evaluation of the parties existing within the Roman Catholic Church and thus the impression is given that the Cardinal's reign was occupied with a war of personalities and not with a struggle between two distinct philosophies.

In spite of its defects, however, we have to take a certain amount of material on trust from Purcell, such as letters which have now disappeared. Quotations from this source have been kept to a minimum, excepting when they can be verified from the extant papers.

Other primary printed sources are as follows:

1. Gwynne, S. and Tuckwell, G. M., *The Life of the Rt. Hon. Sir Charles W. Dilke, Bart., M.P.*, 2 vols. (John Murray, 1917). This contains a number of references to Manning culled from the Dilke and Chamberlain Papers.

2. Leslie, S., *Henry Edward Manning: His Life and Labours* (Burns, Oates, ed. 1954). This was the first really independent estimate of Manning since Purcell and although Leslie used the latter a great deal, he incorporated new material (especially on Manning's relations with the American bishops) and he had a few letters from Tillett in his possession. His work, however, was popular biography and he was guilty of a number of factual errors as well as errors of interpretation and especially in regard to educational policy. His chapter on Ireland in particular was very confusing.

3. Walsh, P. J., *William J. Walsh, Archbishop of Dublin* (Longmans, 1928). This contains a number of valuable letters taken largely

from the archives of Archbishop's House, Dublin. It is a sound biography, although somewhat tinged with political bias.

4. Morley's *Gladstone* is also of great importance not only for its direct references to Manning but also for its value as a source for the general political history of the period.

5. Manning's own works have proved a mine of information and especially his Charges as Archdeacon of Chichester and Pastorals as Archbishop of Westminster.

The writer found the Roman Catholic newspapers and periodicals of the day—especially *The Month*, *The Dublin Review*, *The Tablet*, and *The Catholic Times*—of great value. Various other journals were consulted when the need arose and they are cited in the notes.

NOTES

Abbreviations

B.M.: British Museum.
G.P. : Gladstone Papers.
M.P.: Manning Papers.
N.P. : Newman Papers.
M. : Manning.
G. : Gladstone.

CHAPTER I: THE 'OLD CATHOLICS' AND PRACTICAL CHRISTIANITY

1. Hay, M. V., *The Jesuits and the Popish Plot* (Sands & Co., London, undated), p. 63.
2. Purcell, E. S., *Life of Cardinal Manning, Archbishop of Westminster* (Macmillan, 1896), I, p. 653.
3. The table is taken from *The Irish in Great Britain* by John Denvir (London, 1892).
4. For the extent of Protestant Irish immigration into Scotland see Handley, J. E., *The Irish in Scotland, 1798–1845* and *The Irish in Modern Scotland* (Cork University Press, 1943 and 1947), *passim*.
5. Denvir, op. cit. p. 99.
6. Ibid. *passim*, also D. Thomson, *England in the Nineteenth Century* (Pelican, 1952), pp. 137 et seq.
7. Ibid. p. 112.
8. Ibid. p. 123.
9. Ward, W., *The Life and Times of Cardinal Wiseman* (Longmans, ed. 1912), II, p. 15.
10. Ibid.
11. Hay, op. cit. p. 109.
12. Ward, op. cit. II, p. 54.
13. Ibid.
14. Thureau-Dangin, P., *The English Catholic Revival in the Nineteenth Century* (Dutton & Co., New York), I, pp. 302 et seq.
15. Ward, op. cit. I, pp. 444 et seq.
16. Lunn, A., *Roman Converts* (Chapman & Hall, London, 1924), p. 103.
17. Ward, W., *W. G. Ward and the Catholic Revival* (Macmillan, 1890), p. 75.
18. Ward's *Life of Wiseman*, op. cit. II, p. 222.
19. Lunn, op. cit. p. 100.
20. Butler, E. C., *Life and Times of Bishop Ullathorne*, (Burns, Oates, 1926), I, p. 153.
21. Ward's *Life of Wiseman*, op. cit. II, pp. 253 et seq.
22. Butler, op. cit. p. 276.
23. Leslie, S., *Henry Edward Manning : His Life and Labours* (Burns, Oates, 1921), p. 151.
24. Ibid. p. 156.
25. Purcell, op. cit. II, p. 257.
26. M.P. An autobiographical note, 1890.
27. Manning, H. E. *A Charge Delivered at the Ordinary Visitation of the Archdeaconry of Chichester, in July, 1842* (London, 1842), pp. 16–17.
28. Ibid.
29. From the Charge of 1843, p. 35.

30. Ibid. p. 28.
31. Ibid. p. 43.
32. Ibid. p. 46.
33. From the Charge of 1845, pp. 43 et seq.
34. Ibid.
35. From the Charge of 1846, pp. 28 et seq.
36. Ibid. pp. 31 et seq.
37. Oxford.
38. From the Charge of 1846, pp. 33 et seq.
39. Ibid.
40. Ibid.
41. Ibid. pp. 45 et seq.
42. Ibid.
43. Ibid.
44. From a pamphlet published privately in 1847.
45. Manning, H. E., *What One Work of Mercy Can I Do This Lent? A Letter to a Friend* (London, 1847), p. 9.
46. Ibid. p. 10.
47. Ibid.
48. From the Charge of 1848, p. 60.
49. Leslie, op. cit. pp. 107 et seq.
50. Ibid. p. 108.
51. Mallet, C. E., *History of the University of Oxford* (Methuen, 1927), III, p. 234.
52. M.P.
53. Manning, H. E., *Pastime Papers* (Ed. Wilfrid Meynell, Burns, Oates, 1892), p. 17.
54. M.P. An autobiographical note, 1890.
55. Ibid.
56. Lunn, op. cit. p. 187.
57. Snead-Cox, J. G., *Life of Cardinal Vaughan* (Burns, Oates, 1910), I, p. 482.
58. Ibid.
59. Denvir, op. cit. p. 250. Italics mine.
60. Brackwell, C., 'The Church of England and Society, 1830–1850', thesis presente for M.A. degree (Birmingham University), May 1949, unpublished, p. 121.
61. Ibid.
62. Ibid. p. 47.
63. Manning, *Pastime Papers*, op. cit. p. 25.
64. Ibid. p. 33.
65. M.P., Diary for 1890, entry for 1 August.
66. From the Charge of 1846, op. cit. p. 47.
67. Leslie, op. cit. footnote.
68. Farrar, in *Review of the Churches*, March 1892.
69. Belloc, H., *Cruise of the 'Nona'* (Constable, London 1955), pp. 54–55.
70. Lunn, op. cit. p. 73.
71. M.P.
72. Ullathorne, B., *Letters* (1886), p. 478.
73. Ibid. *Letters* (1888), p. 479.
74. Purcell, op. cit. I, p. 40.
75. M.P. Autobiographical note, undated.
76. *The Month*, Nov. 1893, No. 353, p. 331. Italics mine.
77. *Dublin Review*, **144** (1894), p. 45.
78. G.P., M. to G. 2.9.67.

CHAPTER II: THE SCHOOLS

1. Beales, A. C. F. in *English Catholics, 1850–1950* (Burns, Oates, 1950), p. 367.
2. Ibid.
3. Purcell, op. cit. II, p. 354.
4. Taylor, I. A., *The Cardinal Democrat* (Kegan Paul, 1908), p. 31.
5. M.P., 1878–82 Journal.
6. Leslie, op. cit. p. 485.
7. The Pastoral of 8 June 1866 is in the M.P., but is also quoted at length in *Manning's Work For Children*, ed. E. St. John (Sheed & Ward, 1929), pp. 21 et seq.
8. *The Times*, 12 June 1866.
9. *The Tablet*, 16 June 1866.
10. Ibid.
11. Ibid.
12. St. John, op. cit. pp. 40 et seq.
13. *The Tablet*, 16 June 1866.
14. St. John, op. cit. pp. 62 et seq.
15. M.P., Talbot to M., 22.6.66.
16. Beales, op. cit. p. 371.
17. Dickens, C., *Household Words*, extract from 'Charnwood', 25 Apr. 1857.
18. Dickens, from *All the Year Round*, 21 May 1859.
19. St. John, op. cit. p. 71.
20. Evennett, H. O., *The Catholic Schools of England and Wales* (C.U.P., 1944), pp. 124 et seq.
21. Ibid.
22. Ibid.
23. Ibid.
24. St. John, op. cit. pp. 89 et seq.
25. G.P., M. to G. 15.3.68.
26. Ibid. M. to G. 16.6.68.
27. Ibid. M. to G. 3.7.68.
28. Ibid. M. to G. 29.7.68.
29. *The Times*, 27 Feb. 1873.
30. Ibid. Letter dated 27 Feb., published 28th.
31. St. John, op. cit. pp. 130 et seq. *et passim*.
32. Beales, op. cit. p. 373.
33. Ward, W., *William George Ward and the Catholic Revival* (Macmillan, 1893), p. 297.
34. Ibid.
35. Taylor, op. cit. pp. 49–50.
36. Butler, op. cit. II, p. 249.
37. Ward, W., *The Life and Times of Cardinal Newman* (Longmans, 1912), II, pp. 332–3.
38. Purcell, op. cit. II, p. 515.
39. Ibid. II, pp. 332–4.
40. Ward, Maisie, *The Wilfrid Wards and the Transition* (Sheed & Ward, 1934), I. p. 220.
41. *Dublin Review*, 1863, pp. 139 et seq.
42. Kerk, F. J., *Reminiscences of an Oblate of St. Charles* (Burns, Oates, 1905), now out of print, pp. 74 et seq.
43. Leslie, op. cit. p. 152.
44. M.P., Diary 1848.
45. Leslie, op. cit. p. 297.
46. Battersby, W. J., *Brother Potamian : Educator and Scientist* (Burns, Oates, 1953), pp. 43 et seq.
47. M.P., M. to Vaughan 20.10.80.

48. Battersby, op. cit. pp. 43 et seq.
49. M.P., M. to Vaughan 31.10.80.
50. Battersby, op. cit. p. 51.
51. M.P., M. to Vaughan 8.11.80.
52. McAniff, M., Pamphlet published for Centenary Celebrations of St. Anne's Ugthorpe (Stokeld, Middlesbrough), p. 15.
53. Beales, op. cit. p. 337.
54. Archer, *Secondary Education in the XIX Century* (C.U.P., 1921), pp. 230 et seq.
55. Anson, P. F., *The Religious Orders and Congregations of Great Britain* (Worcester, 1949), and Steele, F. M., *The Convents of Great Britain* (1925), *passim*.

CHAPTER III: THE ACT OF 1870 AND ITS CONSEQUENCES

1. Grove, R. B., 'An Investigation into Public Opinion and the Passing of the Education Act, 1870.' An M.A. Thesis in Education of the University of London, 1949 (unpublished), p. 68.
2. Garvin, J. L., *The Life of Joseph Chamberlain* (Macmillan, 1932), I, p. 88.
3. Purcell, op. cit. II, pp. 492–3.
4. Howard, C. H. D., in *Manning: Anglican and Catholic*, ed. FitzSimons (Burns, Oates, 1957), p. 110.
5. McEntee, G., *The Social Catholic Movement in Great Britain* (Macmillan, 1927), p. 41.
6. Leslie, op. cit. p. 174.
7. G.P., M. to G. 11.2.68.
8. Ibid. M. to G. 11.3.68.
9. Manning, H. E., article in *The Nineteenth Century*, Dec. 1882.
10. Garvin, op. cit. I, p. 92.
11. G.P., M. to G. 10.4.69.
12. Ibid. M. to G. 24.2.70.
13. Ibid. M. to G. 7.3.70.
14. Garvin, op. cit. I, p. 106.
15. Purcell, op. cit. II, p. 493.
16. G.P., M. to G. 25.3.70.
17. Grove, op. cit. p. 197.
18. Beales, op. cit. p. 376.
19. Purcell, op. cit. II, pp. 436 et seq.
20. G.P., M. to G. 6.4.70.
21. Ibid. G. to M. 26.3.70.
22. Ibid. G. to M. 26.3.70.
23. Ibid. G. to M. 16.4.70.
24. Garvin, op. cit. I, p. 114.
25. G.P., M. to G. 10.7.70.
26. Butler, op. cit. II, p. ii.
27. Ibid, pp. 146 et seq.
28. M.P., Ullathorne to M. 7.10.70.
29. Garvin, op. cit. I, p. 116.
30. M.P., M. to Ullathorne 7.10.70.
31. Butler, op. cit. II, pp. 146 et seq.
32. Purcell, op. cit. II, pp. 494–5 n.
33. Beales, op. cit. p. 273.
34. Ibid. p. 376.
35. G.P., M. to G. 25.10.71.
36. G.P., M. to G. 1.11.71.
37. *The Times*, 22 May 1929.
38. Ibid. 30 April 1929.

16

39. *The Universe*, 8 Aug. 1930.
40. Ibid.
41. *The Times*, 8 May 1929.
42. G.P., M. to G. 27.9.71.
43. *Dublin Review*, Jan. 1868, pp. 131 et seq.
44. Grove, op. cit. p. 68.
45. Purcell. op. cit. II, p. 493.
46. *The Tablet*, 25 Feb. 1870, pp. 265 et seq.
47. *Catholic Times*, 22 Jan. 1870, p. 6.
48. Ibid. 5 Mar. 1870, p. 2.
49. Ibid. 24 Sept. 1870, p. 4.
50. Beales, op. cit. p. 374.
51. Purcell, op. cit. II, p. 494.
52. Ibid. II, p. 493, and also McEntee, op. cit. p. 42.
53. Garvin, op. cit. I, p. 122.
54. Ibid. II. p. 124.
55. Howard, C. H. D., *English Historical Review*, Oct. 1950, pp. 477 et seq.
56. Grove, op. cit. p. 290.
57. Beales, op. cit. p. 379.
58. Manning, H. E., in *The Nineteenth Century*, 12 (1882), 958 et seq.
59. Snead-Cox, op. cit. II, p. 91.
60. M.P., M. to Vaughan, 23.10.85.
61. Ibid. M. to Vaughan 14.11.85.
62. McEntee, op. cit. p. 45.
63. Howard, C. H. D., in *English Historical Review*, Jan. 1947, LXII.
64. O'Brien, C. C., *Parnell and his Party* (Oxford, 1957), p. 105.
65. M.P., M. to Vaughan 20.12.85.
66. G.P., M. to G. 5.3.86.
67. Ibid., M. to G. 25.9.87.
68. Ibid., M. to G. 10.11.87.

CHAPTER IV: HIGHER EDUCATION

1. Manning, H. E., *A Charge Delivered at the Ordinary Visitation of the Archdeaconry of Chichester, in July 1846* (London), pp. 33 et seq.
2. Purcell, op. cit. II, p. 289.
3. M.P., M. to Talbot 22.4.64.
4. Mallet, op. cit. II, p. 378.
5. *Dublin Review*, 1863, op. cit. pp. 139 et seq.
6. Snead-Cox, op. cit. II, pp. 76 et seq.
7. Armytage, W. H. G., *Civic Universities* (Benn, 1955).
8. Evennett, H. O., in *The English Catholics, 1850–1950*, op. cit. p. 293.
9. The Charge of 1849, pp. 18 et seq.
10. Albion, G., in *The English Catholics*, op. cit.
11. M.P., M. to Talbot 22.4.64.
12. Newman Papers (Copy), J. H. N. to Ullathorne 23.9.64.
13. Ward's *Life of Newman*, op. cit. II, pp. 62–63.
14. Ibid.
15. Ibid. II, p. 80.
16. Lunn, op. cit. p. 107.
17. Gasquet, J. R., *Cardinal Manning* (London, 1895), pp. 61 et seq.
18. Butler, op. cit. II, p. 10.
19. Evennett, op. cit. p. 297.
20. N.P. (Copy), J. H. N. to Ullathorne, 23.9.64.

21. Ward's *Newman*, op. cit. II, p. 67.
22. Purcell, op. cit. II, pp. 296 et seq.
23. The Speech of the Rev. R. A. Coffin, C.SS.R., Provincial, to the Diocesan Synod, preserved in MS. at St. Mary's, Clapham, S.W.4. Unpublished.
24. Ward's *Newman*, op. cit. II, pp. 121 et seq.
25. Ibid. II, p. 123.
26. M.P., Vaughan to M. 29.3.67.
27. M.P., M. to Talbot 1.2.67.
28. M.P., Ullathorne to M. 14.7.66.
29. M.P., Vaughan to M. 10.4.67.
30. M.P., Vaughan to M. 29.3.67.
31. Purcell, op. cit. II, p. 303.
32. Howard, C. H. D., in *The English Catholics*, op. cit.
33. The Charge of 1849, op. cit. pp. 66–67.
34. The Charge of 1846, op. cit. p. 38.
35. Purcell, op. cit. II, p. 266.
36. Coffin Papers, Douglas to Coffin 1.8.70.
37. *Dublin Review*, July 1863, p. 59.
38. Purcell, op. cit. II, p. 294.
39. *Letters and Notices* (Manresa Press), XXI, pp. 3 et seq.
40. From *Pastoral Letter of the Archbishop and Bishops of the Province of Westminster in Provincial Council Assembled*, 1872, p. 120.
41. *English Catholics*, op. cit. pp. 134–5.
42. N.P., M. to N. 12.4.55.
43. M.P., Clifford to M. 7.11.67.
44. Ward's *Newman*, op. cit. II, pp. 195 et seq.
45. Ibid. p. 196.
46. Purcell, op. cit. II, p. 496.
47. M.P., Journal, Bk. No. 4, pp. 100 et seq.
48. Albion, G., in *The English Catholics*, op. cit.
49. Purcell, op. cit. II, p. 497.
50. N.P., M. to N. 12.6.73.
51. N.P. (Copy), N. to M. undated.
52. N.P., M. to N. 21.11.73.
53. N.P., N. to M. 24.11.73.
54. G.P., M. to G. 1.3.73.
55. Purcell, op. cit. II, p. 496.
56. M.P., M. to Vaughan 22.11.80.
57. McEntee, op. cit. pp. 102 et seq.
58. Purcell, op. cit. II, p. 497.
59. M.P., Journal, Bk. No. 4, pp. 100 et seq.
60. *Manchester Guardian*, 24.4.79.
61. M.P., Journal, Bk. No. 4, pp. 108 et seq.
62. M.P., Ullathorne to M. 7.7.78.
63. M.P., M. to Ullathorne 5.8.78.
64. M.P., M. to Ullathorne 23.8.78.
65. Ullathorne Papers, W. and J. Gibson to Ullathorne 8.1.79.
66. U.P., Ullathorne to W. and J. Gibson undated.
67. U.P., Arnold & Co. to Ullathorne 23.5.79.
68. U.P., Ullathorne to Arnold & Co. 25.5.79.
69. Purcell, op. cit. II, pp. 504 et seq.
70. Evennett, op. cit. pp. 305–8.
71. M.P., M. to Vaughan 20.10.80.

72. Butler, op. cit. II, p. 36.
73. Barry, W., *Cardinal Newman* (Hodder & Stoughton, 1927), p. 97.
74. Extract from Vaughan's address to the Westminster Archdiocese on his appointment as Manning's successor—in Wardley Hall Archives, Vol. 2, 7, p. 440.
75. Wardley Hall Archives, Vol. 2, p. 560.
76. Manning, H. E., *Miscellanies*, I, pp. 75 et seq.
77. Purcell, op. cit. II, pp. 543–4.

CHAPTER V: THE CONDITION OF THE PEOPLE.

1. M.P., autobiographical note, dated 1880.
2. Fitzsimons, J., in *The English Catholics*, op. cit. p. 137.
3. G.P., M. to G. 25.3.68.
4. G.P., M. to G. 16.6.68.
5. G.P., M. to G. 3.7.68.
6. G.P., M. to G. 29.7.68.
7. G.P., M. to G. 12.7.72.
8. Purcell, op. cit. II, p. 640.
9. Ibid. p. 641.
10. G.P., M. to G. 21.12.72.
11. G.P., M. to G. 26.12.72.
12. Purcell, op. cit. II, pp. 640–1.
13. Manning, H. E., 'The Rights and Dignity of Labour', in a collection entitled *Socialism* in the National Central Library, B.P. 165924–B.P. 165950, p. 10.
14. Gwynne, S. and Tuckwell, G. M., *The Life of the Rt. Hon. Sir Charles W. Dilke Bart.*, *M.P.* (John Murray, 1917), I, p. 267.
15. Ibid. I, p. 506.
16. Ibid. p. 509.
17. Ibid. II, p. 19.
18. Ibid. p. 242.
19. Manning's Charge of 1849, op. cit. p. 39.
20. *Fortnightly Review*, **49** (1888), 153 et seq.
21. Llewellyn Smith, H. and Nash, Vaughan, *The Story of the Dockers' Strike* (T. Fisher Unwin, 1889), p. 28.
22. Ibid. p. 19.
23. Ibid. p. 125.
24. Purcell, op. cit. II, p. 665.
25. Smith and Nash, op. cit. p. 133.
26. Ibid. p. 146.
27. Ibid. p. 148.
28. *Morning Post*, 15 September 1889.
29. Mason, Canon, in *Memoirs of Archbishop Temple*, II, p. 148.
30. Leslie, op. cit. p. 373.
31. de Pressensé, F., *Cardinal Manning* (London, 1897), p. 209.
32. Snead-Cox, op. cit. I, p. 477.
33. *Dublin Review*, July 1891, pp. 163 et seq.
34. Crawford, V. M., *The Church and the Worker* (C.S.G., Oxford, 1945), p. 36.
35. G.P., M. to G. 27.8.90.
36. Smith and Nash, op. cit. p. 143.
37. Burns Papers, Diary for 1891.
38. Lunn, op. cit. p. 122.
39. Browne, H. J., *The Catholic Church and the Knights of Labor*, a Ph.D. Dissertation (Catholic Univ. of America Press, 1949), pp. 341 et seq.

40. Crawford, V. M., *Catholic Social Doctrine, 1891–1931* (C.S.G., Oxford, 1933), pp. 34–40.
41. Capecelatro, Cardinal, *Christ, the Church and Man* (St. Louis, 1909), pp. 73 et seq.
42. George, H., *The Condition of Labour* (ed. 1891), p. 121.
43. Ibid. front page.
44. Walsh, P. J., *William J. Walsh, Archbishop of Dublin* (Longmans, 1928), pp. 226 et seq.
45. Tracy-Ellis, J., *The Life of James, Cardinal Gibbons, Archbishop of Baltimore, 1834–1921* (Milwaukee, U.S.A., 1952), II, p. 489.
46. Ibid. p. 554.
47. Hicks, J. D., *The American Nation* (ed. 1941), pp. 181 et seq.
48. Browne, op. cit. pp. 68–69.
49. Ibid. p. 60.
50. Tracy-Ellis, op. cit. II, pp. 493–4.
51. Browne, op. cit. p. 181.
52. Tracy-Ellis, op. cit. II, pp. 506 et seq.
53. M.P., Keane to M. 10.2.87.
54. Tracy-Ellis, op. cit. II, pp. 508–9.
55. M.P., Keane to M. 28.2.87.
56. M.P., Gibbons to M. 14.3.87.
57. M.P., M. to Keane, 15.4.87.
58. M.P., Keane to M. 23.4.87.
59. *The Tablet*, 30 April 1887.
60. M.P., Keane to M. 22.3.87.
61. M.P., Keane to M. 23.4.87.
62. Tracy-Ellis, op. cit. II, p. 632.
63. M.P., Vaughan to M. 17.10.80.
64. M.P., Leo XIII to M. 17.1.91.
65. M.P., Walsh to M., 24.3.91.
66. M.P., Leo XIII to M. 11.5.91.
67. *Dublin Review*, July 1891, p. 167.

CHAPTER VI: IRELAND AND GLADSTONE.

1. Gladstone Papers, M. to G. Christmas 1890.
2. Charlton, L. E. O. (ed.), *Recollections of a Northumbrian Lady* (Jonathan Cape, 1949), pp. 225 et seq.
3. Gwynn, D., in *Manning, Anglican and Catholic* (ed. Fitzsimons, Burns, Oates, 1951), p. 118.
4. M.P., Cullen to M. 8.4.67.
5. M.P., Cullen to M. 8.4.67.
6. M.P., M. to Ullathorne, 17.2.69.
7. Denvir, op. cit. pp. 209–10.
8. G.P., M. to G. 5.4.67.
9. G.P., M. to G. 22.9.67.
10. G.P., M. to G. 15.1.68.
11. G.P., M. to G. 11.2.68.
12. Leslie, op. cit. p. 193.
13. G.P., M. to G. 11.3.68.
14. M.P., Cullen to M. 15.3.68.
15. Purcell, op. cit. II, p. 517.
16. G.P., M. to G. 24.3.68.
17. Manning, H. E., *Ireland: A Letter to Earl Grey* (Longmans 1868), *passim*.

18. Morley, J., *The Life of William Ewart Gladstone* (London, 1903), II, pp. 141-3.
19 Ibid. p. 142.
20. Gwynn, op. cit. p. 125.
21. Butler, op. cit. I, p. 140.
22. M.P., M. to Anderdon 2.4.68.
23. G.P., M. to G. 28.3.68.
24. G.P., M. to G. 8.4.68.
25. Gwynne and Tuckwell, op. cit. I, p. 75.
26. G.P., M. to G. 3.11.69.
27. Sheehy-Skeffington, F., *Michael Davitt, Revolutionary, Agitator and Labour Leader* (T. Fisher Unwin, London, 1908), pp. 64 et seq.
28. Morley, op. cit. II, p. 284.
29. M.P., M. to G. 19.5.71.
30. G.P., M. to G. 27.7.71.
31. G.P., M. to G. 23.8.72.
32. G.P., G. to M. 26.8.72.
33. G.P., M. to G. 11.2.68.
34. G.P., M. to G. 3.11.69.
35. M.P., Cullen to M. 13.10.71.
36. Leslie, op. cit. p. 207.
37. Davitt, op. cit. p. 192.
38. O'Brien, C. C., *Parnell and his Party, 1880-90* (Oxford, 1957), p. 68, n. 2.
39. Walsh, op. cit. pp. 108 et seq.
40. *The Tablet*, 16 April 1921.
41. Gwynn, op. cit. pp. 119 et seq.
42. Morley, op. cit. III, pp. 62, 63.
43. Walsh, op. cit. p. 139.
44. Gwynne and Tuckwell, op. cit. I, p. 374.
45. Ibid. p. 375.
46. Ibid. II, p. 131.
47. Garvin, op. cit. I, p. 596.
48. Walsh, op. cit. p. 151.
49. Gwynne and Tuckwell, op. cit. II, pp. 149 et seq.
50. Ibid. II, p. 31.
51. Walsh, op. cit. p. 156.
52. Gwynne and Tuckwell, op cit. II, p. 150.
53. Gwynn, op. cit. p. 135 et seq.
54. Ronan, M. V., *The Most Rev. W. J. Walsh, D.D., Archbishop of Dublin* (Bray, 1927), p. 5.
55. Garvin, op. cit. I, pp. 596-7.
56. O'Brien, op. cit. p. 92, n. 2.
57. Ibid. p. 95.
58. *Irish Historical Studies*, 8 (Sept. 1953), 342.
59. Gwynne and Tuckwell, op. cit. II, pp. 129-30.
60. Garvin, op. cit. I, p. 599.
61. O'Brien, op. cit. p. 96.
62. *English Historical Review*, **62** (Jan. 1947), *passim*.
63. M.P., Walsh to M. 27.12.85.
64. Walsh, op. cit. pp. 262 et seq.
65. *Irish Historical Studies*, 8 (Sept. 1953), 342.
66. *English Historical Review*, **62** (Jan. 1947), 49.
67. G.P., M. to G. 7.11.85.

68. Letter in National Library of Ireland, M. to Sir Charles Gavan-Duffy 19.8.87. Italics mine.
69. G.P., M. to G. 25.9.87.
70. Denvir, op. cit. p. 396.
71. G.P., M. to G. 5.12.90.
72. Walsh, op. cit. pp. 226 et seq.
73. *English Catholics, 1850–1950*, op. cit. p. 486.
74. *Pall Mall Gazette*, 4 April 1887.
75. *The Tablet*, 8 April 1887.
76. Walsh, op. cit. p. 263.
77. *The Times*, 20 July 1881.
78. Gwynne and Tuckwell, op. cit. I, p. 375.
79. Ibid. p. 177.
80. M.P., Walsh to M. 23.2.86.
81. Walsh, op. cit. p. 212.
82. *Pall Mall Gazette*, 4 April 1887.
83. Walsh, op. cit. p. 265.
84. Ibid. p. 212.
85. Ibid. *passim*.
86. Davitt, M., *The Fall of Feudalism in Ireland* (Harper, New York, 1904), p. 407.
87. McEntee, op. cit. pp. 55 et seq.
88. Walsh, op. cit. pp. 408 et seq.
89. O'Brien, op. cit. pp. 287–8.
90. M.P., Walsh to M. 6.12.90.
91. O'Brien, op. cit. p. 286.
92. M.P., M. to Walsh 4.12.90.
93. Ibid. Walsh to M. 14.12.90.
94. Walsh, op. cit. p. 262.

CHAPTER VII: PHILANTHROPY

1. Manning, H. E., in *The Nineteenth Century*, XXIII, Jan.-June 1888, pp. 321 et seq.
2. Carter, H., *The English Temperance Movement: A Study in Objectives* (Epworth Press, London, 1933), I, pp. 95–96. Italics mine.
3. Handley, J. E., *The Irish in Scotland, 1798–1845* (Cork Univ. Press, 1943), p. 235.
4. *English Catholics, 1850–1950*, op. cit. p. 282.
5. Tynan, K., *Father Mathew* (London, 1908), *passim*.
6. Ibid. p. 88.
7. Ibid. p. 89.
8. Manning, H. E., *The Temperance Reformation, the United Kingdom Alliance, and Local Option* (Simpkin, Marshall & Co., London, 1882), p. 5.
9. Purcell, op. cit. II, p. 595.
10. Ibid. pp. 597–8.
11. Gwynn, op. cit. p. 282.
12. Carter, op. cit. I, p. 142.
13. G.P., M. to G. 27.10.68.
14. Manning's Speech of 4 Sept. 1882 at Newcastle on behalf of the United Kingdom Alliance (Simpkin, Marshall & Co., London, 1882), p. 7.
15. Taylor, I. A., *The Cardinal Democrat: Henry Edward Manning* (Kegan Paul, London, 1908), p. 91.
16. *The Month*, Feb. 1879, p. 292, quoting Sir James Paget.
17. Taylor, op. cit. pp. 103–4.
18. Ibid. p. 104.

19. Carter, op. cit. I, p. 161.
20. Ibid. p. 162.
21. Ibid. p. 204.
22. Hutton, A. W., *Cardinal Manning* (Methuen, 1892), p. 168.
23. Purcell, op. cit. II, p. 603.
24. Booth, B., *Echoes and Memories* (Salvationist Publishing & Supplies Ltd., London, 2nd edn. 1928), pp. 76–78.
25. Purcell, op. cit. II, pp. 653 et seq.
26. Booth, op. cit. pp. 117 et seq.
27. Ibid. p. 125.
28. Purcell, op. cit. II, pp. 653 et seq.
29. Booth, op. cit. pp. 141 et seq.
30. *The Zoophilist*, XI (1891–2), pp. 230–1.
31. McEntee, op. cit. p. 78.
32. *The Zoophilist*, op. cit. pp. 230 et seq.
33. Ibid.
34. Ibid. p. 228.
35. Ruskin, J., *Works* (ed. Cook & Wedderburn, London, 1901), XXXVI, pp. lxxxvi-lxxxvii.
36. Ibid.
37. Ibid. XXXVII, pp. ccxl-ccxli.
38. Ibid. XXXVI, p. ccciii.
39. Ibid. XXXVII, pp. ccccxix-ccccxx.

CHAPTER VIII: EPILOGUE

1. Purcell, op. cit. II. pp. 234, 697, 699.
2. Ruskin, op. cit. XXXVII, pp. cccxxiii-cccxxiv.
3. Ibid. p. cccxxi.
4. Booth, op. cit. pp. 76–78.
5. Ibid.
6. Ibid.
7. Manning in *The Nineteenth Century*, XXIII (Jan.-June 1888), pp. 321 et seq.
8. *The Month*, April 1879, pp. 465 et seq.
9. Leslie, op. cit. p. 495.

BIBLIOGRAPHY

B.O.W.   — Burns, Oates (and Washbourne), London.
C.U.P.   — Cambridge University Press.
C.S.G.   — Catholic Social Guild.
C.T.S.   — Catholic Truth Society.

ALBION, G. 'Manning and the See of Westminster', in Fitzsimons, op. cit.
AMHERST, W. J. *The History of the Catholic Emancipation and the Progress of the Catholic Church in the British Isles* (1886)
ANSON, P. F. *The Catholic Church in Modern Scotland* (B.O.W., 1937)
—— *The Religious Orders and Congregations of Great Britain and Ireland* (Worcester, 1949)
ARCHER, R. L. *Secondary Education in the XIX Century* (C.U.P., 1921)
ARMYTAGE, W. H. G. *Civic Universities* (Benn, 1955)
BARFF, F. S. *An Introduction to Scientific Chemistry* (1872)
BARRY, W. *Cardinal Newman* (Hodder & Stoughton, 1927)
BATTERSBY, W. J. *Brother Potamian : Educator and Scientist* (B.O., 1953)
—— 'Educational Work of the Religious Orders of Women, 1850–1950' in Beck, op. cit.
—— 'Secondary Education for Boys' in Beck, op. cit.
BEALES, A. C. F. 'The Struggle for the Schools' in Beck, op. cit.
BECK, G. A. (ed.). *The English Catholics, 1850–1950* (B.O., 1950)
BELLESHEIM, A. *History of the Catholic Church of Scotland* (Blackwood, Edinburgh, 1890)
BELLOC, H. *The Cruise of the 'Nona'* (Constable, 1928)
BENNETT, J. 'The Care of the Poor' in Beck, op. cit.
BODLEY, J. E. C. *Cardinal Manning and Other Essays* (Longmans, 1912)
BOOTH, B. *Echoes and Memories* (Salvationist Press, 1926)
BRACKWELL, C. 'The Church of England and Society, 1830–1850'. Thesis presented for M.A. degree in History, Birmingham University, 1949. Unpublished
BROWNE, H. J. *The Catholic Church and the Knights of Labor*, a Ph.D. Dissertation (Washington, 1949)
BUTLER, C. *Life and Times of Bishop Ullathorne* (2 vols., Burns, Oates, 1926)
Cambridge Modern History. Ed. W. W. Ward, 1910. Vol. XII
CAPECELATRO, Cardinal. *Christ, the Church and Man* (St. Louis, 1909)
CARTER, H. *The English Temperance Movement : A Study in Objectives* (2 vols., Epworth Press, 1933)
CHARLTON, L. E. O. (ed.) *Recollections of a Northumbrian Lady* (Cape, 1949)

CRAWFORD, V. M. *Catholic Social Doctrine, 1891–1931* (C.S.G., 1945)
—— *The Church and the Worker* (C.S.G., 1945)
Curriculum and Examination in Secondary Schools (H.M.S.O., 1943)
DAVITT, M. *The Fall of Feudalism in Ireland* (New York, 1904)
DENVIR, J. *The Irish in Great Britain* (1897)
DE PRESSENSE, F. *Cardinal Manning* (1897)
DICKENS, C. 'Charnwood', in *Household Words*, 25 April 1857
——*All The Year Round*, 21 May 1859
DISRAELI, B. *Lothair* (1870)
DWYER, J. J. 'The Catholic Press, 1850–1950', in Beck, op. cit.
EVENNETT, H. O. 'Catholics and the Universities', in Beck, op. cit.
——*The Catholic Schools of England and Wales* (C.U.P., 1944)
FITZSIMONS, J. (ed.) *Manning, Anglican and Catholic* (B.O.W., 1950)
GARVIN, J. L. *The Life of Joseph Chamberlain* (4 vols., Macmillan, 1932)
GASQUET, J. R. *Postscript to 'Cardinal Manning'* (C.T.S., 1896)
GEORGE, H. *The Condition of Labour* (1891)
GREGORY, J. C. *A Short History of Atomism* (A. & C. Black, 1931)
GRETTON, R. H. *Modern History of the English People, 1880–1898* (Secker, 1910)
GROVE, R. B. 'An Investigation into Public Opinion and the Passing of the Education Act, 1870.' An M.A. Thesis in Education of London University. Unpublished.
GWYNN, D. 'Manning and Ireland' in Fitzsimons, op. cit.
—— 'The Irish Immigration' in Beck, op. cit.
GWYNNE, S. and TUCKWELL, G. M. *The Life of the Rt. Hon. Sir Charles Dilke, Bart., M.P.* (2 vols., Murray, 1917)
HANDLEY, J. E. *The Irish in Modern Scotland* (Cork, 1947)
—— *The Irish in Scotland, 1798–1845* (Cork, 1943)
HAY, M. V. (ed.) *The Blairs Papers, 1603–1660* (Sands, 1929)
—— *The Jesuits and the Popish Plot* (Kegan Paul, 1934)
HICKS, J. D. *The American Nation* (Boston, 1941)
HOWARD, C. H. D. 'Documents relating to the Irish "Central Board" Scheme, 1884–5' in *Irish Historical Studies*, vol. VIII, March 1953
—— 'Joseph Chamberlain and the "Unauthorised Programme" ' in *English Historical Review*, October 1950
——'Joseph Chamberlain, Parnell and the Irish "Central Board" Scheme, 1884–5' in *Irish Historical Studies*, vol. VIII, September 1953
—— 'Manning and Education' in Fitzsimons, op. cit.
—— 'The Parnell Manifesto of 21 November, 1885, and the Schools Question' in *English Historical Review*, January 1947, vol. LXII
HUTTON, A. W. *Cardinal Manning* (Methuen, 1892)
JOHNSTON, T. *The History of the Working Classes in Scotland* (Forward Publishing Company, Glasgow, 2nd edn. 1929)

KERK, F. J. *Reminiscences of an Oblate of St. Charles* (B.O., 1905)

LAWSON, J. P. *The Roman Catholic Church in Scotland, its Establishment, Subversion, and Present State* (Edinburgh, 1836)

LESLIE, S. *Cardinal Gasquet : A Memoir* (B.O., 1953)

—— *Henry Edward Manning : His Life and Labours* (B.O.W., 1921)

—— 'Manning and Newman' in Fitzsimons, op. cit.

—— 'Some Birmingham Bygones' in *Dublin Review*, vol. CLXVI, 1920

LEYS, M. D. R. *European Catholics and the Social Question* (C.S.G., 1943)

LILLY, W. S. (ed.) *Characteristics, Political, Philosophical, and Religious* (1885)

LUNN, A. *Roman Converts* (Chapman & Hall, 1924)

McANIFF, M. Pamphlet published for Centenary Celebrations of St. Ann's, Ugthorpe (Stokeld, Middlesbrough)

McENTEE, G. P. *The Social Catholic Movement in Great Britain* (New York, 1927)

McGRATH, F. *Newman's University, Idea and Reality* (1951)

MACKENZIE, C. *Catholicism and Scotland* (Kegan Paul, 1938)

MALLET, C. E. *History of the University of Oxford*, vol. III (Methuen, 1927)

MANNING, H. E. *Essays on Religion and Literature* (1874)

—— *Four Great Evils of the Day* (New York, 1899)

—— *Ireland : A Letter to Earl Grey* (Longmans, 1868)

—— *Miscellanies* (3 vols., B.O.W., 1877)

—— *Pastime Papers*, ed. Wilfrid Meynell (B.O.W., 1892)

—— *The Rights and Dignity of Labour* (1874)

—— 'Sermons and Charges.' A collection bound for Manning's personal use and preserved at St. Mary of the Angels, Bayswater—also his Pastorals in the same collection

—— *What One Work of Mercy Can I Do This Lent? A Letter To A Friend.* (Edwards & Hughes, 1847)

—— *The Temperance Reformation : The United Kingdom Alliance and Local Option.* Two speeches by his Eminence Cardinal Manning at Newcastle-on-Tyne, 4 and 5 September 1882 (Simpkin, Marshall & Co., 1882)

—— Various writings and articles in newspapers, journals and reviews, as specified in the text and chapter notes

MARCHANT, Sir James. *Anthology of Jesus* (Cassell, 1936)

MAY, J. L. *The Oxford Movement* (Lane, 1933)

METLAKE, G. (pseud. for John Joseph Laux) *Christian Social Reform* (Dolphin Press, Philadelphia, 1912)

MORLEY, J. *Life of Gladstone* (3 vols., 1903)

O'BRIEN, C. C. *Parnell and his Party* (Oxford, 1957)

'OLDCASTLE' (pseud. for Wilfrid Meynell). *Cardinal Archbishop of Westminster* (1886)

'OLDCASTLE'. *Memorials of Cardinal Manning* (1892)
—— *Sayings of Cardinal Manning* (1892)
PARTINGTON, J. R. *A Text-Book of Inorganic Chemistry* (1934)
Pastoral Letter of the Archbishop and Bishops of the Province of West-minster in Provincial Council Assembled (1872)
PECK, W. G. *The Social Implications of the Oxford Movement* (Scribners, 1933)
PURCELL, E. S. *Life of Cardinal Manning, Archbishop of Westminster* (2 vols., Macmillan, 1896)
—— (ed.) *Life and Letters of Ambrose Phillips de Lisle*, n.d.
RONAN, M. V. *The Most Rev. W. J. Walsh, D.D., Archbishop of Dublin* (Dublin, 1927)
RUSKIN, J. *Works* (ed. Cook & Wedderburn, 39 vols., 1901)
SANDFORD, E. G. (ed.) *Memoirs of Archbishop* [Frederick] *Temple* by Seven Friends (2 vols., 1906)
SHEEHY-SKEFFINGTON, F. *Michael Davitt, Revolutionary Agitator and Labour Leader* (Unwin, 1889)
SMITH, H. L. and NASH, V. *The Story of the Dockers' Strike* (Unwin, 1889)
SNEAD-COX, J. G. *Life of Cardinal Vaughan* (2 vols., Burns, Oates, 1910)
STEELE, F. M. *The Convents of Great Britain* (Sands, 1925)
ST. JOHN, E. *Manning's Work for Children* (Sheed & Ward, 1929)
STRACHEY, L. *Eminent Victorians* (new edn., Chatto & Windus, 1948)
SWEENEY, M. V. 'Diocesan Organisation and Administration', in Beck, op. cit.
TAYLOR, I. A. *The Cardinal Democrat : Henry Edward Manning* (Kegan Paul, 1908)
THUREAU-DANGLIN, P. M. P. *The English Catholic Revival in the Nine-teenth Century* (2 vols., New York, Dutton & Co., 1915)
TIERNEY, M. A. (ed.) *Dodd's Church History of England* (1843)
TRACY-ELLIS, J. *The Life of James, Cardinal Gibbons, Archbishop of Baltimore, 1834–1921* (2 vols. Bruce Publishing Company, Mil-waukee, 1952)
TYNAN, K. *Father Mathew* (Macdonald & Evans, 1908)
ULLATHORNE, B. *From Cabin Boy to Archbishop* (Autobiography, B.O., 1891)
—— *Letters* ed. by Mother Francis Raphael, O.S.D. (B.O. 1892)
Vivisection, Publications of the Victoria Street Society for the Protection of Animals from (1887), *Cardinal Manning as an Anti-Vivisectionist* and *The Cardinal Archbishop of Westminster on Vivisec-tion*.
WALSH, P. J. *William J. Walsh, Archbishop of Dublin* (Longmans, 1928)
WARD, D. 'Manning and his Oblates', in Fitzsimons, op. cit.
WARD, M. *The Wilfrid Wards and the Transition* (Sheed & Ward, 1934)

WARD, W. *Ten Personal Studies* (Longmans, 1908)
—— *The Life and Times of Cardinal Wiseman* (2 vols. ed., Longmans, 1912)
—— *W. G. Ward and the Catholic Revival* (Macmillan, 1893)
—— *William George Ward and the Oxford Movement* (1890)
—— *The Life of John Henry Newman* (2 vols., Longmans, 1913)
WARD, W. G. *The Ideal of a Christian Church* (1844)
WHEELER, G. 'The Archdiocese of Westminster' in Beck, op. cit.
WHITE, G. *Cardinal Manning* (R. Washbourne, 1882)
Zoophilist, The, vol. XI, 1891–2

APPENDIXES

I. Newman-Manning Correspondence at Bayswater

Part A

The lists in the left-hand columns are of the letters in the care of Professor Chapeau at Bayswater. In the right-hand columns are those published by Purcell or others. The unpublished letters are marked with a *. Those marked † are lost since Purcell's handling of them (in fact, we do not really know if they existed at all).

Part A (1835–1845)

Letters at Bayswater			Letters published by Purcell in Volume I of his Life of Manning
			Newman to Manning
—	.	.	4 Sept. 1836 (p. 223)
19 Oct. 1836	.	.	10 Sept. 1836 (p. 223—misdated by P.)
24 Feb. 1837	.	.	pp. 224–5
12 Apr. 1837	.	.	pp. 226–7
12 Jan. 1838	.	.	p. 142
28 Jan. 1838	.	.	—
6 Mar. 1838	.	.	pp. 228–9
*4 Apr. 1838	.	.	—
*6 Jun. 1838	.	.	—
9 Aug. 1838	.	.	p. 137
*29 Aug. 1838	.	.	—
18 Oct. 1838	.	.	p. 153
—	.	.	24 Oct. 1838 (p. 137)
1 Sept. 1839	.	.	pp. 233–4
*9 Sept. 1839	.	.	—
*14 Sept. 1839	.	.	—
			Newman to Keble and others
—	.	.	†3 Jan. 1841 (p. 186)
*22 July 1841	.	.	—
14 Oct. 1843	.	.	—
25 Oct. 1843	.	.	—
31 Oct. 1843	.	.	—
—	.	.	†24 Dec. 1843 (p. 254)
—	.	.	†16 Nov. 1844 (p. 258)
—	.	.	†9 Feb. 1845 (p. 305)

Manning to Newman

—	.	.	.	†7 Apr. 1835 (p. 219)
—	.	.	.	†15 Sept. 1835 (p. 219)
26 Oct. 1837	.	.	.	p. 225
*2 Nov. 1837	.	.	.	—
*22 Nov. 1837	.	.	.	—
*9 Jan. 1838	.	.	.	—
2 Mar. 1838	.	.	.	pp. 227–8
16 Mar. 1838	.	.	.	pp. 230–1
12 Aug. 1839	.	.	.	p. 157
23 Oct. 1839	.	.	.	pp. 231–2
*1 Mar. 1840	.	.	.	—
24 Dec. 1840	.	.	.	—
*6 Feb. 1845	.	.	.	—
—	.	.	.	†14 Oct. 1845 (pp. 309–10)

Note

Purcell writes (I, p. 309 n. 17) about Manning's letter of 14 Oct. 1845: 'This letter alone was preserved of those written since 1840. All the rest, even the one described at the time as "a great gift", were destroyed by Newman consequent to his correspondence with Archbishop Manning in 1866.' Purcell here is wrong, as appears from J.H.N.'s correspondence at the Birmingham Oratory (see Appendix III), and from the list in Part B of this Appendix.

Part B (1852–1890)

Letters at Bayswater

Newman to Manning (or others)	*Manning to Newman (or others)*
8 June 1852	17 May 1865
14 Oct. 1852	1 Nov. 1865
17 Aug. 1854	2 Nov. 1865
19 Aug. 1854	3 Nov. 1865
16 Apr. 1854	17 Apr. 1867
19 Oct. 1855	7 Aug. 1867
10 Dec. 1855	14 Aug. 1867

Part B (1852–1890) (continued)

Newman to Manning (or others)	Manning to Newman
5 Feb. 1856	14 Aug. 1867
1 Apr. 1856	24 Aug. 1867
9 Apr. 1856	29 Aug. 1867
11 Jan. 1857	4 Sept. 1867
25 June 1857	9 Feb. 1875
30 Sept. 1857	2 Aug. 1878
6 Oct. 1857	4 Feb. 1879
21 Dec. 1857	20 Feb. 1879
21 Dec. 1857	22 Feb. 1879
14 July 1863	23 Feb. 1879
22 June 1864	8 Mar. 1879
19 Mar. 1865	Easter Day 1880,
9 May 1865	25 Sept. 1881
31 May 1865	9 May 1884
9 Feb. 1866	
Easter Day, 1866	
15 Apr. 1867	
28 July 1867	
31 July 1867	
10 Aug. 1867	
18 Aug. 1867	
18 Aug. 1867	
2 Sept. 1867	
14 Oct. 1867	
28 Jan. 1870	
Easter Eve, 1875	
4 Feb. 1879	
5 Feb. 1879	
4 Mar. 1879	
11 Mar. 1879	
20 Mar. 1879	
9 Apr. 1879	
19 May 1879	
5 June 1879	

Other correspondence at Bayswater is between Manning and Ulla-thorne and Manning and Vaughan. There are also letters from Fr. Mills, the Bishop of Hexham, Fr. Neville, Fr. Oakeley, Cardinal Franchi, the Duke of Norfolk, and a number of unclassified letters.

II. The Gladstone Papers

The chief letters in the Gladstone Papers at the British Museum dealing with social topics are as follows:
(Add. MSS. 44249–44250)

5 Apr.	1867	M. to G.
22 Sept.	1867	M. to G.
11 Feb.	1868	M. to G.
11 Mar.	1868	M. to G.
15 Mar.	1868	M. to G.
24 Mar.	1868	M. to G.
28 Mar.	1868	M. to G.
8 Apr.	1868	M. to G.
16 June	1868	M. to G.
29 July	1868	M. to G.
27 Oct.	1868	M. to G.
10 Apr.	1869	M. to G.
14 July	1869	M. to G.
3 Nov.	1869	M. to G.
21 Nov.	1869	M. to G.
21 Feb.	1870	M. to G.
7 Mar.	1870	M. to G.
25 Mar.	1870	M. to G.
26 Mar.	1870	G. to M.
16 Apr.	1870	G. to M.
10 July	1870	M. to G.
27 July	1871	M. to G.
27 Sept.	1871	M. to G.
25 Oct.	1871	M. to G.
1 Nov.	1871	M. to G.
12 July	1872	M. to G.
23 Aug.	1872	M. to G.
26 Aug.	1872	G. to M.
21 Dec.	1872	M. to G.
26 Dec.	1872	M. to G.
15 Jan.	1873	M. to G.
1 Mar.	1873	M. to G.
7 Nov.	1885	M. to G.
5 Mar.	1886	M. to G.
19 Jan.	1887	M. to G.
25 Sept.	1887	M. to G.
10 Nov.	1887	M. to G.
27 Aug.	1890	M. to G.

17

22 Nov. 1890 M. to G.
27 Nov. 1890 M. to G.
5 Dec. 1890 M. to G.
Christmas 1890 M. to G.

III. MANNING-NEWMAN LETTERS AT BIRMINGHAM

Correspondence from Manning to Newman at the Birmingham Oratory (said by Purcell (I, p. 309 n. 17) to have been destroyed).

22 Feb. 1835
12 July 1837
21 July 1837
25 July 1837
15 Jan. 1840
8 Oct. 1843
25 Oct. 1843
27 Oct. 1843
4 Dec. 1843
13 Nov. 1844
23 Nov. 1844
5 Feb. 1845
14 Oct. 1845
23 Oct. 1845
6 Apr. 1851
27 July 1851
6 Aug. 1851
26 Aug. 1851
28 Sept. 1851
30 Oct. 1851
30 Apr. 1855
23 Jan. 1857
21 Aug. 1857
20 May 1858
25 June 1861
26 Jan. 1862
27 May 1865
29 June 1865
10 Jan. 1866
12 June 1866
10 Aug. 1866
21 Nov. 1873
5 Apr. 1875

25 Feb. 1879
?   1880
8 May   1880
30 Sept. 1889
22 Feb. 1890

The following letters are preserved at the Birmingham Oratory and all refer to the bestowing of the Cardinal's Hat on Newman:

29 Jan. 1879 Manning to Ullathorne
no date   Card. Nina to M. (with translation)
3 Feb. 1879 Ullathorne to Manning
4 Feb. 1879 Manning to Newman and Newman to Manning
4 Mar. 1879 N. to M. and again on 5 Mar.
8 Mar. 1879 M. to Newman
15 Mar. 1879 Nina to M.
24 Mar. 1879 M. to Newman
16 Apr. 1879 M. to Newman
15 May 1879 Nina to M.
16 May 1879 M. to N.

IV. MANNING LETTERS AT BRISTOL[1]

Letters from Manning and others to Archbishop Errington are preserved at St. Ambrose, Leigh Woods, Bristol, 8. Those referring to the negotiations for the appointment of a Delegate-Apostolic for Scotland in 1868 are as follows:

26 Feb. 1868 Manning to Errington
5 Mar. 1868 Manning to Errington
13 Mar. 1868 Clifford to Errington
23 Mar. 1868 Errington to Manning
25 May 1868 Clifford to Errington
26 June 1868 Manning to Errington
7 July 1868 Turner to Errington
29 July 1868 Manning to Errington
10 Aug. 1868 Turner to Errington

[1] See my article in the *Innes Review* for Autumn 1957, entitled 'Documents Relating to the Appointment of a Delegate-Apostolic for Scotland, 1868', for a full account of these letters.

INDEX

Aberdeen University, 115
Academia of the Catholic Religion, 126–8
Acton, Lord, 67, 69 and n.
Aeschylus, 115
Agricultural Workers' Union, 129, 132–3
Albert, Prince Consort, 90
Albion, G., 'Manning and the See of Westminster', 92, 109
Allen, Dr. Henry, 76
Allen, William, Cardinal, 1, 2
Allies, T. W., 29
Amalgamated Society of Engineers, 132
America, United States of, Manning's influence in, 149–54, 215
American Quarterly Review, the, 140
Ampleforth Journal, the, 95
Ampleforth School, 58
Anderdon, John, 172, 177
Anne, family, 162
Anson, P. F., *The Religious Orders and Congregations of Great Britain and Ireland*, 41 n.
Anstruther, Sir Robert, 205
Anti-Vivisection Act, 1877, 20, 209
Antwerp, 142
Arch, Joseph, 132–3, 137
Archer, R. L., *Secondary Education in the Nineteenth Century*, 63
Argyll, Duke of, 49
Armagh, Archbishop of, 169
Arnold, Matthew, 28; *Culture and Anarchy*, 28
Arnold, Thomas (elder), 90, 115 n.
Arnold, Thomas (younger), 90 n., 115 n.
Association for Promoting State-directed Colonization, 48
Athanasianism, 90
Atomic Theory, Dalton's, 116
Australia, 15, 142

Bagshawe, Mgr. E. G., Bishop of Nottingham, 23, 205
Bain, Alexander, *Education as a Science*, 28
Balliol College, Oxford, 117
Barff, Professor F. S., 115–16, 125; *An Introduction to Scientific Chemistry*, 116

Barnabo, Cardinal, 93, 99–100
Barnardo, Dr., 48–49
Barry, Father William, 41; *Cardinal Newman*, 125
Battersby, W. J., *Brother Potamian, Educator and Scientist*, 56, 57 n., 58
Bayswater Journal, Manning's, 18 n.
Bayswater, St. Mary of the Angels, 16, 18–19, 31
Beales, A. C. F., 'The Struggle for the Schools', 31, 73
Beaumont College, 54, 58
Beaumont, Lord, 5
Bedford College, London, 58
Beever, Miss Susan, 213
Bell, Rev. Andrew, 29, 30
Belloc, Hilaire, 22; *The Cruise of the Nona*, 141
Benedict, St., Rule of, 212
Bennett, J., in *The English Catholics, 1850–1950*, 42 n.
Benson, E. W., Archbishop of Canterbury, 21, 145–6
Bentham, Jeremy, 27
Benthamite philosophy, 28
Besant, Walter, 214
Bessborough Commission, 1880, 180
Beverley, Diocese of, 79; Bishop Briggs of, 9 n.; Bishop Cornthwaite of, 103
Biblical Commission, 117
Bilsborrow, J., Bishop of Salford, 124
Birkhead, Rev. George, 1 n.
Birmingham, 22, 23, 65, 67, 81, 83, 120
Birmingham League, 67, 86
Birmingham Oratory, 58, 93, 98, 110
Bishop, Rev. William, Vicar Apostolic of Chalcedon, 1
Bismarck, Prince, 130 n., 138
Blackwell, Rev. George, 1 n.
Bodley, J. E. C., 138 and n., 214
Bonaparte, Prince Lucien, 209
Booth, Mrs. Bramwell, 208
Booth, William Bramwell, 207–9, 214, 215
Booth, William, General, 19, 207, 214; *In Darkest England and the Way Out*, 207
Borthwick, Algernon, 137
Boulton, S. B., 142
Brassey, T., later 1st Earl, 135, 143

Braye, Alfred Lord, 115
Braye, Lord, 123
Brentford, Catholic school at, 59
Briggs, J., Bishop of Beverley, 9 n.
Bright, John, 18, 23
Bristol, (Anglican) Bishop of Gloucester and, 209
Bristol, reformatory at, 39
British Association, 116, 117
Bruce, H. A., Licensing Bill (Act), 1871, 205-6
British and Foreign Schools Society, 29, 77
Brown, G., Bishop of Liverpool, 9 n.,
Brown, T. J., O. S. B., Bishop of Newport and Menevia, 9 n., 10, 38, 77-78
Brown, J., Bishop of Shrewsbury, 9 n.
Browne, H. J., The Catholic Church and the Knights of Labor, 157
Browning, Elizabeth Barrett, 212
Browning, Robert, 49
Brothers of Charity of St. Vincent de Paul, 41
Brothers of the Christian Schools, 42
Buckle, G. E., 29
Buffon, G. L. L., 116
Burgess, T., Bishop of Clifton, 9 n.
Burke, Edmund, 153
Burne-Jones, Edward, 212
Burns, John, 141 et seq., 148, 214
Bute, Marquis of, 79, 119, 209-10
Butler, Bishop, of Limerick, 180
Butler, C., The Life and Times of Bishop Ullathorne, 10, 38 n., 95, 125
Butler, Josephine, 208
Butt, J., Bishop of Southwark, 42, 60
Butt, Isaac, Land Tenure in Ireland, 177-8
Buxton, Sydney, later Lord, 142, 147
Byron, Lord, 17

California, U.S.A., 118
Cambridge University, 58, 87 et seq., 90-93
Camden Society, Cambridge, 115
Camoys, Lord, 6
Canada, 48, 154
Canning, George, 18
Capecelatro, Cardinal, Archbishop of Capua, 149; Christ, the Church and Man, 149
Capel, Mgr. T. J., 55, 56, 109, 117-25, 216

Capuchins, 194, 200
Cardinal Manning Secondary Modern School for Boys, 53
Cardinal Vaughan Grammar School, 53
Carlingford, Lord, 183
Carlisle, Lord, 163
Carlyle, Thomas, 28, 32
Carnarvon, Lord, 185, 187
Carter, H., The English Temperance Movement, 200, 203, 206
Caswell, Father, 98 and n.
Catesby, Mgr., in Lothair, 118
Catholic Academies, 51
Catholic Conference 1893, 23
Catholic Directory, The, 2 n.
Catholic Education Council, Westminster, 38 n.
Catholic Poor Schools Committee, 30
Catholic Poor Schools Society, 29
Catholic Times, the, 78, 79, 80, 81, 189
Census of 1841, 3
Chadwick, Sir, E., 27
Chamberlain, Joseph: Nonconformist agitation in Birmingham, 63, 65; views on education, 75, 81, 83-84, 85; Irish 'Central Board' scheme, 181, 185-9; on Errington Mission, 183; resigns on Coercion Bill, 187
Champion, H. H., 144
Chapeau, Prof. A., 171
Charlton, Mrs., 162
Charnwood Forest reformatory, 39
Chartism, 132
Chatard, F. S., Bishop of Vincennes, 153
Chelsea, Catholic School in, 41, 59
Chesterton, G. K., 74-75
Chichester, Manning Archdeacon of, 11, 18, 87
Childers, H. C. E., 187
Children's Acts, 20
Christian Brothers of France and Ireland, 30
Christian Mission, 207
Christian Remembrances, The, 20
Christian Socialist Movement, 24, 129, 214-15
Church, R. W., Dean of St Paul's, 50
Cistercians, 39
Citeaux, Rule of, 212
Civil Service Commission, 115
Clapham, Catholic School in, 55, 59
Clarke, Dr. R. F., 52, 113, 117

Clarendon Commission, 1861, 58
Clarendon, 4th Earl of, 69
Clifford, W. J. H., Bishop of Clifton: 'Old Catholic' nominee for Westminster, 9, 53; Manning's opponent in Hierarchy, 10, 38; supports Newman, 98; against university ban, 101–8; connexion with Jesuits, 112; on Capel's appointment, 120; on Prior Park, 104–7, 113, 114; on Errington Mission, 183
Clifford, Sir Charles, 31–32
Clifford of Chudleigh, family, 2, 10, 38, 210
Coercion Act, 1881, 180
Coercion Bill, 1885, 187
Coffin, Fr. R. A., later Bishop of Southwark, 42, 97–98, 100, 101
Colenso, Dr. T. W., later (Anglican) Bishop of Natal, 90, 118
Combination Laws, 131
Committee for the Relief of Paris, 211
Committee for the Unemployed, 211
Compton, Lord, 139
Comte, Auguste, 30
Congreve, Richard, 30
Cornthwaite, R., Bishop of Beverley, 79, 103
Corrigan, M. A., Archbishop of New York, 151 et seq., 191 n.
Cowper-Temple clause, in Education Act, 72–76, 85
Cox, J. G. Snead-, 192
Crawford, V. M., Catholic Social Doctrine, 149
Crimean War, 17
Criminal Law Amendment Act, 1871, 132
Croke, T. W., Archbishop of Cashel: influence of H. George on, 150; and the Land League, 179–80; and Dublin appointment, 181–4; and Central Board, 186 et seq.; and Persico Mission, 195 et seq.; and Parnell, 197; friendship with Manning, 214
Cross Commission, vii, 26, 59, 85–86
Cross, Sir Richard, 85, 208
Cullen, Cardinal, Archbishop of Dublin, 163 ff., 177, 179, 181

Daily Chronicle, the, 144
Daily News, the, 144
Daily Telegraph, the, 55, 56 n., 124
Dalgairns, Father, 50 and n.
Dalton's Atomic Theory, 116

Dames of Nazareth, 59
Danell, James, Bishop of Southwark, 42
Darboy, Mgr. G., Archbishop of Paris, 130 n
Darwin, Charles, 115; Origin of Species, 31; Antiquity of Man, 31
Daughters of the Cross of Liège, 41
Davitt, Michael, 150–1, 174, 179, 183, 191, 196
Deaf and Dumb Schools Act, 1893, 72, Defective and Epileptic Children Act, 1899, 72
de Grey, Lord, 66
de la Salle Brothers, 53, 55–57
de Mun, A. A. M., 149
Denbigh, 8th Earl of, 193
Denvir, J., The Irish in Great Britain, 4–5
Derby, 15th Earl of, 161, 166, 171 n.
Descurtins, G., 149
Devas, Charles Stanton, 117, 125
Devas, Rev. F., 117
de Vere, Aubrey, 104
Dickens, Charles, 39, 40, 214
Digby, Kenelm, family, 115
Dilke, Lady, 138
Dilke, Sir Charles: and trade unions, 132; friendship with Manning, 137–9; and Ireland, 173, 181, 193; and Errington Mission, 182–5, 193; and Central Board Scheme, 185 et seq.; resigns on Coercion Bill, 187
Disraeli, Benjamin, Lord Beaconsfield: and Second Reform Bill, 27; Lothair, 51 n., 118, 169 n.; and Cowper-Temple clause, 74; leader of Conservatives, 166; and Ireland, 167–9, 175, 177; his Irish University Act, 179
Dock Labourers' Union, 147
Dock Strike, 1889, 2, 136, 140–8
Dodd's Church History of England, 54
Döllinger, J. J. I., 94
Donnelly, Dr. N., Bishop of Canea, 181–3
Douay College, 2 n.
Douglas, Rev. Lord Archibald, 41
Douglas, Father Edward, 101
Doutreloux, Mgr., Bishop of Liège, 148
Downey, R., Archbishop, 217
Downside School, 58
Dublin, Newman's University in, 102, 104, 111 n., 125; Trinity College, 99, 168, 173, 175, 177; University College, 168, 175

Dublin Review, the, 24, 51, 77, 88, 89, 94, 95 n., 102, 146, 160
Durham Letter, 6

Ealing, Catholic School at, 59
East Ham, reformatory at, 39
Ecclesiastical Titles Bill, 5, 6
Education Act, 1870, 26, 35, 46, 61–86, 175
Education, Privy Council Committee on, 29; Roman Catholic view of, 44; Utilitarian and Secularist views of, 43, 44
Eliot, George, 30
Elizabeth I, Queen of England, 1, 2
Ellicot, C. J., (Anglican) Bishop of Gloucester and Bristol, 209
Elliot, Sir F., 209
Eltham, Catholic School at, 41
Endowed Schools Bill (Act), 1869, 63–65
Enfield, Orphanage at, 41
English College, Rome, 2 n, 5, 80
English Historical Review, the, 84
Errington, G., Bishop of Plymouth, 9, 9 n., 10, 101 n., 217
Errington, George (later Sir), 84, 182, 184
Errington Mission, 138, 181–4, 185, 188, 193
Evennett, H. O., 100, 125; *The Catholic Schools of England and Wales*, 44; 'Catholics and the Universities', 91, 96
Exhibition, Great, 1851, 54; Paris, 1867, 54

Faber, F. W., 7, 8, 100
Fabre, Edouard, Archbishop of Montreal, 154
Factory Acts, 27
Farrer, F. W., Archdeacon, 21
Fawcett, Henry, 173
Fenianism, 24, 79, 161 et seq., 200
Ferry, Jules, 41, 85
Finchley, Industrial School at, 41, 59
Fitzsimons, J., *Manning, Anglican and Catholic*, 129
Florençe, 118
Formby, Father, 72
Forster, W. E., 86, 182, 193 (*see* Education Act, 1870 and Endowed Schools Bill, 1869)
Fortnightly Review, the, 139
France, Manning's social work in, 215
French anti-clerical laws, 41

French Revolution, 3, 28
Froude, J. A., 49, 209

Gainsborough, Earl of, 31
Garibaldi, 24, 166
Garvin, J. L., *The Life of Joseph Chamberlain*, 71, 81, 183, 185
Gasquet, Dr. J. R., 50
Gavan-Duffy, Sir Charles, 190
Gay-Lussac, J. L., 116
General Election, 1885, 83, 187
George, Henry, 149–53, 155, 191, 192 n.; *Progress and Poverty*, 152, 191 n.; *Social Problems*, 150
Germanic liberalism, 89, 94
Germanic, the, 157
Gibbons, Cardinal J., of Baltimore, 22, 512, 154–8, 210
Gibson, W., 122
Giffen, Robert, 139
Girton College, Cambridge, 58
Gladstone, Rt. Hon. W. E.: friendship with Manning, 16–18, 24, 176, 198 n., 214; Irish disestablishment, 20, 173; distrusted by 'Old Catholics', 23; Third Reform Bill, 27; Poor Law Bill, 45–46, 129 et seq.; and Metaphysical Society, 49; and Education Bill (Act), 61–86; and university education, 112; and prisons, 131; and trade unions, 132 et seq.; and dock strike, 147; Irish Land Acts, 174–5, 180; Irish University Bill, 1873, 175; Irish Home Rule, 177, 189; Coercion Act, 1881, 180, 186; and Errington Mission, 182–5, 193; defeated at 1885 Election, 187–9; on Papal Infallibility, 189; First Home Rule Bill, 189
Glasgow, Earl of, 209
Glennon, J. J., Archbishop of St. Louis, 158
Glossop, Lord Howard of, 78
Gloucester and Bristol, Anglican Bishops of, 209
Golden Square, London, Catholic School in, 59
Goldwell, Thomas, Bishop of St Asaph, 1
Gordon, W., Bishop of Leeds, 124
Gordon Riots, 5
Gormanston, Lord, 170
Goschen, B. J., 206
Gospel of St. John, 115
Goss, A., Bishop of Liverpool, 38, 42

Grandison, Cardinal, in *Lothair*, 169 n.
Grand National Consolidated Trades Union, 131
Grant, T., Bishop of Southwark, 9, 9 n., 10, 17, 36, 38, 42
Granville, 2nd Earl, 182, 183, 187
Great Exhibition, 1851, 54
Green, J. R., 28
Green, T. H., 28
Gregory, Joshua C., 116 n.; *A Short History of Atomism*, 116
Gregory XV, Pope, 1
Grey, 3rd Earl, 150, 169, 171 et seq.
Grey, Lord de, 66
Grosvenor Square, 20, 100
Gualdi, Don Enrico, 194
Guardian, The, 6 n.
Gwynn, Prof. Denis, in *Manning, Anglican and Catholic*, 163, 173, 203

Hallam, Henry, *Constitutional History of England*, 29
Hamilton, Sir W., 112
Hammersmith, Seminary, 21; Catholic Reformatory, 30; Training College for Men, 30, 37, 49; Industrial School, 39; Orphanage, 41; Poor Law School, 41; Convent, 59; St. Mary's Normal College, 118; Nazareth House, 137
Hampstead, Poor Law school at, 41
Harcourt, Sir W., 183, 193
Harper, Father, S.J., 127
Harrison, Frederick, 30
Harrison, Rev. William, 1 n.
Harrow Road, Orphanage in, 41
Harrow School, 17 n.
Hartington, Lord, 183, 190
Handley, J. E., *The Irish in Scotland, 1798–1845*, 200
Healy, Mgr. J. A., Bishop of Portland, 155
Hedley, J. C., O.S.B., Bishop of Newport, 95, 123, 160, 203
Hedonistic calculus, 27
Hendren, J. W., O. S. F., Bishop of Clifton and, later, Nottingham, 9 n.
Herbert, Sydney, 17
Hicks, Rev. Leo, 113 n.
Hierarchy, restoration of, 5, 6; Low Week meeting of, 1864, 92–93; 1866, 102; 1868, 121; 1873, 110, 120
Highgate, Passionist Monastery at, 95
Hinckley School, 58
Hinsley, Cardinal, 217

Hogarth, W., Bishop of Hexham, 9 n., 10
Holden, Father Henry, 2
Homerton, Poor Law School at, 41
Homes for Destitute Boys, 47–8
Hope, J. R. (later Hope-Scott), 108, 170
House of Commons Committee on Temperance, 201
Howard, E., 38
Howard, Cardinal, 188 n., 193
Howard, C. H. D., 182; *Manning: Anglican and Catholic*, 61, 77, 84, 101, 186, 187, 188
Howard, Lord, of Glossop, 78–79
Hughes, T., 132
Humboldt, A. von, 28
Hutton, A. W., *Cardinal Manning*, 206
Hutton, R. H., 49
Huxley, T. H., 49, 50, 74, 75, 81
Hygienic Movement, 52, 60

Idealist Movement, 28
Ilford, St. Nicholas's Industrial School at, 39, 40
Iliad, the, 115
Index, the, 152
Indian education, 28
Industrial Revolution, 4, 29, 31, 51
Industrial Schools, Walthamstow, 30, 39 n.; North Hyde, 35; Norwood, 35; Ilford, 39, 40; Hammersmith, 39; Finchley, 41; Isleworth, 41; Tower Hill, 41; Liverpool, 42
Inglis, Sir Robert, 176
Innes Review, 217 n.
Inopportunism, 95, 102
Institute of Preventive Medicine, 210
International Prison Congress, 131
Ireland, viii, 3–5, 15, 24, 104, 161–198; Royal University of, 117, 179; temperance campaign in, 201
Irish Catholicism, 3; immigrants in Britain, 3–5, 18, 30, 32; in Bayswater, 18; Church, disestablishment of, 20, 164, 168–173; Parliamentary Party, 84; education, 104, 164, 168–9, 175; Land Bills, 133, 174–5; Land League, 150, 151, 179–80, 182, 196; land question, 165–6, 174–5, 195; Home Rule, 167, 177 et seq.; University Bills, 175, 179; Ladies' Land League, 179; Central Board scheme, 180 et seq.; temperance campaign, 200–1

Isleworth, Industrial School at, 41, 59

James,I, King of England, 54
Jessel, Sir George, 128
Jesuits, 53, 98, 102 n., 104 et seq.;
  Manning's relations with, 53–57, 108–
  113; and University education, 104 et
  seq.; opposition to London University,
  112 et seq.; opposition to Knights of
  Labour, 154; and temperance, 204
Jews, social work in East London, 32
John, St., the Gospel according to, 115
Johnson, Rev. L., 127
Joseph, Father, 194
Jowett, Benjamin, 89–90, 98

Keane, J. J., Bishop of Richmond, U.S.A.,
  155–7
Keating, Archbishop F. W., 217
Kensington, University College at, 12, 26,
  38 n., 93, 108, 114–125, 216
Kershaw, Canon R., 127
Kingsley, Charles, 24, 52, 129, 214
Knights of Labour, 22, 149–52, 153–7,
  166 n.
Knowles, James, 49 n.

Labour Party, English, 30
Labour Representation League, 132
Lacordaire, H. D., 94
Lacy, R., Bishop of Middlesbrough, 124
Lady Margaret Hall, Oxford, 58
Lancaster, Joseph, 29, 30
Land Bills (Acts), Irish, 133, 174–5, 180
Langdale, Charles, 29
La Retraite nuns, 59
Lavington, Manning vicar of, 11, 18, 133
Lawrence, Fr., O.C.R., 40
Lawson, Sir Wilfrid, 203
League of the Cross, 202–6
Leeds, Diocese of, 42, 124
Leeds Mechanics Institute, 23, 126, 134
Leo XIII, Pope, 22, 123, 147, 150, 158–60,
  185, 194, 195, 198, 217
Lefevre, L. J. Shaw-, 187
Leslie, Sir Shane, The Life and Labours of
  Cardinal Manning, vii, 10, 18 n., 62,
  129, 143 n., 144, 159, 165 n., 178, 186,
  191 n., 192 n., 206
Lewes, George Henry, 30
Leyburn, Bishop John, 2

Leytonstone, Catholic school at, 41
Liberal Party, 45, 70, 84
Licensing Bill (Act), 1871, 205–6
Liège, Social Congress at, 1890, 148, 159
Liénart, Cardinal Achille, Bishop of Lille,
  149 n.
Limerick, Bishop of, 195 n.
Lincoln, Abraham, 18
Linnaean Society, 115
Livesay, Joseph, 200
Liverpool, Diocese of, 38, 42; reformatory
  at, 39; industrial school in, 42
Llandaff, Lord (Henry Matthews), 23
Local Option, 204
London, 22 n., 32; Bishop of, 21, 90, 142,
  145; University, 58, 105, 111–14, 125;
  School of Medicine for Women, 58;
  Working Men's Association, 132;
  Committee on Distress in, 139; Lord
  Mayor of, 142 et seq.; Hospital, 148;
  Trades Council, 148
Louvain University, 116
Lowe, Robert, 27
Lubbock, Sir John, 143
Lunn, Arnold, Roman Converts, 8 n., 19,
  94
Lyell, Sir Charles, Principles of Geology, 31
Lynch, Archbishop, of Toronto, 154
Lythgoe, Father, 54

Macaulay, T. B., 28
McCabe, Cardinal, Archbishop of Dublin,
  179, 181
McCarthy, Tom, 141, 144
McClosky, Cardinal, 151
McEntee, Dr. Georgina P., The Social
  Catholic Movement in Great Britain, 6 n.,
  62, 84, 144, 196, 209
McGlynn, Dr. E. (the McGlynn case),
  151–3, 155, 191 n.
McGrath, Fergal, Newman's University,
  Idea and Reality, 125
Mainz, 149
Manchester, 166, 189
Manchester Guardian, the, 118
Manchester Statistical Society, 117
Mann, Tom, 141, 144
Manning, Henry Edward, Cardinal,
  Archbishop of Westminster: member
  of Cross Commission, vii, 26; appoint-
  ed Archbishop of Westminster, 1865, 9,
  10; and the middle classes, 11, 14; on

personal sanctification of clergy, 11; University College at Kensington, 12, 14, 26, 114-25, 216; and agricultural labourers, 13, 16; views on science, 13-14, 87, 111, 210; and Ireland, 15, 84, 161-98; at Bayswater, 16, 18, 31; friendship with Gladstone, 17-18, 176, 198; and Irish immigrants, 18; and Irish Church disestablishment, 20, 168-73; rejects plan for new cathedral, 32; founds Westminster Diocesan Education Fund, 35-36; campaign to rescue Catholic children from workhouses, 42; relations with Dr. Barnardo, 48-49; and Metaphysical Society, 49-51; St. Charles's College, 52-53; antagonism to Jesuits, 53-57; education for the wealthy, 58; education for girls, 58-60; schools for handicapped children, 60; against admission of Catholics to Oxford and Cambridge, 87 et seq.; plans for Catholic University, 102-14; relations with Newman and Jesuits, 109-14; appointment and dismissal of Mgr. Capel, 117-24; the 'workers' Cardinal', 124; educational policy summarized, 126; Academia of the Catholic Religion, 126-8; work for French relief, 130; work for prisons, 131; and trade unions, 131 et seq.; views on labour and capital, 135-6; interest in housing, 138; interest in colonization, 139; and the dock strike, 142-8; and social reform abroad, 148 et seq.; influence in U.S.A., 149-54; and Knights of Labour, 154 et seq.; influence on Leo XIII, 158-60; and Irish education, 168-9, 175, 179; and Irish land question, 174-5; and the Temporal Power, 176; and Irish Home Rule, 177, 188 et seq.; and Dublin Archbishopric, 181-5; and Chamberlain's 'Central Board' Scheme, 185-9; supports Tories at 1885 Election, 187-9; with Walsh against 'Old Catholics', 191 et seq.; against Parnell, 196-8; and temperance movement, 200-7; his League of the Cross, 202-6; and Salvation Army, 207-8; Social Purity Crusade, 207-8; anti-vivisectionism, 209-11; and Ruskin, 211-12; his personality, 213-17; becomes Cardinal, 217; his death, 198, 217. Writings: Bayswater Journal, 18 n.; Charges, of 1843, 11-12; 1845, 13, 134; 1846, 13-14; 1848, 16; Ireland : a Letter to Earl Grey, 169, 171 et seq.; Manning Papers (Correspondence), vii, Pastime Papers, 18; Pastoral Letters, on education, 32, 33-34, 42, 46, 47, 78, 124; on poverty, 136; 'Law of Nature, Divine and Supreme, The', 140; Rights and Dignity of Labour, The, 23, 126, 134; Temperance Reformation, The, 201; What One Work of Mercy Can I Do This Lent? A Letter to a Friend, 15; 'The Work and Wants of the Catholic Church in England', Dublin Review, 51.

Manning, Monsignor William, 51
Mansion House Friends Relief Fund, 129
Mansion House, London, 130, 142
Mason, Canon, in Memoirs of Archbishop Temple, 145
Marist Brothers, 57
Martineau, Harriet, 30
Martineau, J., Types of Ethical Theory, Study of Religion, 30 n., 49
Marx, Karl, 30
Mary, the Blessed Virgin, 3
Marylebone Board of Guardians, 35
Mathew, Dr. D., in English Catholics, 1850-1950, 172 n., 192 n.
Mathew, Father, 20, 200-1
Matthews, Henry, Lord Llandaff, 23
Maurice, F. D., 24, 49, 129, 214
Maynooth College, 84, 175, 179, 180, 181
Mazzinianism, 165 n.
Mechanics Institutes, 23, 27, 51, 126, 127, 134
Mermillod, Cardinal, Bishop of Geneva, 149
Metaphysical Society, 49-51, 116, 126, 211
Middlesbrough, Bishop of, 124
Millite doctrine, 23
Mill, James, 27
Mill, John Stuart, 27
Mill Hill, Catholic school at, 40
Miners' Association, 132
Minto, 4th Earl of, 209
Mivart, Prof. St. George, 41, 50, 115-16, 125; The Appendicular Skeleton of the Primates, 116
Montalembert, G. R., 94
Month, The, 102, 112, 204-5
Moran, P., Archbishop of Sydney, 182-3, 188 and n.
Morley, John, 49, 171

Morley, Samuel, 132
Morning Post, the, 144
Morris, Father John, 54
Mount St. Bernard Abbey, 39
Mount St. Mary's College, 54, 58
Mount-Temple, Lord, 209
Most Holy Sacrament, nuns of the, 59
Mundella, A. J., 132, 209

Napoleon Bonaparte, 130
Nash, V., H. L. Smith and, *The Story of the Dockers' Strike*, 141 et seq.
National Association for Promoting State-Directed Colonization, 139
National Association of United Trades for the Protection of Labour, 132
National Education League, 76
National Education Union, 76
National Society for Education, 29, 77
Nazareth House, Hammersmith, 137
New Hall Convent, 59
New Learning, 51
New Statesman and Nation, the, 69 n.
Newman, John Henry, Cardinal: enters Roman Catholic Church, 7; his Lives of the Saints, 7; candidate for Westminster, 10; advocates traditional education, 13; no experience of poor, 18; on temperance reform, 22; his *Development of Christian Doctrine*, 31; on Metaphysical Society, 50; his orthodoxy suspected, 78; his *Discourses on the Scope and Nature of a University Education*, 88 n., 91–92; and proposed Oratory at Oxford, 93–102, 123; on Papal Infallibility, 95; and University in Dublin, 104, 111, 125, 168; on Catholic University, 108; relations with Manning, 109–14, 216–17; on London University, 111 et seq., 125; and Gladstone on Ireland, 180–1; and Dublin Archbishopric, 182; and Ruskin, 212; becomes Cardinal, 216
Newnham College, Cambridge, 58
Newport, Bishop of, 122
Nightingale, Florence, 16, 17
Nineteenth Century, the, 140, 146
Nonconformist Academies, 27
Norfolk, Duke of, 5, 6, 79, 119 n., 121, 124, 183, 188, 192, 193, 194, 216
North Hyde, Industrial School at, 35
Northampton, Bishop of, 124

Northern Press and Catholic Times, the, see *Catholic Times*
Norwood, Industrial School at, 35
Nottingham, Diocese of, 42, 120, 205
Nugent, Father, 42

Oakeley, F., 100
Oblates of St. Charles, 18, 41, 51
O'Brien, C. C., *Parnell and his Party*, 179, 185, 197
O'Connor, Arthur, 197
Odger, George, 132
Odyssey, the, 115
'Old Catholic' Church, 3 n.
Old Hall, St. Edmunds, 21
Old Hall Green, 58
O'Neill, Charles, 127
Opportunists, 61
Oratorian Order, 8, 57
Oratory, Oxford, Newman's proposed, 93–102
Oratory, Birmingham, 58, 93, 98 and n. 110
Oscott College, 58, 114
Owen, Robert, 131
Oxford Mission, 95
Oxford Movement, viii, 3, 59, 114
Oxford, proposed Oratory at, 93–102
Oxford University, 58, 87 et seq., 90–93

Paley, F. A., 114–5, 125
Pall Mall Gazette, the, 144, 194, 208
Papal Curia, 157, 210
Papal Encyclicals, *Rerum Novarum*, 145, 146, 159–60, 217; *Quadragesimo Anno*, 145; *Immortale Dei*, 159; *On the Condition of Labour*, 160
Papal Infallibility, 18, 95
Paris, Archbishop of, 30 ; Committee for the Relief of, 211; Commune, 75, 130 n.; Exhibition, 1867, 54; Siege of, 130
Parnell, Charles Stewart, 84–85, 178, 182, 186, 187, 188–91, 196; his *Manifesto*, 187
Partington, J. R., *A Text Book of Inorganic Chemistry*, 116
Passionist Monastery, Highgate, 95
Pastoral Letters, Manning's, 32, 33–34, 42, 46, 47, 78, 124, 136; Bishops', 103, 114, 119

Pattison, Mark, 49
Pau, 118
Paul, St., 24
Peace Congresses, 24, 166
Peel, Sir Robert, 27
Penal Laws, 7, 88
Permissive Bill, 1868, 203-7
Perry, Father, S.J., 127
Persico, Mgr., 194-6
Persico Mission, 191
Petre, Lord, 31, 38, 53, 118, 119, 121
Phillimore, Robert, 170-1
Pigott forgeries, 196
Pisa, 88
Pius IX, Pope, 1, 9, 10, 32, 99, 118, 123, 217
Poole, Sister Imelda, 96
Poor Law Bill (Act), 1868, 45-46, 129-30
Poor Law Amendment Act, 1866, 43
Poor Servants of the Mother of God, 41
Poor School Sisters, of Notre Dame, 41, 59
Popes, Sixtus V, 1; Pius IX, 1, 9, 10, 32, 99, 118, 123, 217; Gregory XV, 1; Leo XIII, 22, 123-4, 147, 150, 158-60, 185, 194, 195, 198, 217
Portobello Road, Poor Law School in, 41
Positivism, 30, 31, 214-15
Potamian, Brother, 55-57
Potter, T. B., 132
Powderley, Terence, V., 153 et seq.
Primrose Dames, 193
Prior Park Seminary, 58; plans for university at, 104 et seq.
Prison Ministers Bill, 1872, 131
Privy Council, Committee on Education, 29, 68; Education Grants, 30, 37
Propaganda Fide, Congregation de, 1 n., 9, 96, 98, 101, 102, 103, 157 and n.
Pugin, A. W. N., 8
Purbrick, Father, 112
Purcell, Edmund S., Life of Cardinal Manning, vii, 17 n., 18 n., 23, 32, 50, 51, 52 n., 61, 67, 80, 89, 97, 100, 109, 113, 117, 126, 144, 164, 191, 202, 203, 206, 207, 208-9, 213
Pusey, E. B., 114

Queen's College, London, 58
Queen's Colleges, Belfast and Cork, 168, 175, 179
Queen's University, Ireland, 179

Raphael, Mother Frances, O.S.D., Letters of Archbishop Ullathorne, 22 n., 166 n.
Ratcliffe School, 58
Rawes, Rev. Henry A., 52
Reade, Charles, 214
Redemptorist Order, 8, 97, 154
Reform Bills (Acts), First, 1832, 17; Second, 1867, 27, 61, 171 n.; Third, 1884, 23, 27
Reform League, 24, 166
Reformatory and Industrial Schools Acts, 1866, 38-39, 40, 72
Reformatories, St. Edward's, East Ham, 39; Liverpool 39; Bristol, 39; Charnwood Forest, 39
Reichzeitung, the, 157
Reisach, Cardinal, 99
Religious Orders in education, 40-41
Rescript of 1867, 124
Revised Code, for education, 49
Rice, James, 214
Richmond, Yorks., 112
Riddell, A., Bishop of Northampton, 124
Rigby, Fr. Nicholas, 57
Riley, Athelstan, 75
Ripon, 1st Marquis of, 216
Roehampton, St. Charles's College at, 53
Romanos Pontifices, Papal Bull, 114
Rome, English College at, 2 n., 5, 80, 217 n.; Manning's visits to, 53, 206 n.; Vaughan's visit to, 99-100; Bishop Clifford at, 101; American College at, 155
Rope, Rev. Henry G., 80
Rosminian Order, 8
Royal Commission on the Housing of the Working Classes, 137-8
Royal Institution, 115
Royal Society, 115
Royal University of Ireland, 117
Ruskin, John, 49, 137, 199, 211-12, 213, 214; his Fors Clavigera, 211-12
Russell, Lord John (later 1st Earl), 5, 6, 77, 91, 161, 166
Russell, Lord Odo (later Lord Ampthill), 69

Sabetti, Aloysius, 154, 155
St. Aloysius' College, Highgate, 58
St. Ambrose, Church of, Bristol, 102 n.
St. Benedict, Rule of, 212
St. Asaph, Bishop of, 1

St. Charles's College, Kensington, 52–53, 120 n., 124
St. Edmund's College, Ware, 50
St. Edward's Seminary, Liverpool, 58
St. James's Hall meetings, 36, 46
St. John, E., *Manning's Work for Children*, 48
St. John, the Gospel according to, 115
St. John's College, Islington, 58
St. Mary's Normal College, Hammersmith, 118
St. Mary's School, Woolhampton, 58
St. Oswald's Mission, 162
St. Paul, 24
St. Pius X, Church of, Kensington, 53
Salford, Diocese of, 42, 124
Salisbury, 3rd Marquis of, vii, 84–86, 138, 181, 185, 187, 191, 206, 208
Salle, de la, Brothers, 53, 55–57
Salvation Army, 19, 21, 202
Sandhurst, Royal Military College, 94
Satolli, Archbishop, 152–3
Schools Enquiry Commission, 58
Scott, Benjamin, 208
Scottish Schools Bill, 64
Scottish Universities, admission of women to, 59
Seager, Charles, 114, 125
'Secularist' education, 43, 63
Seddon, Father, 48
Sedgwick, Adam, 90
Seghers, Archbishop, of Oregon, 153
Selborne, 1st Earl of, 49
Servites, 41
Severn, Mrs. Arthur, 212
Seville, English College at, 2
Shaftesbury, 7th Earl of, 209, 210–11
Shelley, Percy Bysshe, 17
Shop Hours League, 139
Shrewsbury, Earls of, 115
Sidgwick, Henry, 49
Simeoni, Cardinal, 151, 157
Sisters of Charity, 40
Sisters of Mercy, 41, 60
Sixtus V, Pope, 1
Slave trade, 20
Social Purity Crusade, 207–9
Smith, H. L., and Nash, V. *The Story of the Dockers' Strike*, 141 n.
Smith, Bishop Richard, 2 n.
Smith, Dr. R. A. L., 69 n.
Snead-Cox, J. G., 192
Society of Arts, 136

Society of Jesus, 53–57, 103, 104–14
Somers, A., 127
Somerville College, Oxford, 58
Southampton, 141 n.
Southend, Catholic School at, 41, 59
Southwark, Bishops of: Grant, 9, 9 n., 10, 17, 36, 38, 42; Danell, 42; Butt, 42, 60; Coffin, 97
Southwark Catholic Rescue Society, 42
Southwark, Diocese of, 55, 120, 122
Spectator, The, 14
Spencer, Herbert, 31, 199
Spencer, 5th Earl, 182, 193
Spinkhill Manor, 2
Stafford, Lord, 38
Standard, the, 203
Stanley, A. P., Dean of Westminster, 49, 90, 98
Stamford Hill, Catholic School at, 41, 59
Stead, W. T., 207–8
Steele, F. M., *The Convents of Great Britain*, 41 n.
Stepney, Orphanage in, 41
Stephen, Leslie, 79, 209
Stephens, Uriah S., 153
Stevenson, Rev. Joseph, 128
Stonyhurst College, 54, 58, 103, 112
Stonyhurst Manor, 2
Stourton, Charles, 103
Strachey, Lytton, 213
Strauss, D. F., *Life of Jesus*, 14
Swing Riots, 134
Synod, Provincial, 1873, 110

Tablet, the, 78, 157, 180, 192, 198, 205
Talbot, Monsignor G., 7, 10, 37, 92, 98, 101, 102
Taschereau, E.-A., Archbishop of Quebec, 154
Tasker, F. W., 52
Taunton Commission, 1864, 58, 63
Taylor, I. A., *The Cardinal Democrat: Henry Edward Manning*, 144, 205
Temperance reform, 22, 200–7
Temple, Frederick, Bishop of Exeter and later London, 21, 90, 142, 145, 205; *Memoirs of*, 145 n.
Tennyson, Alfred, Lord, 49
Tests, religious, repeal of, 2, 101, 102, 103, 176
Thompson, Gordon, 117
Throckmorton, family, 115

Throckmorton, Sir John, 6 n.
Tierney, Rev. M. A., Ed., *Dodd's Church History of England*, 54 and n.
Tilbury, 140 n.
Tillett, Ben, 141 et seq.
Times, The, 34, 35, 36, 43, 46, 139, 140, 142, 144, 167, 183, 192
Tolpuddle trial, 1834, 132
Totteridge, Poor Law School at, 41
Tower Hill, Industrial School at, 41
Townsley, John, 98
Tracy-Ellis, Prof. John, 157 n.
Tract 90, 7,
Trades Parliamentary Association, 139
Trelawny, Sir John, 131
Trevelyan, Sir Charles, 132
Trinity College, Dublin, 99, 168, 173, 175, 177, 179
Turner, W., Bishop of Salford, 9n.
Turner, Rev. Sydney, 42
Tynan, Dr. P., 181-2
Tyndall, J., 49

Ullathorne, W. B., O.S.B., Bishop of Birmingham: protests against ultramontanism, 7; Vicar Apostolic, 9 n., 10; on Australian convict settlements, 15; *Letters* quoted, 22 n., 166 n.; distrust of Gladstone, 23; on education, 38, 65-66, 70-71; and Newman, 93 and n., 97, 98, 100, 102; and Capel, 119-23; on Ireland, 164, 165 n., 171
Unemployed, Committee for the Relief of, 211
Union Society, Oxford, 17
Unions of Stevedores, 141
Unita Catholica, 157
United Ireland, 183
United Kingdom Alliance, 200-6
Universalis Ecclesiae, Letters Apostolic, 1
Universities, question of admitting Catholics to, 87-90
University College, Dublin, 168, 175
'University Commission, The', 91
University education, Bishops' pastoral letter on, 103
Ushaw College, 58, 96
Utilitarian philosophy, 27, 28, 30, 31, 43
Utrecht, 3 n.

Valladolid, English College at, 2 n.

Vaterland, the, 157
Vatican Council, 61, 62, 65, 69, 72, 79, 103, 130, 175
Vaughan, Herbert, O.S.C., Bishop of Salford, later Cardinal, Archbishop of Westminster: and Salvation Army, 19; on rich and poor, 23, 24; supports Manning on education, 38, 55, 57, 85, 86; and Dr. Barnardo, 49; on Newman's proposed Oratory, 98-100; connexions with 'Old Catholics', 112; opposed by Jesuits, 114; removal of university ban, 124; tributes to Manning, 126, 158-9; criticism of Manning, 146; and Ireland, 185, 192, 195; opposed to Walsh, 198; on temperance, 206-7
Vaughan, William, Bishop of Plymouth, 101 n.
Vaux of Harrowden, family, 2
Vavasour, family, 2
Vere, Aubrey de, 104
Victoria Street Society, 209
Victoria University, 59
Villiers, Charles Pelham, 45-46, 130
Virgin Mary, the, 3
Vogelsang, K. von, 149
Voluntary Schools Association, 83
Von Ketteler, W. E., Bishop of Mainz, 149

Wales, Prince of, 138
Walsh, P. J., *William J. Walsh, Archbishop of Dublin*, 166 n., 184 n.
Walsh, W. J., President of Maynooth, later Archbishop of Dublin: appointed to Dublin, 84, 181-6; influenced by George, 150, 151; and McGlynn case, 151 et seq.; tributes to Manning, 159, 198; and Irish Land Bill, 180; and Irish movement, 188, 190; against 'Old Catholics', 191-8; on Parnell, 197
Walthamstow, Industrial School at, 30, 39 n.
Wandsworth, Training College at, 49
Ward, Maisie, *The Wilfrid Wards and the Transition*, 51
Ward, W. G., 7, 49, 50 and n., 92, 93, 125 n., 214
Ward Wilfrid, vii, 7, 34, 125; his *William George Ward*, 7, 49; *The Life and Times of Cardinal Wiseman*, 7, 50; *The Life of John Henry Newman*, 50 n., 51, 52, 94
Ware, St. Edmund's College, 50

Wareing, W., Bishop of Northampton, 9 n.

Weld, family, 2

Weld, Father, 107, 108, 112

Westminster Diocesan Education Fund, 35–39, 46–47, 49, 76

Westminster Gazette, the, 52

Westminster, 1st Marquis of, 162

Wilberforce, Bishop, 171

Winchester, Bishop of, 90, 209

Windthorst, L., 149

Wiseman, Nicholas, Cardinal, 1st Archbishop of Westminster: English Hierarchy restored under, 1, 5, 6–7; imports religious Orders, 8; reconciliation of 'Old Catholics', Irish, and Converts, 8–9; quarrels with Hierarchy, 10; and

Crimean War, 17; founds Catholic Poor Schools Society, 29; proposed memorial to, 31; schools under, 39, 49; university ban under, 92; Newman's attitude to, 100; founds Academia of the Catholic Religion, 126; and Ireland, 161–3

Wood, Sir Evelyn, 209

Woolwich, Catholic School at, 41, 59

Woolwich, Royal Military Academy, 94

Worcester College, Oxford, 114

Wordsworth, Charles, 17

Zetland, Earl of, 5

Zoological Society, 115

Zoophilist, The, 211

PRINTED IN GREAT BRITAIN AT
THE UNIVERSITY PRESS
ABERDEEN